Positive Approaches to Corrections: Research, Policy, and Practice

Roger J. Lauen, Ph.D.

American Correctional Association
4380 Forbes Boulevard
Lanham, MD 20706

rector
Gabriella M. Daley, Director, Communications and Publications
Leslie A. Maxam, Assistant Director, Communications and Publications
Alice Fins, Publications Managing Editor
Michael Kelly, Associate Editor
Mike Selby, Production Editor

Printed in the U.S.A. by McArdle Printing Company, Inc., Upper Marlboro, MD.

ISBN 1-56991-065-0

This publication may be ordered from:

American Correctional Association
4380 Forbes Boulevard
Lanham, MD 20706-4322
1-800-222-5646

Library of Congress Cataloging-in-Publication Data

Lauen, Roger J.
     Positive approaches to corrections : research, policy, and
  practice / Roger J. Lauen
       p.   cm.
    Includes bibliographical references.
    ISBN 1-56991-065-0 (pbk.)
    1. Corrections—United States. I. Title.
  HV9466.L28 1997
  365'.973—dc21   96-50994
                                                            CIP

Table of Contents

PREFACE by James A. Gondles, Jr. v

INTRODUCTION by Paul Gendreau, Ph.D. vii

FOREWORD ix

SECTION 1: POLICY 1

CHAPTER 1 A Statement of the Correctional Problem 5

CHAPTER 2 The Political Context of Corrections 31

CHAPTER 3 The Role of the Media in the Presentation of Crime 39

CHAPTER 4 Crime: Rates, Theories, Descriptions 53

CHAPTER 5 Drugs, Alcohol, and Prison Use 75

CHAPTER 6 Race and Prison Use 87

CHAPTER 7 The Triangle: Collaboration Among Practitioners,
Policymakers, and the Research/Academic Community 95

CHAPTER 8   Developing A New Agenda for Corrections 105

SECTION 2: PRACTICE 117

CHAPTER 9   Risk Assessment: Making Critical Decisions 119

CHAPTER 10   Identifying and Meeting the Treatment Needs
of Offenders 135

CHAPTER 11   Responsivity: Tailoring Treatment and Supervision
to the Unique Characteristics of Each Offender 165

CHAPTER 12   Continuous Client, Staff, and Program Evaluation 173

CHAPTER 13   Doing Community Corrections Right 197

CHAPTER 14   In Summary 223

REFERENCES 229

INDEX 249

INDEX OF AUTHORITIES CITED 254

Preface

The American Correctional Association is pleased to present *Positive Approaches to Corrections: Research, Policy, and Practice* by Roger Lauen. This book discusses many of the issues facing corrections and provides some fresh ideas for solutions. By reading this book, practitioners, policymakers, researchers, and students will find guidance to meet the unique challenges they face in corrections.

Dr. Lauen has researched a wealth of information and has determined that things can work in corrections. He shows us how things can work in easily understandable prose and clear charts that are corroborated by scores of researchers and correctional practitioners. Lauen believes that offenders should be treated and supervised by using risk and needs assessment instruments (instead of being classified based on their offense), and he discusses several methods that have proven successful. He presents this approach as a way to make corrections more efficient and cost effective.

We know that offenders commit different crimes for different reasons, and they will respond to correctional treatment, regardless of the sanction imposed, according to their individual traits and characteristics. Dr. Lauen believes that by recognizing the complexity of the psychology involved in criminal conduct, and by matching offenders with treatment consistent with their characteristics, correctional efforts can be more successful. He emphasizes the importance of cooperation among researchers, policymakers, and practitioners, discusses some of the hurdles that get in their way, and offers ways out of these dilemmas.

Positive Approaches to Corrections: Research, Policy, and Practice is an important addition to the many products and services that the American Correctional Association offers. We welcome your comments. If you are not already a member of ACA, please join us so that you may participate more fully in the advancement of your career and improvement in the field of corrections.

James A. Gondles, Jr.
Executive Director
American Correctional Association

Introduction

Two major problems that obfuscate thinking clearly about criminal justice issues in the United States are the predominance of the "common sense" perspective and the parochialism of many policymakers in the system. Proponents of common sense, in my opinion, are essentially anti-intellectual in the sense that they are ideologically driven, hence accept only "evidence" often of a specious nature—that suits their purposes. Thus, how often do we hear that "common sense" tells us that the solution to the crime problem is only such and such (in other words—more deterrence)? In regard to the second point, I frequently encounter a lack of interest, disdain, or even fear of considering different approaches to long-standing criminal justice problems (such as crowding) that emanate from either other states or especially other countries.

In this text, *Positive Approaches to Corrections: Research, Policy, and Practice*, Roger Lauen demonstrates a healthy respect for evidence and a willingness to avoid a hidebound perspective—the way we have done things in the last twenty years is the way it should be. The first eight chapters are oriented toward policymakers. Of particular interest to this observer are the presentation of long-term trends on prison sentences, incarceration (Chapter 1); the political context (Chapter 2); the role of the media (Chapters 3 and 7). Indeed, Chapter 3 struck home because the media presentation of crime issues is, to my mind, the major stumbling block to witnessing any rational change in criminal justice policies at the sociopolitical level.

Chapters 9-13 are intended for practitioners. Here, the reader is brought up to date on how to assess criminal behavior. The most productive strategy for protecting the public, benefitting the offender (better supervision and treatment), and being fiscally responsible is to assess the offender risk properly. I was also drawn to Chapters 12-13; several sound points are contained therein (such as staff factors). Finally, part 1 of Chapter 14 bears repeating time and time again. The correctional enterprise is fraught with minefields—conceptually, philosophically, and operationally—but we always seem to engage in undue masochism by forgetting there are very real limits to our authority. We cannot be all things to all people.

In closing, Roger Lauen, has provided the reader with a refreshing perspective on how to manage significant components of the corrections enterprise. The evidence is certainly there to support his various contentions. Let us hope more policymakers and practitioners use it.

Paul Gendreau, Ph.D.
Professor of Psychology and Director,
    Centre for Criminal Justice Studies
Kimberley Placentine DeFrancis
University of New Brunswick
New Brunswick, Canada

Foreword

The field of corrections is not easy to understand, analyze or predict. The field does not have a single unifying set of ideas. In the academic world, criminology is taught in a variety of disciplines (sociology, psychology, political science, public policy, and public administration). To "get a handle" on corrections is not easy.

Because incidents in life can seldom be attributed to one great all-encompassing doctrine, we instead must seek out the numerous and varied underlying influences. In corrections or any other social environment, events often have numerous causes, effects, and meanings, all of which interact to form the resulting exprience or development. In using analysis to understand such occurrences, the focus should be to recognize the great diversity of causes, effects, meanings, and the interactions of the three, and not to generalize by reducing all of this to one or two simple conclusions.

It also could be said that the aim of correctional legislation or the aim of a criminal sanction always should be to capture the variety of causes, effects, and meanings and trace their interaction. Unfortunately, that is not usually the case. When elected officials speak out on crime, they almost always speak unidimensionally. "Crime is rampant in our streets." "We need to come down hard on these street criminals." "Mandatory prison terms for anyone using a gun," and so on. This is the clarion call. The call is for more social control, not more understanding. These calls deny the multiplicity of causes and complexity of crime and its remedies.

Changes in the Corrections Field

The originial idea for this book was to write a third edition to a previous book, *Community-Managed Corrections* (first edition 1988, second edition 1990). Reflecting on what has transpired since 1990, I concluded that an entirely new book was needed. Changes in the field of adult corrections since the first edition of *Community-Managed Corrections* in 1988 are innumerable. The following chart illustrates what has happened to the adult corrections population in the last few years.

CHART 1: Adult Inmate Population in the United States: 1985 - 1995

	1985	1995	Percentage Increase	Percentage Held
State Prisons	452,372	1,004,608	122	63
Federal Prisons	37,669	99,466	164	6
Local Jails	254,986	490,442*	92	31
Totals	745,027	1,594,516	114	100

*1994; 1995 data was not available for jails.

Source: Bureau of Justice Statistics 1995.

Never before in the history of our country has the incarcerated population increased at this rate in such a short period. Additionally, similar rates of growth have occurred in probation, parole, community corrections, and in the juvenile system.

Other changes in the corrections field included the introduction and use of objective measures and tools to assess risk and treatment needs for classification of offenders, as well as a wide variety of treatment strategies, and many new ways of supervising offenders in noninstitutional settings. Only some of these changes were helpful. Getting an accurate fix on what type of offender one is dealing with is essential for practitioners. Without this kind of knowledge, some offenders are given too much supervision, others not enough; some are court ordered into Alcohol Anonymous programs when they have a psychological dependence on marijuana but no alcohol addiction.

The relentless expansion of the criminal justice network has had devastating impacts on African-American and Latino individuals and neighborhoods. Incredibly high rates of incarceration among racial and ethnic minorities have resulted in social dislocations on a massive scale and, in turn, are having profound effects on families and children.

Other Changes Within the Last Decade

During this last decade (1985-1995), my perspective has undergone significant change. In 1985, I predicted that state and local governments would stop prison expansion because of the prohibitive costs. The figures in Chart 1 illustrate how wrong that prediction was. State governments are being caught in a two-way firestorm. As the federal government abdicates its responsibility for many social programs and delegates them to the states, state revenues are being curtailed due to taxpayers' revolts (Proposition 13 in California; Amendment 1 in Colorado; Measure 5 in Oregon). In spite of greater demands for spending for the poor, the elderly, and the sick, state governments have continued to increase prison budgets 10 to 25 percent per year and more. With no new revenue sources, increased prison money comes out of education funding and other vital social programs.

In 1985, I held on to the belief of many sociologists and criminologists that crime was caused in large part by poverty and not much else. Fix poverty and crime would dry up and blow away. That was intellectually naive and embarrasingly, not very scientific. With the help of research-oriented clinical psychologists, my understanding of crime causation and remedies that emerge from that literature is much improved. To stay abreast, one must read a lot, attend conferences, and network with colleagues.

Also in 1985, I was full of optimism regarding the potential of community corrections as a means of humanizing the field of adult corrections, providing treatment needs to adult offenders and reducing prison use. Hope still remains, but the bubbling optimism is gone.

Today, we know that community corrections cannot operate or be improved in a vacuum. If jail and prison use increase 10 percent a year, community corrections populations also will increase. This increase will occur whether the field is ready for it or not, whether adequate staff is there or not, and whether program space is available or not. Corrections is a system; a change in one component has an impact on some or all other facets of the system.

From what I have observed firsthand and from the body of "what works" literature (see Chapter 12 for a summary of evaluation literature), the quality of community corrections in many parts of the country is poor. Low-risk offenders are placed in residential programs. High-risk offenders are placed in nonresidential settings. Community corrections staff, especially staff working in private for profit programs, are low paid and use their private employment as a temporary parking spot until higher paid public employment comes their way.

In the last few years, I have been an expert witness in lawsuits against community corrections programs, some of the very programs that I helped establish twenty years ago. This has been a painful experience. In my opinion, the choice was to use the courts as a vehicle for improvement or stand by and watch the quality of services decline. Again, in my opinion, most state legislators did not care about the quality of community corrections services; they only viewed community corrections as a less expensive place to put adult offenders. The executive branch cared but was under media and legislative pressure to provide bed space for jail and prison crowding. This pressure diverted their attention away from monitoring and quality control. By default, the courts became the vehicle for system improvement. However, this is not an appropriate use of the courts. The executive branch must do a better job of monitoring program quality, and the legislature must establish reasonable corrections policy and do this collaboratively with the judiciary and the executive branch. This is not being done now in most places, but it must be the long-range objective.

Another significant systems problem occurred because thousands of adult offenders in community corrections programs would have been placed in some form of probation or parole program had community corrections not been established in the 1970s and 1980s. This became known as widening the net of social control. When the criminal justice net widens, low-risk offenders are placed into correctional settings that provide more supervision than needed, medium-risk offenders are placed in correctional settings in which they do not get the level of supervision or treatment services they need, and high-risk offenders are crowded together with low- and medium-risk offenders.

Additionally, widening the net contributes to already crowded court rooms, large probation and parole caseloads grow to unmanageable proportions, stress levels among detention officers increase to dangerous levels, verbal altercations among prison inmates increase and become more ominous, the entire system is under crisis mode. If widening the net of social control resulted in less street crime, it might well be worth the investment. Thus far, there is little empirical support to show that as more people are forced under the corrections umbrella, our streets and communities are safer.

Fear of crime has far outstripped the actual incidence of crime. Crime fear is so palatable that eager, opportunistic elected officials prey on it and exploit it for their own benefit. Politicians promise to combat crime with longer prison sentences. "Get tough" bidding wars among politicians are not uncommon just weeks before election time. A catchy political cliche introduced in the State of Washington (three strikes and you're out) moves with the speed of a prairie fire to California, New York, and Florida. Colorado passed a three-strikes law two years ago even though a habitual-offender law had been on the books for over a decade. The public yearns for public safety the same way they invest in get-rich schemes, sweepstakes, and lotteries. The public hopes that something, anything, will be done to deliver us to the promised (safe streets) land.

Print and television media bombard us daily with gory stories of death, rape, drug busts, and destruction of property. The purposeful misrepresentation of violent crime by print and TV media serves their pecuniary interests. However, we do have more violent crime than other comparably industrialized, first-world countries. Why are we so cursed? Aren't first-world countries supposed to be better (read safer) than second and third-world countries? Why, when we travel to Germany, Canada, France, Japan, even Mexico, does everything seem so civilized, so safe, so hospitable?

What Can Be Done?

The purpose of this book is to lay out a plan to return to a more sane, less frightened, more reasonable and balanced corrections system. Prison dependence is a result of a variety of public policy choices made by public and elected officials (Chapter 2), which in turn is driven by a host of other factors, such as the presentation of crime by the media (Chapter 3), the public's fear of crime and purposeful manipulation and misrepresentation of that fear, large scale social conditions, racial fears and policies (Chapter 6), and the efficacy of correctional intervention. To "correct" the "problem," we must address, analyze, assess, and present recommendations for improvement on all these matters.

The factors that surround the correctional situation are not all bad. There are some promising signs. The Campaign for an Effective Crime Policy has emerged within the last three years. This is a very impressive group of public officials, elected officials, and criminal justice specialists who are unified in their belief that fundamental change in the entire crime, criminal justice, and corrections systems is long overdue. They have issued a call for a rational debate on crime and punishment. Some of the elements of their proposed policy include the following:

1. Establishment by the United States President of a national commission on crime to address the causes, prevention, and reduction of crime and delinquency

2. Allocating sufficient amounts of money for drug treatment

3. Reexamining mandatory sentencing

4. Reexamining the federal sentencing guidelines

5. Expanding community corrections and providing adequate funding for it

6. Allocating sufficient funds for research and examining: the length of prison sentences, the impact of criminal justice policy on racial and ethnic minorities and women, and the relationship between crime, poverty, unemployment, and victimization

7. Expanding crime-prevention programs

8. Requiring fiscal-impact statements on prison-related legislation

9. Encouraging public-private partnerships for crime reduction and getting the federal government to provide leadership and training in planning, coordinating of effective anti-crime strategies, including problem-oriented or community policing

Whether this group can effect systems change remains an unknown. However, there is no doubt that without the likes of this group, it is unlikely that systems improvement will occur.

Another promising sign is that a small number of public school advocates are beginning to realize that prisons are getting state funds that schools used to get. Some are beginning to organize at the local level for K-12 education. Others are organizing university faculty to give higher education a higher priority than new prison construction.

Value-free Science and Pressing Public Policy Demands

As a graduate student in the late 1960s, I was drawn into a controversial, but engaging debate on value-free versus value-laden science. The long-standing tradition had been value-free science, in other words, dissecting, analyzing, interpreting information without interjecting any of your own personal values or opinions. The new school of thought was that everyone has values, including scientists, and it is dishonest not to acknowledge these values in the course of conducting a study, teaching students, or writing a report. Therefore, in actuality, everything is value laden.

I was persuaded to join the value-laden school of thought. The precept of this school was to conduct ourselves objectively and professionally, using the canons of the scientific method, and simultaneously be quite explicit about our values. The value-free school of thought was adamantly against this posture viewing the value-laden school as advocates for certain causes or issues. The idea of being an advocate was inconsistent with the role of scientist. To use the legal analogy, you either can be an advocate for society and be a prosecutor or an advocate for the accused and be a defense attorney. There is no middle ground. This advocacy debate continues today. The well-known researcher Joan Petersilia states:

> Researchers tend to shy away from suggesting policy and program implications because they fear the spectors of "advocacy" and subjectivity. . . . Explanation of the meaning and implications of a study's findings does not constitute advocacy, nor does it violate scientific objectivity, as long as the findings and analysis lead logically to the conclusions and implications drawn.
>
> (Petersilia 1996)

Chapter 7 explains some changes that researchers and academicians need to pursue to connect with both policymakers and practitioners. If and when this is done, the anxiety about advocacy and science should subside as meaningful collaboration occurs among all the major actors who shape corrections policy.

The critical issues of the 1960s—the war in Vietnam, the civil rights struggle, and political upheavals—seemed so urgent that a careful, analytical, and scientific approach to problems was difficult, and at times, almost seemed inappropriate. Unfortunately, most of these issues have not gone away in the last thirty years. The race issue is still an urgent matter. In the field of corrections, racial disproportionality among jail and prison populations is one of the most critical issues. The cold war has ended, but social class and racial strife continue. South Central Los Angeles exploded in anger in 1992 just as it did in 1965. Can a value-laden, social scientific approach to these issues be of any help?

The obvious answer is affirmative and the pages that follow constitute my affirmative answer. Whether this value-laden approach is convincing and persuasive, only the reader will decide. My thoughts are not as optimistic as those included in *Community-Managed Corrections* (1988) but are much more grounded in the realities of the fiscal austerity and the general ideological conservatism of the late 1990s. The urgency to address these problems, however, is exactly the same as it was during the turbulent 1960s.

Indebtedness, Gratitude, Acknowledgements

Working in the corrections field, like working in any other, means collaboration, cooperation, and asking for and receiving support from co-workers. Thirteen years ago, as the state director of community corrections for Colorado, I met a caseworker in a residential program in Boulder, Brad Bogue. For reasons that still remain somewhat of a mystery, we "hit it off." After years of effort, Brad has worked his way up the ladder to become an influential leader in adult corrections in Colorado. In the interim thirteen years, my relationship with Brad has evolved from mentor, to co-learner, to student, to collaborator. His imprint on this book has been significant and for that I am grateful. If he had a less hectic schedule, he would have been a co-author of this book.

Penny Collins Brown is another person who deserves "honorable mention." I met Penny about sixteen years ago. She then was a supervisor in a halfway house. Since that time, Penny has been the director of three different residential community corrections programs, a state parole officer, the owner/operator of a small restaurant, the chief executive of a 600-bed county jail, an undersheriff, and now a superintendent of a juvenile detention facility. This synopsis explains the depth and breadth of her talents. The truly amazing thing is how well she has done all of these jobs. Her dedication to her work has been an inspiration to me. The future of the corrections field depends on recruiting, rewarding, and sustaining people like Penny Collins Brown.

In addition to the usual imperatives of death and taxes, writers also must come to grips with editors. My editor is Alice Fins, publications managing editor of the American Correctional Association. I was hoping for an uncritical cheerleader; what I discovered in Alice is a helpful, savvy, English professor. She maintained her patience and sense of humor through not one, but two, major rewrites of this manuscript. I applaud her editorial skills and am very appreciative of her assistance and that of her staff.

There are many others I have worked with whom I would like to acknowledge. Some are Paul Hoffman, Mario Salinas, Ted Rubin, Carol Lease, Adam Brickner, Betty Marler, Paul Katsampos, and several others. I am grateful to them all for their dedication, support, and critique when I needed it.

Roger J. Lauen

Section 1: Policy

There are two intended audiences for this book. They are: policymakers and correctional practitioners. For this book, policymakers are public and elected officials. More specifically, policymakers include: state legislators; judges; high level administrative types, such as the governor, the state director of corrections, and other influential types in the executive branch. Also included in this group are staff people who work for policymakers, such as people who attend meetings on behalf of policymakers and prepare legislative bills, policy papers, and proposals.

In years past, policymakers would not be included in this type of book. This book would be viewed as only relevant to correctional insiders, such as probation officers, parole board members, prison wardens, and the like. As recently as the 1970s, corrections budgets made up only a very small fraction (2 to 5 percent) of the general fund expenditures of most state governments and because of this, policymakers, the media, and the general public did not care much about correctional policy, goals, or objectives.

Things have changed within the last decade. Public expenditures for prisons and other correctional programs have increased three and four times as fast as public education, even faster than health care. Today, some state prison budgets are as large as the higher education budget. As a result, correctional policy is now on center stage.

From an elected official's standpoint, the only viable perspective on crime and punishment is tough, tougher, and toughest. Using criminal offenders as the base for a political campaign, as George Bush did with Willie Horton in 1988, is a simple and effective political script. Why consider any other approaches?

Actually, there are several reasons to consider political scripts that are something other than the "get tough" approach. The findings are now in, and they show:

- Correctional costs are sky high.

- Correctional expenditures are so high that they are competing with education funding and other important state and local services.

- The promise of safer streets by the "get tough" advocates has not materialized. Violent crime nationally and in most large urban areas is the same or up, not down.

- Violent crime for youthful offenders is up significantly, demonstrating the futility and uselessness of deterrence theory for young procriminal types.

- The over promising (more prisons = less crime) by legislators and district attorneys is just another contributing factor in the public's cynicism about political institutions.

The second compelling reason not to play the "get tough" card is that individual offenders are no less criminal after they serve a "tough" sentence than a "lenient" sentence. Most boot camp graduates have just as much trouble adjusting to community life as normal probationers do. The only difference between a "tough" and a "lenient" sentence is cost. "Tough" costs more, in most cases, a lot more.

Still another reason that "getting tough" is not a good idea is that "tough" legislation, "tough" governors and "tough" judges usually are following their personal ideologies or what they perceive as the public's crime fears. Personal or political ideology is not a good basis from which to formulate crime and corrections policy. Using theory is a much better way to go. Crime causation theory is based on social learning principles. "Get tough" legislation and policies are typically based on simplistic (do the crime and you'll do the time), unidimensional ideology and do not assume that people can learn and change.

For these and other reasons, "get tough on crime and criminals" may be the easiest route to political fame and fortune but has been disastrous for state and local budgets. Independent of the impact on crime or political careers, the impact of "get tough" legislation and policy on the daily practices of professionals in the criminal justice system is almost immediate. Some of this impact is incremental, some profound. For these reasons, a separate section of this book is dedicated to policymakers.

Chapter 1

A Statement of the Correctional Problem

This chapter presents the critical issues that are impinging on the field of corrections. Suggestions for improvement of these issues are offered throughout the book but especially in Chapters 8 and 13 and in Part II, which is intended especially for the practitioner.

We Got Tougher, but We Missed the Bad Guys

In our rush to "get tough" during the 1980s and 1990s, prison sentences were doubled and tripled in length (see Chart 1.2, page 11), and the number of offenses for which mandatory prison and life in prison sentences resulted has increased dramatically. The public purpose of this "get tough" movement was to capture and incapacitate the violent and dangerous offender, which in turn was supposed to make our streets safer. Contrary to conventional wisdom and the public's perception of criminal justice practices, most violent criminals are still on the street, not in prison.

ACA Public Correctional Policy on Sentencing

INTRODUCTION:

Changes in U.S. sentencing policies have been a major cause of an unprecedented prison population expansion in the past twenty years. The cost of constructing and operating prisons at a time of decreasing revenues is getting the attention of more and more elected officials who have to make difficult budget decisions. In addition, the absence of a noticeable reduction in adult crime rates as incarceration rates have climbed, raises serious questions about the efficacy of America's sentencing policies.

Sentencing policy today takes many forms. In some venues legislatures have taken authority over that policy, leaving little discretion in the sentencing of individual offenders to the judiciary. Under these circumstances "sentencing" discretion is shifted to the prosecutors and takes the form of plea bargaining and charge selection. In others, judges and parole boards retain wide discretion on a case-by-case basis. In still others, sentencing commissions have been given responsibility for defining how offenders are punished. Regardless of the form, sentencing policy directly affects what the correctional practitioner does on a daily basis, and to the extent that this policy fails in fairness and rationality, then our practice is adversely affected.

For that reason, we, as members of the American Correctional Association, have a vested interest in the sentencing policies which we must carry out. As implementors of these policies we have a unique vantage point from which to provide input on their effectiveness and consequences. If we do not provide that voice of our collective experience on this matter, then sentencing practices nationwide will fail to be as soundly based as they should be in this important public policy area.

The objectives of punishment, retribution, deterrence, incapacitation, and rehabilitation, while legitimate social goals, should be applied to the sentencing process which attempts to control crime as much as possible, at the lowest cost to taxpayers, in the least restrictive environment consistent with good public safety.

POLICY STATEMENT:

It is important for correctional professionals and their association to take an active role in voicing concerns and providing input into the establishment of sound sentencing policies. The American Correctional Association should actively promote the development of sentencing policies. Those policies should:

A. Be based on the principle of proportionality. The punishment imposed should be commensurate with the seriousness of the crime and the harm done;

B. Be impartial. Both the individual discretion exercised in sentencing and the policies that define how offenders are to be punished must be impartial with regard to race, ethnicity, gender, and economic status;

C. Include a broad range of options for punishing, controlling, and treating offenders;

D. Be purpose driven. Policies must be based on a clearly articulated understanding of the purposes they purport to have. They should be grounded in knowledge of the relative effectiveness of the various sanctions we impose in our attempts to achieve these purposes;

E. Encourage the evaluation of sentencing policy on an ongoing basis. The monitoring of the use of the various sanctions should be done to determine their relative effectiveness based on the purpose (s) they are intended to have. Likewise monitoring should take place to ensure that the sanctions are not applied based on race, ethnicity, gender or economic status;

F. Recognize that the criminal sentence must be based on multiple criteria. Consideration should be given to such factors as the harm done to the victim, the past criminal history, the need to protect the public, and the opportunity to provide programs for offenders as a means of reducing the risk for future crime;

G. Allow for recognition of individual case differences. Sentencing policy should provide the framework to guide and control discretion according to established criteria and within appropriate limits, but must allow for tailoring of sentences within those limits to fit each case presented to the court;

H. Have as a major purpose restorative justice—righting the harm done to the victim and the community. The restorative focus should be both process and substantively oriented. The victim or their representative should be included in the "justice" process. The sentencing procedure should address the needs of the victim, including their need to be heard and as much as possible to be and feel restored to whole again;

I. Community-based programs should be utilized for those offenders who, consistent with public safety, can be retained there;

J. Be linked to the resources needed to implement the policy. The consequential cost of various sanctions should be assessed. Sentencing policy should not be enacted without the benefit of a fiscal impact analysis. Resource allocations should be linked to sentencing policy so as to ensure adequate funding of all sanctions including total confinement and the broad range of intermediate sanction and community-based programs needed to implement those policies.

This Public Correctional Policy was unanimously ratified by the American Correctional Association Delegate Assembly at the Congress of Correction in St. Louis, Missouri, August 10, 1994.

The offense of conviction. Most convictions represent a negotiated plea and may not accurately reflect the original charge. However, quite often the original charge or charges reflect prosecutorial decisions and may not accurately reflect the actual offense. The prison inmate's offense of conviction provides a window on state criminal statutes, mandatory prison laws, police and prosecutors' priorities, and judges' sentencing patterns. Chart 1.1 illustrates the types of offenders in state prisons (by sentences served, not admissions) and the growth among those types of offenders since 1980.

CHART 1.1: Estimated number of prisoners in state prisons by most serious offense of conviction: 1980 to 1993

Offense Type	1980	1985	1990	1993	Percent Increase 1980 to 1993
All Offenses	295,819	451,812	684,544	828,371	+181
Violent*	173,300	246,200	313,600	394,500	+128
Larceny/Theft	14,300	27,100	34,800	34,700	+143
Auto Theft	3,500	6,300	14,400	20,400	+482
Public Order**	12,400	23,000	45,500	52,100	+320
Drugs	19,000	38,900	148,600	186,000	+878

*Violent offenses include: murder, rape, robbery, assault.

**Public order offenses include: weapons' violations, drunk driving, escape, court offenses, obstruction of justice, commercialized vice, morals and decency charges, and liquor law violations.

Source: Bureau of Justice Statistics 1994.

As is evident by examining Chart 1.1, increases occurred in all offense categories; however, the significant increases are in the nonviolent property, drug, and public order offenses. Offenders serving sentences for violent crimes increased the least of all categories.

The characteristics of offenders admitted to prison can also provide a perspective on sentencing practices and criminal justice policy priorities. In 1992, only 28.5 percent of all of the adults admitted to state prisons had been convicted of any violent crime. Almost three out of four adults admitted to state prisons

(70.5 percent) had been convicted of property, drug, or public order crimes (Bureau of Justice Statistics 1994). During the 1980s and 1990s, we got "tough" on criminal offenders, but we captured a higher proportion of the least serious offenders in the criminal justice net than we did of the dangerous and violent offenders.

An Example of Inappropriate Use of Prison

Rose Medina is locked up in a Colorado prison. She is about forty years old. Her sentence: life without parole. Unless the courts overturn her sentence or the governor commutes her sentence, she will die in prison. Her last offense of conviction: forgery. Her offense of conviction before that one: forgery. Her offense before that one: forgery. Rose was caught, charged, and convicted under a habitual offender law. During her last trial, her defense attorney was negotiating with the District Attorney for a sentence that was mutually agreeable to both sides. The best deal he got from the District Attorney was a twenty-year sentence. Rose thought twenty years in prison for forgery was ridiculous. She turned it down. With no agreement, the District Attorney persuaded the court to go for the maximum allowable sentence, life without parole. A young, insecure sentencing judge attempting to "make her mark" in a very conservative community agreed with the District Attorney's recommendation. Needless to say, there is a lot of room for a change of policy regarding prison use (See Chapter 8 for suggestions for change).

Making Prison Sentences Longer

Rose Medina's situation is instructive of what has happened to state criminal statutes and the impact of those new statutes on state prisons within the last ten years. Until about 1975, no one convicted of forgery, regardless of their prior record, received a life sentence without parole. That is no longer the case. Life sentences are becoming increasingly common. Also, until the early 1980s, the only offense that resulted in a life sentence was murder. That also is no longer the case.

The Colorado criminal statutes for murder provide an example of the increasing length of stay in prisons. In 1973, a life sentence was subject to the indeterminate sentencing structure. This meant that the state parole board decided when lifers were to be released from prison. The actual time served by lifers in 1973 was twelve-calender years, on average. In 1981, the legislature, upon the urging of local prosecutors, decided to lengthen prison sentences for murder. The law was changed to provide for a twenty-year minimum; after this, the parole board would consider release. In 1985, sentences for all offenses were doubled. Hence, murderers had to serve forty years in prison. Then in 1989, prosecutors and an ambitious state senator who was planning to run for higher office, changed the life sentence for murder to life in prison with no possibility for parole. Since 1993, Colorado legislators have been trying to figure out how to institute the death penalty for offenders convicted of murder.

The same process of gradually lengthening prison sentences has occurred for other offenses such as burglary, drug offenses, robbery, and rape. In the 1970s, a first-time burglar in Colorado served about eight-to-ten months in prison, a second-time burglar about twelve-to-fourteen months. Today, burglars receive ten-year sentences, and serve about 60 percent of that sentence. This is a dramatic increase in prison time served.

Chart 1.2 compares sentence length for adults in prison across the country between two important time periods, just prior to the national introduction of the "get tough on crime" era of the 1980s and about ten years after the "get tough" era was in effect. The Bureau of Justice Statistics has conducted two surveys of the length of prison sentences. The first survey included the length of prison sentences in twelve states in the late 1970s and early 1980s (Bureau of Justice Statistics 1984). The second survey included a sample of 300 counties and the length of prison sentences in those jurisdictions in 1992 (Bureau of Justice Statistics 1995). Comparing two surveys of noncomparable samples is hazardous. However, this comparison is not comparing apples and oranges; it is somewhat equivalent to comparing red apples to green apples. The comparison in a general way shows what has happened to the length of prison sentences during this twelve-year time span.

The percentage increase in length of time served in prison explains why prisons are crowded in the 1990s. A 90 percent increase in the time served for murder is a dramatic increase, but has less impact on prison crowding than a comparable increase for inmates serving time for rape. The reason: there were almost two-and-a-half times as many adults sent to prison for rape (21,655) as there were for murder (9,079). What appears to be a relatively small (23 percent) increase in the prison sentence length for burglary, becomes a prison management nightmare of

114,630 burglars admitted into state prisons in 1992 alone (Bureau of Justice Statistics 1994).

CHART 1.2: Length of Stay* in State Prisons (adults): 1980 versus 1992 (in months)

Type of Offense	1980 Sample**	1992 Sample***	Percent Increase
Murder	58	110	90
Rape	43	82	91
Robbery	38	54	42
Aggravated Assault	26	42	62
Burglary	22	27	23
Larceny	15	17	13
Drugs	17	21	24

*Prison time is actual time served, not sentence imposed.

**The 1980 sample included mean (arithmetic average) time served for these offenses.

***The lengths of time served for the 1992 sample estimates time served, calculated by the Bureau of Justice Statistics to be 38 percent of the length of the sentence imposed by the sentencing court.

Source: Bureau of Justice Statistics 1984 and 1995.

Corrections Populations: 1975 to 1994

Chart 1.3 illustrates the growth in corrections over the past twenty years. It only includes figures for the states; it does not include juveniles, those in the Federal Bureau of Prisons, or those in many types of community corrections programs.

CHART 1.3: Adults Under Correctional Supervision in the States: 1980 to 1994

Correctional Type	1980	1985	1994
State Prisons	305,458	452,372	958,704
Local Jails	158,394*	343,569*	459,804*
Probation	1.07 million	1.8 million	2.8 million
Parole	196,786	260,578	671,000

*Dates for jail inmate populations are: 1978, 1988, and 1993.

Source: Bureau of Justice Statistics, Special Report on Jail Inmates, Prisoners, Probation and Parole.

Chart 1.3 shows that the growth in all sectors of adult corrections is remarkable. No other country in the world ever has experienced anything comparable in a fifteen-year time span, unless one compares our present use of prisons with conditions of war. Perhaps the rate of growth in prisons was somewhat comparable under Stalin in the USSR between 1930 and 1950, or in South Africa under the apartheid system between 1950 and 1990.

Rates of Incarceration: 1930 to 1990

Taking a longer view of incarceration policies in the United States, Chart 1.4 illustrates the rate (number of adults locked up per 100,000 people in the general population) of incarceration from 1930 to the present. This chart includes both state and federal prisoners. Federal prisoners historically have accounted for about 5 percent of all adults in prison. Hence, the vast majority of inmates in Chart 1.4 are in state prisons.

CHART 1.4: Incarceration Rate for Adults in State and Federal Prisons: 1930 to 1994

Year	1930	1940	1950	1960	1970	1980	1990	1994
Rate of Incarceration (per 100,000 population)	104	131	109	117	96	138	293	387

Source: Bureau of Justice Statistics 1994.

There are four interesting features of Chart 1.4: (1) The incarceration rate was stable for almost forty years (about 100 inmates per 100,000), the incarceration rate was low for almost forty years. (2) The incarceration rate in 1940 was quite similar to the rate in 1980. (3) In the last ten-to-fifteen years, this stability has disappeared; incarceration rates almost quadrupled between 1970 and 1990. (4) The incarceration rate increased more from 1990 to 1994 than it did during the fifty-year period of 1930-1980.

ACA Public Correctional Policy on Crowding and Excessive Workloads in Corrections

INTRODUCTION:

Overpopulation of correctional programs and facilities can negate the effectiveness of management, program, security, and physical plant operations and can endanger offenders, staff, and the public at large. High population density within correctional facilities may be associated with increased physical and mental problems, more frequent disciplinary incidents, higher rates of assault and suicide, and decreased effectiveness in programs and services. When the population of a correctional program or facility exceeds capacity, maintaining safe and reasonable conditions of confinement and supervision becomes increasingly difficult, and may become impossible. Excessive workloads in institutional and community corrections dilute effectiveness of supervision and support services and threaten public safety.

POLICY STATEMENT:

The number of offenders assigned to correctional facilities and community services should be limited to levels consistent with recognized professional standards. Correctional agencies should:

A. Establish and maintain safe and humane population and workload limits for each institution and service program based on recognized professional standards;

B. Develop, advocate, and implement, in coordination with the executive, legislative, and judicial branches of government, emergency and long-term processes by which offender populations can be managed within reasonable limits;

C. Anticipate the need for expanded program and facility capacity by using professional population projection methodologies that reflect both demographic and policy-related factors influencing correctional population growth;

D. Advocate for the full development and appropriate use of pretrial/adjudication release, probation, parole, community residential facilities, and other community services that are appropriate for offenders that, as a consequence, reduce the number of offenders in crowded facilities; and

E. Develop, advocate, and implement plans for necessary additional facilities, staff, programs and services.

This Public Correctional policy was unanimously ratified by the American Correctional Association Delegate Assembly at the Winter Conference in Orlando, Florida, January 20, 1985. It was reviewed and amended January 16, 1991, at the Winter Conference in Louisville, Kentucky. It was reviewed without change January 16, 1996, at the Winter Conference in Philadelphia, Pennsylvania.

Prison Use in the United States Versus Other First-world Countries

How does the United States fare when compared to other, similar countries in its prison use? Chart 1.5 illustrates the rate of incarceration for first-world industrialized countries.

CHART 1.5: Rates of Incarceration in First-world Industrialized Countries

Country	Incarceration Rate	Year
United States	398	1989, year end
Canada	109	July 1986
New Zealand	106	1989
Scotland	95	1990
England and Wales	93	1990
France	82	1990
West Germany	78	1990
Australia	75	1990
Sweden	58	1990
Italy	57	1990
Norway	57	1990
Netherlands	44	1990

Source: Young and Brown 1993. The USSR is not included in this list. Perhaps Young and Brown did not consider the USSR a first-world industrialized country or because statistics were unavailable from the USSR.

The average rate of incarceration for all first-world countries listed, excluding the United States is 78 per 100,000. Hence, the United States' rate is more than five times that of our "sister" countries. The 1996 rate of incarceration in the United States is approximately 590 per 100,000 when adult county jail populations (jail rate is about 185/100,000) are included with state and federal prisons (Bureau of Justice Statistics 1995). The United States' rate is even higher if juvenile offenders are included.

Young and Brown (1993) caution against cross-national comparisons because of a lack of common definitions of terms. Some countries count pretrial (remand) populations along with sentenced populations; in the United States, we do not. Some count misdemeanors and felons together, most do not, including the United States. However, even taking these problems into account, the United States relies more heavily on incarceration, than other first-world, industrialized countries.

Much has been written about why the incarceration rate in the United States is so much higher than than in comparable first-world, industrialized countries, but there is no concise conclusion or consensus that explains why the United States' rate is so out of sync with the rest of the world (Young and Brown 1993). The United States does have a much higher rate of violent crime, but crime and incarceration rates are unrelated. While the United States pursues a very reactive and punitive policy toward crime, other countries, especially Northern European countries, attempt to address the sources of crime, engage in crime prevention, and use rehabilitative approaches for criminal offenders (Currie 1985, Young and Brown 1993).

Macroeconomics and Crime and Justice

Is there any connection between economics and prison use? Generally, the progressives on the left side of the ideological continuum answer affirmatively; the conservatives say no. Quite a bit of academic and research work exists on this topic.

Culture determines a society's penal climate. For example, countries that have a highly individualistic and competitive ethos, premised on notions of meritocracy and equal opportunity, and have substantial gaps between rich and poor are likely to be comparatively severe in their penal outlook. Also, the greater a society's tolerance of inequality, the more extreme is their scale of punishment (Young and Brown 1993). From this perspective, the individualistic society views punishment as a negative reward, just as positive rewards in the form of higher incomes and more social status are bestowed on those who succeed in business or professional careers (Young and Brown 1993).

In the United States, the top 1 percent of the population own almost 40 percent of all the wealth. By contrast, the top 1 percent of the British population own about 18 percent of the wealth. The bottom 20 percent of the population in the United States earn only 5.7 percent of all after-tax income paid to individuals (Bradsher 1995). These income distribution figures are constantly in flux. However, as Chart 1.6 shows, since 1979, the wealthiest people in America have increased their riches.

CHART 1.6: The Rich Are Getting a Lot Richer: Changes in Average Family Income, 1979 to 1994

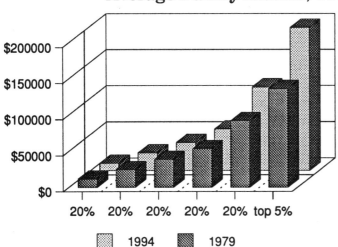

Source: U.S. Census Bureau, all income in 1994 dollars.

In the words of Elliott Currie, a criminologist at the University of California at Berkeley:

> The evidence for a strong association between inequality and crime is overwhelming. Denying it requires what we might politely describe as a highly selective interpretation of the facts. And we are unlikely to relinquish our status as the most violent of developed societies if we do not confront that hard and uncomfortable reality.
>
> (Currie 1985)

Currie states that the inequality associated with high rates of crime involves more than differences in income alone. This income and crime connection is complex and multifaceted.

The distribution of income and wealth is very skewed in this country. In developing countries, it is even more maldistributed than in the United States. However, in most other first world countries, especially in Northwestern Europe, the opposite is true: there is a much more equitable distribution of income and wealth (Crossette 1996). As shown in Chart 1.5, in most European countries, prison use is considerably less than in the United States. This concentration of wealth among an extremely small segment of the United States population lends credence to Young and Brown's thesis that a society's tolerance of inequality is highly correlated with punitive corrections' policies.

More Prisons Have Not Reduced Crime

One of the most important societal purposes of correctional supervision, if you believe pronouncements by public and elected officials, is crime reduction or crime containment. Given the historically unprecedented increase in correctional supervision since 1980, we might reasonably have expected the crime rate to decline in approximate proportion to the numbers of adults under correctional supervision (see Chapter 4 for an in-depth discussion on crime trends). Using the most current crime philosophy, deterrence, one also assumes that criminals take heed of corrections policy; the tougher the prison/punishment/incapacitation system is, the less inclined criminals are to commit crimes.

Unfortunately, these policy assumptions are incorrect. As prison, jail, and other corrections populations increase, crime rates have remained quite stable. Violent crime constitutes a very small (8 to 12 percent) proportion of all crime, but commands most of the public's attention, especially through print and television media (see Chapter 3). Society's most severe sanction, incarceration, should be aimed at the most violent and dangerous offenders, but as Chart 1.1 shows, most offenders "doing time" are nonviolent property and drug offenders. Huge increases in jail and prison use have not made a dent in violent crime. Crime victims report increases in violent crime. Police reports of crime show increases in some areas, slight decreases in other areas, and a stable pattern in still other areas. Chapter 4 provides a more detailed analysis of crime patterns. Hence, there does not appear to be any relationship between corrections' policy and crime rates, especially violent crime rates.

Pennsylvania: A Case Example

For many years in Pennsylvania, experts used crime rates to predict future prison bed needs. However, during the 1980s, other factors were recognized. Between 1985 and 1990, the general adult population in the state increased 4 percent, reported index crimes increased 6 percent, adult arrests increased 32 percent, the adult probation population increased dramatically, the local jail population increased 126 percent, but state prison inmates increased a whopping 152 percent. Hence, the direct correlation between crime and imprisonment was not valid (at the time of this study and still is not), and the prison population prediction formula had to be revised. Other factors, such as the political climate of the state legislature, had to be taken into account.

In spite of only minor increases in crime in Pennsylvania during the 1980s, the use of prison as a correctional sanction increased dramatically. In 1980, 32 percent of convicted offenders received a prison sentence; ten years later, 64 percent of the convicted offenders were sent to prison. In 1980, the average length of a prison sentence was slightly more than twenty-seven months; in 1990, the average length had increased to thirty-four months. These criminal justice system changes were policy-level changes unrelated to the number and types of crimes committed.

Analyses of offenders during this period (1980 to 1990) revealed the following: offenders were returning to prison at a greater rate than previously recorded, and drug law violators were being sent to prison with greater frequency and given longer sentences than before. Using deterrence-theory reasoning, violent crime should have decreased as prison use increased. Unfortunately, the opposite happened. Violent crime rates and state prison populations rose simultaneously. Hence, a massive increase in prison use had no impact on violent crime.

The implications for risk and classification decisions are obvious. If Pennsylvania policymakers instead had increased criminal sanctions only on high-risk, high-needs offenders, they might have saved the state millions of dollars of capital construction costs for new prisons and tens of millions of dollars in increased operating costs for prisons in future years. For example, between fiscal year 1981-1982 and fiscal year 1992, state costs for human services increased at an uneven rate. Education costs went up 56 percent, health costs were up 66 percent, welfare costs rose 81 percent, transportation costs were up 85 percent. Correctional expenditures, by stark contrast, increased *263 percent* during the same period!

In its zeal to "get tough" on offenders, the legislative brush used to change the criminal code was unnecessarily broad. The new "get tough" policies included low-risk drug users and technical rule violators on parole. Had objective risk assessment instruments been used to identify low-risk offenders, they could have been statutorily excluded from prison. Had they done that, prison expansion probably could have been avoided altogether (Center for the Study of Law and Society 1992).

The impact of more prisons on the crime debate has been raging for several years. The literature on this debate was presented in the first and second editions of *Community-Managed Corrections* (Lauen 1988, 1990). Advocates for increasing the number of prisons contend that crime rates would have been much higher if prison populations had remained stable. They provide little or no evidence to support such a claim, but claim it nonetheless.

Privatization Movement

In the early nineteenth century, numerous prisoners were either leased to private companies that set up shop in prisons or were used by prison officials to produce finished goods for a manufacturer who supplied raw materials to the prisons. This arrangement continued well into the twentieth century. Neither private employers nor public prison officials were concerned much about the well being of prisoners, which led to widespread abuse of prisoners and poor working conditions inside of prison. The organized labor movement brought attention to this issue, and the publicity surrounding prisoner abuse led Congress during the late 1930s to pass laws designed to prohibit the manufacture and movement of prison-made goods in interstate commerce (National Institute of Justice 1985 and Roberts 1997).

ACA Public Correctional Policy on Correctional Industry

INTRODUCTION:

Correctional industry programs, whether operated by the public or private sector, aid correctional systems in reducing idleness, lowering costs, and providing opportunities for offenders to gain job skills, training, and economic self-sufficiency and to participate in programs of victim compensation and institution cost-sharing.

POLICY STATEMENT:

Correctional industry programs, operating under sound management principles and effective leadership, should:

A. Be based on statutes and regulations that support the development, manufacturing, marketing, distribution, and delivery of correctional industry products and services;

B. Be unencumbered by laws and regulations that restrict access to the marketplace, competitive pricing, and fair work practices except as necessary to protect the offender and system from exploitation;

C. Provide evaluation and recognition of job performance to assist in promoting good work habits that may enhance employability after release;

D. Provide training and safe working conditions, for both staff and offenders, similar to those found in the community at large;

E. Ensure that the working conditions in an industry operated by public or private organizations are comparable with those in the industry at large, and that compensation to inmates is fair;

F. Recognize that profit-making and public service are both legitimate goals of an industry program;

G. Support reinvestment of profits to expand industrial programs, improve overall operations, maintain and upgrade equipment, and assist in the support of inmate training programs that enhance marketable skills, pre-release training, and job placement services; and

H. Integrate industry programs, public or private, with other institutional programs and activities under the overall leadership of the institution's chief administrator.

This Public Correctional Policy was unanimously ratified by the American Correctional Association Delegate Assembly at the Congress of Correction in San Antonio, Texas, August 23, 1984. It was reviewed January 17, 1991, at the Winter Conference in Louisville, Kentucky, without change. It was reviewed January 18, 1995, at the Winter Conference in Dallas, Texas, with no change.

The current debate regarding the use and role of private companies in the corrections business has shifted within the last fifteen years. Prior to 1980 approximately, the debate was about a reasonable division of labor between public financed and run corrections programs and the role of private firms performing a few functions in a cooperative manner with the public sector. Today, the debate has shifted to whether to dramatically reduce the role of the state and to redraw the line between what is properly and historically governmental and what is private. What this means in an increasing number of localities is a wholesale transfer of ownership and operation of corrections programs and the very authority to operate such programs (McDonald 1992).

ACA Public Correctional Policy on Private Sector Involvement in Corrections

INTRODUCTION:

Although most correctional programs are operated by public agencies, there is increasing interest in the use of profit and nonprofit organizations as providers of services, facilities, and programs. Profit and nonprofit organizations have resources for the delivery of services that often are unavailable from the public correctional agency.

POLICY STATEMENT:

Government has the ultimate authority and responsibility for corrections. For its most effective operation, corrections should use all appropriate resources, both public and private. When government considers the use of profit and nonprofit private sector correctional services, such programs must meet professional standards, provide necessary public safety, provide services equal to or better than government, and be cost-effective compared to well managed governmental operation. While government retains the ultimate responsibility, authority, and accountability for actions of private agencies and individuals under contract, it is consistent with good correctional policy and practice to:

A. Use in an advisory and voluntary role the expertise and resources available from profit and nonprofit organizations in the development and implementation of correctional programs and policies;

B. Enhance service delivery systems by considering the concept of contracting with the private sector when justified in terms of cost, quality and ability to meet program objectives;

C. Consider use of profit and nonprofit organizations to develop, fund, build, operate, and/or provide services, programs, and facilities when such an approach is cost-effective, safe, and consistent with the public interest and sound correctional practice;

D. Ensure the appropriate level of service delivery and compliance with recognized standards through professional contract preparation and vendor selection, as well as effective evaluation and monitoring by the responsible government agency; and

E. Indicate clearly in any contract for services, facilities, or programs the responsibilities and obligations of both government and contractor, including but not limited to liability of all parties, performance bonding, and contractual termination.

This Public Correctional Policy was ratified by the American Correctional Association Delegate Assembly at the Winter Conference in Orlando, Florida, January 20, 1985. It was reviewed August 15, 1990, at the Congress of Correction in San Diego, California, with no change. It was reviewed January 18, 1995 at the Winter Conference in Dallas, Texas, with no change.

This move toward privatization came about primarily because the public sector was having difficulty keeping up with the increasing demand for prisons. A secondary factor was the claim that private prisons could be run less expensively and more efficiently than public ones.

Colorado's state constitution, like many, perhaps most states, requires legislators to stay in the black and not incur public indebtedness. In the early 1980s in Colorado, the legislature decided to expand the prison system but was unable to find money to do so. They turned to private financial institutions for money to build prisons. A financial gimmick called "certificates of participation" were developed to get around the state prohibition of public indebtedness. In spite of the fact that there was no public discussion regarding this important change in public policy, the build now/pay later arrangement was instituted in 1982 and continued until about 1992. This arrangement stopped only when it became public that the state was paying hundreds of millions of dollars in interest payments to private financial firms.

Private prisons now exist in at least thirteen states, but less than 2 percent of all inmates are housed in them (Ramirez 1994). However, most states contract with private firms to supervise and treat adult and juvenile offenders in various community programs. From these early examples of privatization, we know that staff salaries are much lower at private prisons than in the public sector. The same pattern exists in the private community corrections sector. Staff in private community corrections programs are paid significantly less than their counterparts in probation and parole. Given this staff-salary differential, private corrections programs have become a training ground for public sector employment. People get a job in a private-for-profit community corrections program and wait for an opening in probation or parole or other parts of the corrections system. Usually, entry-level employment criteria are less demanding in the private sector than in probation or parole. Some of the impacts of this public/private differential on private programs include the following: staff turnover rates in private programs are high, staff morale is low, and the general quality of services is low (McDonald 1989, Lauen 1994, Sullivan and Purdy 1995).

Do private prisons reduce public corrections costs? Some claim they do (Logan and McGriff 1989). Others claim they do not (Immarigeon 1985).

Independent of the cost issue, the emergence of private prisons creates yet another interest group committed to building more prisons. As a result, private prison lobbyists join district attorneys, crime victims' groups, private construction companies, correctional officers' unions, private financial institutions, county officials seeking to place a prison in their economically marginal hometown, and many others who have a financial, political, or organizational self-interest in advocating more prisons (Butterfield 1995).

The national prison debate needs fewer people with a financial or political self-interest and more people with a public perspective. Further, this issue needs a broader range of participants, more public discussion including more open forums for the public to hear arguments pro and con and in which the public can ask questions and get straight answers. When and if this occurs, a wider range of the public will demand higher quality services, improved public safety, more effective correctional programs for inmates and community corrections clients and hopefully, restrict prison use for violent and dangerous offenders.

Where Does the Money Come From for All These New Prisons?

The national and local political mood in late 1995 was to lower taxes and lower the federal deficit by decreasing the cost of the public sector. The result is less public money available to do what the public sector has historically done—pay for services to the poor, the elderly, the indigent, as well as public services such as road construction and maintenance, schools, mental health care, and other areas. As strong as the "less government is better government" mood is, the "get tough on criminals" mentality is far stronger, as seen in the priorities for public spending. In 1991, Americans spent $20.1 billion to build and run prisons for 1.1 million inmates. During the same year, Americans spent about the same amount of money ($22.9 billion) for 13.5 million people on Aid to Families with Dependent Children or welfare (Feldman 1992).

The fiscal conservatism that now dominates both major political parties seems to apply to all public expenditures—except prisons. State general fund appropriations for corrections increased from $8 billion in 1987 to $14 billion in 1991 (Hunzeker 1992). In 1996, it is at least $20 billion and climbing. In California alone, between fiscal year August 1982 and August 1990, state expenditures for prisons increased 321 percent, from $419 million to $1.76 billion (Blue Ribbon Commission 1990). For a total correctional-expenditure figure, it is necessary to add local county jails, federal prisons, and local, state, and federal juvenile institutions. This author's conservative estimate of the current total correctional expenditures is at least $30 billion a year.

At the present time, the federal government is borrowing money to continue operating, and state governments are cutting back public expenditures due to taxpayers' resistance to raising new revenues. Yet, the question remains: from where is all the money coming to build and operate more prisons? The short answer is that the old revenue sources, such as income taxes, property taxes, and sales taxes are no longer the primary sources for prisons. The longer, more complicated answer is that the new source of prison revenue is coming from other existing governmental services, usually public education funding.

ACA Resolution on Fiscal Responsibility for Correctional Legislation

WHEREAS, the percentage increase of the correctional population of the United States during the last decade far exceeds the percentage increase of crime or of the general population;

WHEREAS, a causative factor of overcrowding and excessive workloads in the corrections system is the passage of additional laws without the accompanying appropriation for implementation;

WHEREAS, the net effect of the above often creates overcrowded facilities and results in court ordered early releases; and

WHEREAS, any legislation that will increase the size of the correctional population must also include fiscal appropriation for implementation;

THEREFORE BE IT RESOLVED, that the American Correctional Association supports the requirement that legislators assess the cost of sentencing laws and other correctional initiatives and provide the necessary funding at the time the laws are passed.

This resolution was adopted by the American Correctional Association Delegate Assembly on August 1991, at the Congress of Correction in Minneapolis, Minnesota. It was reviewed and reaffirmed August 10, 1994, at the Congress of Correction in St. Louis, Missouri.

California is an example of a state that already has begun the shift of funding from pubic education to prisons. State spending for corrections increased 25 percent from fiscal 1990-1991 through 1993-1994 (to $3.3 billion), while funds for higher education declined by 25 percent (to $4.4 billion). The $4.4 billion in higher education funds supports 139 public colleges and universities that enroll about 2 million students. The $3.3 billion prison budget supports 120,000 adult inmates. At the present time, existing higher education programs are being cut, while new prisons are being built each year (Salahi 1994, Gottfredson 1995).

In Indiana, over the last fifteen years, the state's share of the University of Indiana's operating budget has fallen from 30 percent to 24 percent. To make up for the loss of state support, student tuition was raised. Tuition used to make up 30 percent of the university's operating budget, but now accounts for 43 percent of it. University president, Myles Brand, attributed the loss of state support to legislators' belief that funds must be concentrated on such "immediate needs" as the prison system (Gottfredson 1995).

The same trend can be seen in Colorado. Between fiscal year 1981 and 1989 in Colorado, state expenditures for social services increased 141 percent, expenditures for K-12 education increased 97 percent, spending on higher education increased 91 percent, and prison expenditures increased 389 percent. Colorado, Indiana, and California are the norm, not the exception.

The cost shift from public education and other existing governmental services to prisons is not publicly announced and has not been scrutinized carefully by legislative or executive branch staff, or the print and TV media. Expenditures for public education are a much better, more productive long-term public investment than prisons. If we continue to rob the schoolhouse to pay for the jailhouse, we will not fulfill our societal promise to educate the public and simultaneously will build correctional institutions that further exacerbate the social isolation that already exists between rich and poor and black and white people.

Another source of funds is the inmate population themselves. In spite of the fact that most jail and prison inmates are poor, elected officials are beginning to charge jail and prison inmates for their keep. Arizona requires inmates to pay a utility fee if they have a television. Connecticut and Missouri charge inmates for the expense of their confinement. New Hampshire compels inmates to repay the cost of state-provided lawyers. Texas demands part of an inmate's wages earned from any work program outside the prison (*New York Times* 1996). The trend to charge inmates for their confinement is driven by political, not fiscal pressures. It is a subcomponent of the "get tough" movement. For those few inmates who enter jail or prison with substantial financial resources, it may be reasonable to ask for some compensation. However, these few inmates will not make a dent in the overall cost to the public of housing, feeding, and guarding more than a million adults now incarcerated.

Quality Control of Correctional Programs by Local and State Officials

The last issue impacting on the field of corrections is the quality control of institutional and community corrections programs. The most important tool for corrections professionals committed to operating high quality programs has been the development of national operating standards. These operating standards were developed by local, state, and federal practitioners, and put into the field in the late 1970s by the American Correctional Association. This accreditation movement was modeled after other accreditation efforts in schools, hospitals, and the airline industry (Keve 1996).

As a former accreditation officer for a local county jail, this author can attest to the effectiveness and comprehensive scope of the national standards. However, an accreditations system is no panacea for program improvement; it is simply a tool and a means to improved operations. Nevertheless, many hundreds of corrections programs around the country have been improved dramatically with the aid and guidance of the American Correctional Association's standards.

Due to the explosion of correctional populations (see Chart 1.3) since 1980, correctional managers have faced intense pressure to open new programs and facilities, make room for more offenders on nonresidential caseloads, squeeze more residential clients into programs that were designed for fewer people, double and triple bunk inmates in jail and prison cells originally designed for one person, and find construction and operating capital for an increasing number of correctional clients.

In the midst of this doubling, tripling, and sometimes quadrupling of correctional clients, a new breed of correctional professional has entered the corrections scene: the private entrepreneur. There is nothing inherently evil about a private entrepreneur, but private entrepreneurs must figure out how to make enough money to make it worth their while. If not, they move to other areas to make money. The emergence of the private entrepreneur in corrections simultaneously obligates the public to monitor the quality of these "outside" programs.

In the estimation of this author, neither private nor public corrections programs are being carefully monitored for quality of service (Lauen 1995). Part of the problem is the explosion of correctional clients. Another part of the problem is that some correctional administrators use the crowded conditions as an excuse for running shoddy programs. Yet another reason is the unwillingness of correctional practitioners and administrators to challenge the dominant "get tough" mood.

Quality control of corrections programs is first and foremost a public sector concern. The public, through legislative decree and executive branch management, must consistently and exhaustively monitor, evaluate, and maintain high-quality correctional programs. For the most part, this is not now being done in most community corrections programs. In select areas, private for-profit community programs are beginning to create a "space monopoly" whereby they exploit the public's need for space by dictating their terms of operation, especially the cost of service. They threaten public officials with program closure if the public does not meet their demands. The demand for program space is so acute that public and elected officials go along with this manipulation and coercion (Purdy and Dugger 1996). Fortunately, this is not a widespread problem, but it provides an example of an unexpected outcome of correctional crowding.

Evaluations of correctional programs can take the form of standards compliance or assessment of a variety of societal objectives, such as crime control, reduction of recidivism, and provision of substance abuse treatment. The American Correctional Association standards and accreditation process has been the primary method of standards compliance around the country. Besides the American Correctional Association standards, little if any effort has been made to carefully assess what specific societal objective a jail or prison is trying to meet. Is it incapacitation only? If so, the only thing to monitor is the quality of daily living conditions. However, most people have tougher, more demanding questions about failure/success rates upon release from jail or prison. If post-release success is a consideration, a whole new set of elements must be monitored, scrutinized, and evaluated. To this author's knowledge, jails and prisons are not being measured against a recidivism standard. Why not? Community corrections programs are measured against a recidivism standard, why not state prisons and local jails?

Orville Pung, a former correctional officer in Minnesota who worked his way up the ranks to the state prison commissioner, is a man of vision. He knew very well that prisons realistically could meet only a very narrow societal objective, namely punishment. To promise anything other than punishment (denial of freedom) was pure folly. However, it takes a dedicated professional to meet even that narrow standard of punishment. Prison food must be good and nutritious, emergency medical care must meet professional standards, all staff and inmates must know about emergency procedures and be competent enough to carry them out. To meet other societal objectives, such as a 10 percent reduction in recidivism from the previous year, is tough and would require a shift in organizational policy.

The point is this: the field of corrections must have narrowly prescribed goals and objectives. These goals and objectives need to be made explicit to all three branches of government and the public at large. Once this consensus is reached, then all correctional programs can and should be continuously monitored and evaluated to ensure compliance. Anything less is a sham and a violation of the public's trust.

ACA Public Correctional Policy on Purpose of Corrections

INTRODUCTION:

In order to establish the goals and objectives of any correctional system, there must be a universal statement of purpose which all members of the correctional community can use in goal setting and daily operations.

POLICY STATEMENT:

The overall mission of criminal and juvenile justice, which consists of law enforcement, courts, and corrections, is to enhance social order and public safety. As a component of the justice system, the role of corrections is:

A. To implement court-ordered supervision and, when necessary, detention of those accused of unlawful behavior prior to adjudication;

B. To assist in maintaining the integrity of law by administering sanctions and punishments imposed by courts for unlawful behavior;

C. To offer the widest range of correctional options, including community corrections, probation, institutions, and parole services, necessary to meet the needs of both society and the individual; and

D. To provide humane program and service opportunities for accused and adjudicated offenders which will enhance their community integration and economic self-sufficiency, and which are administered in a just and equitable manner within the least restrictive environment consistent with public safety.

This Public Correctional Policy was unanimously ratified by the American Correctional Association Delegate Assembly at the Congress of Correction in Chicago, Illinois, August 11, 1983. It was reviewed January 17, 1990, at the Winter Conference in Nashville, Tennessee, with no change. It was reviewed January 18, 1995, at the Winter Conference in Dallas, Texas, with no change.

Summary

It is not likely that all these issues and problems can be dealt with, not to mention solved. However, those of us who are attempting to improve the field of adult corrections must have a good grasp on all the factors that are impacting the field at any given time. The list of factors in this chapter is quite daunting and the task of making changes and improvements in the field is an extremely challenging one.

Chapter 2

The Political Context
of Corrections

Some History of Crime Policy

Most historians peg the beginning of modern criminology to the Enlightenment Period, in the late eighteenth century. Cesare Beccaria's name inevitably is associated with this early period. Beccaria usually is hailed as someone who brought the field of criminology and criminal justice out of the dark ages and into modern, more civilized thought.

Beccaria was highly ideological in his views and after the publication of his treatise (*Dei delitti e delle pane*), was denounced as atheistical and seditious. In contemporary terms, Beccaria was a libertarian. His core beliefs included:

1. Restrictions on individual liberties imposed by criminal law should be kept to an absolute minimum.

2. The nature of the offense should be clearly and precisely defined so as to avoid discretionary interpretations and arbitrary action.

3. Punishments should be no more severe than strictly necessary to dissuade the offender, and others who might be tempted to follow, from repeating the offense.

4. Punishments should be laid down according to a rational tariff to prevent judicial tyranny.

5. Punishment should be inflicted swiftly and surely to achieve maximum effectiveness (West 1985).

A careful reading of the United States Constitution reveals that most of Beccaria's beliefs were incorporated into our federal laws. However, in due course, many of Beccaria's objectives were abrogated due to the crush of criminal cases impinging on the criminal justice system and "tinkering" with criminal statutes in such as way as to punish the powerless and protect the powerful. As a result, one of the basic tenants, swift punishment, was lost and the entire concept of deterrence is inoperable. In spite of this, deterrence continues as one of the most enduring correctional justifications for criminal sanctions.

What Is Best: Ideology or Theory?

The larger issue is the role of ideology in the formation of corrections' policy. Is ideology the best way to go? Are there other approaches that might serve society's interests of public safety and adherence to societal norms in a fair, equitable manner?

Ideologies, according to Donald West, a British criminologist who specializes in juvenile delinquency and was a principal investigator of the Cambridge Study on Delinquency Development, are global and simplistic, more like articles of faith, supposedly true for all times and places, and not to be challenged by fresh observations. Ideological appeals play well in the political arena, where sound bites are the norm and careful examination of the facts is the exception. This is why, in an era of corporate downsizing, there is a loss of real monetary value as the cost of living increases, and a shift from high-paying manufacturing jobs to low-paying service jobs, along with globalization of labor markets wherein manufacturing jobs move from $10 to $20 an hour at United States sites to $1 to $5 an hour in foreign countries, and simplistic calls for public safety and order are popular. The working man and woman are scared and economically insecure.

There is a better way: to rely on theory, not ideology. Theory is a much better way to discuss and formulate corrections policy. Theories, unlike ideologies, are partial explanations, to be adhered to temporarily until such time as improved theories emerge capable of more fully explaining phenomena of criminal behavior. Theories, then, are plastic, flexible, and ever changing. They may incorporate new ideas, especially ideas that have withstood the test of empirical scrutiny and testing. Less definitive ideas generated from theory do not lend themselves to political sound bites, yet it is in the political arena where most corrections policy is being made now.

By contrast, ideologically based policies, whether radical or conservative, are inflexible, indiscriminate, and neglectful of empirical inquiries, which is antithetical to the research community whose business it is to test ideas as a means of building sound theories. Basic knowledge of crime causation and effective correctional intervention cannot be developed without pilot programs and fairly sophisticated evaluation designs, random assignment to control and experimental groups, and data collections. These efforts cost money and take time. In the political arena, these types of experiments are not seen as "tough," and the outcomes are not definitive. Also, theory construction through rigorous research takes several years; political time frames are very short, one year, usually less. Hence, research and theory construction and politics are on different tracks.

Are Elected Officials in Touch With Their Constituents Regarding Crime Issues?

Do the views of state legislators accurately reflect the opinions of constituents? If so, representative democracy is working; if not, something is fundamentally flawed in our system of government. As it turns out, the answer depends on the nature of the issue. Elected officials were accurately "in touch" with their constituents on civil rights issues, but "out of sync" with constituents on foreign affairs and social welfare issues (Miller and Stokes 1963). That was twenty years ago.

More recently, Bill Bradley, in an autobiographical account of his years as a United States Senator, admitted that the words that came out of his mouth were not his but fabrications of what he thought his audience would like to hear. In his words, "For much of my career I had no authentic political voice. I had been campaigning all over the country not to change the world or shake up my audiences but to please the roomful of people to whom I was speaking" (Toner 1996). Elected officials work hard to stay in touch with what the political pundits and pollsters tell them, which may or may not reflect the needs or wishes of the public.

Are Policymakers Leading, Following, or Manipulating?

Do public and elected officials know what the public wants out of the corrections system? If they know what the public wants, are they delivering whatever that is? When these issues were measured carefully by survey research, the findings were quite instructive (Pasewark 1981, Gottfredson and Taylor 1982, Doob and Roberts 1982, Canadian Sentencing Commission 1987, Roberts and Grossman 1990, Schoen 1995). While policymakers (legislators, judges, high-level administrators) feel that the public prefers the goal of incapacitation (preferring prison over other correctional alternatives), the public assigns incapacitation their second-lowest priority. Similarly, while policymakers feel that the public supports the goal of retributive justice (an eye for an eye), this goal actually is given the lowest priority by the public (Gottfredson and Taylor 1982). Given this lack of correspondence between policymakers and their constituents' views, it was no surprise to discover that policymakers think that the public would not be supportive of rehabilitation programs, when in fact the public strongly supports such an approach (Gottfredson and Taylor 1982, American Correctional Association 1995).

Ironically, when policymakers' views on correctional goals were measured against constituents' views, there was overall agreement. Lack of agreement only emerged when the policymakers' perceptions of their constituents' attitudes were measured (Gottfredson and Taylor 1982). Without a clear and precise notion of what the public wants, policymakers are not in a position to deliver the type of corrections system and services that the public wants.

For political survival purposes, public and elected officials have a self-interest in appearing "tough on crime," which may play a significant role in maintaining the gap between elected officials' attitudes and beliefs and their perceptions of the public's attitudes and beliefs. Any other public posture other than "tough on crime" is viewed as political suicide. A "get tough on criminals" stance in political campaigns is easy to develop and deliver, plays well in the media, and wins elections. The ethical issue is whether elected officials are making any systematic attempt to understand the public's feelings or are they manipulating the public's crime fears for short-term political gain and thereby avoiding the complex and long-term causes of crime? Dealing with the symptoms (as seen in the annual FBI crime reports) holds little prospect of reducing the actual rate of criminal activity.

Further, elected officials hold out incarceration as the standard against which all other correctional placement options are measured. If an offender receives a probationary sentence, elected officials, and parts of the public, are likely to view this as "getting off" and not sufficiently punitive. Given this, some parts of the public and most elected officials advocate incarceration in jails and prisons as the "only" appropriate legal sanction for criminal offenders (Schoen 1995).

The Public's Perception of Crime, Criminal Offenders, and Corrections

If the public knows very little about crime and crime causes, a punitive or reactive response to crime should be of little surprise. As it turns out, this is precisely the case. For example, the public overestimates the victimization rate (the number of people in the general population who are crime victims) for violent crime. While the actual violent crime rate is fewer than four incidents per hundred residents each year (in Ohio), only one citizen in twenty perceived the rate to be that low (Knowles 1984).

In Canada, approximately 5 percent of all reported crimes involve violence. However, when asked to estimate this percentage, three-quarters of the public estimated that violent crime to be 30 to 50 percent of all crime (Doob and Roberts 1983). Also in Canada, most people believe (erroneously) that the murder rate has increased since capital punishment was abolished (Doob and Roberts 1982).

The crime/prison debate, if nothing else, is perceptions of reality, not reality itself. Between 1980 and 1996, most of the public and many policymakers thought that crime was growing by leaps and bounds, when, in fact, this was not the case. However, based on that misperception or the purposeful manipulation of that perception, hundreds of new jails and prisons were built.

The public's knowledge of sentencing also is lacking. If the public thinks that a ten-year sentence for robbery actually will be much less, their belief in the system's sense of justice will be minimal. A survey conducted by the Canadian Sentencing Commission found widespread ignorance of sentencing by the public. For three high-frequency offenses (assault, burglary, and robbery) most people estimated sentences to be much more lenient than was the case. For example, in Canada, approximately 90 percent of offenders convicted of robbery are sent to prison. When the public was asked about the incarceration rate for this crime, fully 75 percent of the respondents estimated it to be under 60 percent (Canadian Sentencing Commission 1987). Hence, the public's knowledge of how much crime occurs, the amount of violent crime, and the workings of the criminal justice system leave much to be desired.

The public's views of crime causes determine their enthusiasm or tolerance for particular crime-control strategies. There will be little support for crime prevention through social development among those who view offending as an individual aberration rather than a consequence of adverse social conditions. As it turns out, the public's understanding of the causes of crime are multidimensional and emphasize economic and environmental factors. Reasons for crime in the public's view range from poor parenting, individual motivation, and unemployment. Reasons given for crime will vary depending on whether the public is asked why crime occurs in general or why particular individuals commit crime. Economic reasons are given as explanations for general criminal activity (Roberts and Grossman 1990). These views of crime causation could explain, at least in part, why the public is receptive to community sanctions and not a heavy reliance on incarceration.

Citizens of both the United States and Canada appear willing to invest more money in nonpunitive, nonrepressive responses to crime. When Americans were asked to choose between spending money on more prisons, police, and judges, or on better education and job training, two-thirds endorsed education and job training (Gallup 1989). When Canadians were given a choice between spending money on prison construction or on developing better alternatives to incarceration, fully 70 percent chose the later (Canadian Sentencing Commission 1987). A 1995 survey found that fully 75 percent of those polled agreed with the statement, "a balanced approach of prevention, punishment and treatment is better at controlling and reducing crime than imprisonment alone" (American Correctional Association 1995).

In spite of this rather enlightened public perspective on social development over more punitive measures, policymakers' perceptions of the public are off the mark. Because the public's knowledge of how the criminal justice system works and the scale and nature of crime is fundamentally incorrect, using the public's feelings as justification for particular policy directives makes little sense—except if you are not at all interested in representing the public's perceptions, understandings, and wishes.

Who Wins and Who Loses?

If there are any "winners" in this "get tough" approach to crime, who are they? Elected officials, especially state legislators, are the first and clear set of winners. Prosecuting attorneys are the second group of winners, due to their professional role of representing the state (on behalf of crime victims) in criminal cases. The political alliance between legislators and prosecutors, oftentimes collaborating with crime victims and occasionally with correctional officers, is what is at the core of the prison construction frenzy. The "get tough" approach is a winning political script.

Also, there is no room for debate between "tough" and "soft" positions on crime and its prevention. Given this clear dichotomy, every prosecuting attorney and elected official is playing the "tough" card. Even the few thoughtful, knowledgeable, and brave elected officials are "tough" at election time and "tough" when it comes time to vote on a high visibility criminal justice policy or proposed bill in the legislature.

Who are the losers? The losers are the general public, crime victims, property owners, taxpayers, jail and prison staff, not to mention the "correctional consumers," the inmates. The general public and crime victims are losers because crime has not changed significantly in spite of the fact that the number of people in prison has tripled in the last fifteen years. The streets are not safer today than they were ten years ago; hence, the promises of safer streets made by prosecuting attorneys and state legislators were bogus.

Jail and prison staff are losers because they work inside the correctional institutions. It was never easy to be a jail or prison correctional officer. Until 1970 or 1980 (depending on which part of the country you were in), jails and prisons usually ran at something less than 100 percent of capacity. Now, it is "normal" to operate a correctional institution at 130 to 150 percent of rated capacity. Operating at overcapacity results in extremely high stress levels. Inmates are agitated because of their crowded living conditions. Staff are agitated because inmates are angry and filing complaints and lawsuits regarding living conditions. With patience and tolerance almost nonexistent, more verbal disagreements and fights occur, and suicide rates, substance abuse, and staff turnover rates are very high.

Jail and prison inmates are the last and largest set of losers. They lose because they now are forced to live with one (sometimes more) additional inmate per cell. This is typically a cell that was designed for one person, not two. What this means is that two adult men (95 percent of the time) live in a space not much larger than a walk-in clothes closet. And they live in the walk-in closet not for a few months as they did as recently as 1980, but for many years.

Adult inmates typically have somewhat more emotional, psychological, and socio-economic problems than the society at large, which means adjustment to these cramped conditions does not happen easily or quickly. The United States Constitution is our legal contract with prison inmates and the Eighth Amendment of the Constitution prohibits jail and prison conditions that constitute cruel and unusual punishment. It does not matter that large segments of the general public are not sympathetic to the impact of crowding on inmates. Many jails and prisons have been found in violation of this Eighth Amendment protection. So, inmates lose, and lose big time. On a secondary level, the public loses again by paying exorbitant legal fees in Eighth Amendment jail and prison lawsuits.

Playing the "get tough" card in the political arena has been such a hit that there seems to be a continuous search for new "get tough" avenues to explore and exploit. The most recent example, the "three strikes and you're out" movement, blew across the country with hurricane force, starting in the State of Washington in 1993. Two years later, the movement touched virtually every state in the country as well as the national congress and many local units of government.

Some public and elected officials are now advocating a purposeful reduction in the quality of life inside of prison as a way of "teaching them a lesson," or "reducing recidivism," or other such wishful thinking. This group suggests the removal of television sets, recreational activities and education programs as a means of making prison a more undesirable place than it already is. What is not understood is that the critical element of incarceration is the loss of freedom, not whether an inmate has an up-to-date weight room. Incarceration is the ultimate punishment because it segregates an individual from all that is meaningful in life. Reducing the quality of prison life will not improve recidivism. If this were the case, the crowded conditions inside of most jails and prisons within the last ten years should have reduced the normal 35 to 50 percent recidivism rates long ago. This has not occurred and will not in the future.

Summary

The current ideology towards crime and criminal sanctions (out of sight out of mind, and eye for an eye, get tough, throw away the key) serves short-term political objectives quite nicely. However, the public's desire to have safe streets continue to go unmet. Not until public and elected officials figure out how to gain and maintain public office on a less ideological, more rational (theory-based) basis will any significant change occur.

Chapter 3

The Role of the Media
in the Presentation of Crime

The Murder News

WSOC in Charlotte began its newscast one evening in the fall, 1995. Lead stories: murder suspect arrested. Drive-by shooting at church. Armed robbery. Truck slams into Pizza Hut. Truck slams into Wendy's. Truck crashes on highway. Truck crashes, spills glue. Couple killed in gasoline fire. Rock climber falls to his death. Man drowns in boating accident. Baby drowns in swimming pool. Cut for commercial (Budiansky 1996).

Americans are bombarded with violent news, much of it about crime. How the media presents crime is of critical importance to the public's understanding of the causes and possible remedies for crime. Public opinion polls have documented the public's fear of crime and have found that crime fears are out of proportion to the actual incidence of crime (Chaiken and Chaiken 1983). A good bit of that fear emanates from the presentation of crime in the print and television media. Independent of the source of crime information, crime fears have far outstripped the actual incidence of crime.

This chapter analyzes how crime-related stories are presented by the media, who is involved in constructing crime stories, what slant the stories take, what impact crime stories have on the public, and finally, we will see if there is an impact, how that impact plays out in correctional terms.

ACA Public Correctional Policy on Violence Reduction

INTRODUCTION:

Of utmost concern to the public and those working both in the criminal and juvenile justice systems is the increasing fear of violence in our society. Particularly troubling is the marked escalation of violence among our youth, especially involving the use of firearms. While national data indicate that the violent crime rate overall has declined in recent years, the severity of violent acts and the perception of potential personal injury have risen sharply. There is a sense that the risk of becoming a homicide victim has grown, that the occurrence of gun-related violence is increasing, and that widespread drug trafficking, substance abuse, and gang activity are directly linked as causal factors to this problem.

POLICY STATEMENT:

Traditionally, the response of the criminal justice system—and recently within some segments of the juvenile justice system as well—has been deterrence, punishment and incapacitation. While research shows that violent behavior is often related to continued exposure to violence in families, schools, communities, and through the entertainment media, the criminal and juvenile justice systems are in a unique position to assume a more active, focused role in violence reduction and prevention. In particular, corrections professionals and agencies can impact violence through their work directly with offenders and indirectly through their support of violence prevention policies. Specifically, corrections professionals and agencies should:

A. Train corrections staff early on in their work with offenders to recognize those risk factors that contribute to violent behavior and to utilize effective intervention strategies and techniques to reduce violence within this population;

B. Design and implement effective substance abuse treatment programs utilizing a wide range of modalities so that a continuum of interventions appropriately addressing substance abuse is available to all offenders in need and seeking help;

C. Provide offenders and their families counseling and parenting skills training programs that emphasize the need to break the "cycle of violence" whereby a childhood history of physical and psychological abuse predisposes the victim to become a perpetrator of violence in later years;

D. Integrate conflict resolution models into institutional and community treatment programs so that offenders and their families can be taught conflict resolution and life skills competency techniques as effective alternatives to violent behavior;

E. Establish victim/awareness programs which bring more balance to the system by allowing victims an increased role in the justice process and by requiring offenders to confront the results of their violent acts, thereby contributing to the restoration of the offender, victim and community;

F. Provide effective community supervision—including comprehensive, integrated parole and aftercare services—that promotes community protection, aids in the development of offender skills and competency, and holds the violent offender accountable;

G. Initiate across all points of processing within the juvenile justice system a comprehensive approach to the prevention, treatment and remediation of violent behavior among youth;

H. Support a long-term crime reduction strategy that draws on interdisciplinary research and addresses the causes of crime and violence in a comprehensive and integrated manner, including providing employment opportunities, strengthening families, building strong neighborhoods, increasing community involvement, enhancing the quality of education and other social institutions;

I. Build partnerships that improve communication and collaboration and share technologies, information, and intelligence among the key stakeholders in the criminal and juvenile justice systems, elected officials, and the community to combat violence;

J. Support firearm control legislation and measures to reduce deaths, injuries, and suicides from firearms and reduce their availability to violent offenders and juveniles; and

K. Support mass media campaigns against violence and efforts to encourage the media and entertainment industries to adopt practices that deglamorize violence.

This Public Correctional Policy was unanimously ratified by the American Correctional Association Delegate Assembly at the Congress of Correction in Nashville, Tennessee on August 21, 1996.

The Paradox of Crime News

There are a number of paradoxes regarding crime news. Not all of the paradoxes are the creation of news agencies, but many are embellished and exaggerated by print and television media. Some of the paradoxes include:

1. Women and the elderly have the highest fear of crime and the lowest probability of becoming crime victims (Will and McGrath 1995).

2. White crime victims get the greatest media coverage in spite of low rates of victimization, relative to nonwhite victims (Will and McGrath 1995).

3. Crime news stories are up (Media Monitor 1995); general crime rates are not.

4. Crime news stories depict random stranger-to-stranger crime when in reality, most person crimes (murder, rape, aggravated assault) are acquaintance-to-acquaintance crimes.

5. Nonviolent property and drug crimes (possession and sales) constitute the vast majority (85 to 90 percent) of all crimes committed, but media presentations of crime are overwhelmingly violent (Barak 1995).

6. In news stories, most crime victims are over thirty when in reality most crime victims are young, under thirty.

7. Media stories depict crime perpetrators and victims as individuals. Rarely, if ever, do crime stories include corporate perpetrators and large classes of victims, in spite of the fact that the economic impact of corporate crime far outstrips street crimes, such as burglary, theft, and robbery (Wright, Cullen, and Blankenship 1995).

Some of these paradoxes are the result of poor information or ignorance. Others are purposeful distortions of reality. The origin of these paradoxes are explored later in this chapter.

The News Content

Choosing particular events over others is an important part of the social construction of crime. The media consistently chooses individual criminal events to portray on the daily news. Deliberate decisions by large corporations, such as the Ford Motor Company's decision to continue building the Ford Pinto, in spite of the fact that the position of the gas tank was hazardous and oftentimes exploded when hit from the rear, are rarely presented by the media (Wright, Cullen, Blankenship 1995). The media has the same problem that criminal justice personnel have: it is difficult, complex, and time consuming to investigate and authenticate corporate misdeeds. It is much easier to pick up the "news" on the police scanner, which is a constant source of criminal activities.

However, listening to the police scanner to the near exclusion of everything else results in a very distorted picture of crime; in other words, the content does not correspond to the actual incidence of crime (Davis 1951, Sheley and Ashkins 1981, Doob 1985, Randall, Lee-Simmons and Hagner 1988). Content studies of television reveal that 87 percent of televised crime consists of murder, robbery, kidnaping, and aggravated assault. The two most dominating media crimes are murder and robbery, with murder constituting nearly one-fourth of all crime portrayed. Even using the FBI's official crime statistics, which are police reports of street crimes and exclude most white collar crimes, violent person crimes only account for about 10 percent of the total of all serious, felony crimes (Barak 1995).

In addition to the crime-laden news media, there are "true crime" genre books and magazines (*True Detective, Bad Blood, Fatal Vision*), movies (*To Catch a Killer*), talk radio, television talk shows, and, increasingly, prime time television crime shows (*NYPD Blue*) (Durham 1995). However, the print and TV media are the prime sources of crime information for most people. Graber (1980) found that 95 percent of a panel of citizens indicated that the mass media was their primary source of crime information. Given this, inaccurate media portrayals of crime may result in public perceptions that reflect significant misunderstandings of complex crime and justice issues (Durham 1995).

In 1994, the three major television broadcast networks (ABC, NBC, CBS) aired nearly 2,000 crime stories, or more than six stories per night. Crime accounted for more news stories than the economy, health care reform, and the midterm elections combined. Since the early 1990s, television's attention to crime has more than tripled. Overall, crime coverage increased from 632 stories in 1991 to 1,949 stories in 1994. In 1991, the average network newscast aired about four crime stories a week. By 1994, that total had risen to two crimes stories every night on each network (Media Monitor 1995).

In 1995, crime news increased 32 percent more than 1994, and 52 percent over the 1993 totals. The rate of the increase in crime stories is quite phenomenal. Chart 3.1 illustrates the number of news stories shown on TV in 1995.

CHART 3.1: TV News Stories in 1995

Topic	Number of Stories
Crime	2,574
Bosnian Conflict	1,101
Health Issues	925
Economy	710
Federal Budget	592
Russia	501
Elections	485
Race Relations	377
Israel	316
Japan	309

Source: Media Monitor 1996.

The Rocky Mountain Media Watch in Denver surveyed 100 local TV programs in 58 cities on a single night, September 20, 1995. They discovered a dreadful sameness about TV programming. The typical half hour "news show" offered about twelve minutes of "news," more than 40 percent of it depicting violent crimes or disasters.

Max Frankel, a veteran news commentator and writer, describes this presentation of the news, as "recklessly disturbing the peace." An unnamed prominent television executive says it is wrong to even think of these half-hour news programs as ventures in "news." He described them as "spot deliverers," meaning they are low-cost noisemakers looking to attract the largest possible audience for ads whose revenues the news station keeps entirely for itself (Frankel 1995).

News stories about crime emphasize the randomness of criminal events (Sacco 1995, Brownstein 1991, Barak 1995). In so doing, the fear of crime is democratized, that is, it places all people on the same plane for risk of victimization. In fact, this is not the case. Most violent crime is not random, but instead is a result of angry outbursts between well-known friends, family members, and lovers.

To be objective and fair, the crime content of news stories should mirror the actual incidence of crime. Yet, crime in the United States has not changed much in the last ten-to-fifteen years (see Chart 4.3). Television networks are presenting crime in a way that would lead the public to believe that crime is much more prevalent and violent than it actually is and has been. The issue is *representativeness*. What is presented to the public is not representative of what the real crime scene is. For example, where are the TV stories about the savings and loan scandal, which cost taxpayers billions of dollars and made many a small group of prominent people extremely wealthy within a few years time? This was a news story for only a very short time. Yet, taxpayers will be paying for this multibillion dollar fraud for years to come.

Why So Many Crime Stories?

Why do news agencies give so much coverage to the topic of crime? There are many reasons, some of which are described below. Yet, not all individuals agree that there should be less crime coverage. According to David Simon, a crime reporter for the *Baltimore Sun*, there should be more crime coverage. However, Simon is not happy with the format and the type of crime news. He thinks that both print and TV media exploit the visual attributes of crime (a body on the ground, a body in a body bag, a cop charging through a door, a victim crying about her loss) and do not give enough attention to the substantive attributes, such as the social, economic, and political factors surrounding a crime event. Without this substantive information, strange (unrepresentative) images are created such as good guy/bad guy dichotomies.

Simon describes how his newspaper editors gave him all the space he wanted when a crime victim was white and the perpetrator was African-American. In another case, when the victim was African-American, the space allocated for the story was minimal. The news editors that Simon reports to know that their economic livelihoods depend on Nielsen and Arbitron ratings. The imagery of violence sells well, that is, it enhances ratings. Therefore, reporters are rewarded financially and professionally for presenting crime stories with this particular slant (Nieman Reports 1994).

Another reason for so many crime stories in the media is that stories are easy to prepare and readily available. The lack of factual complexity associated with the ordinary crime story generally means that it can be easily written and edited by news workers. Additionally, the routine crime story is a rather uncomplicated matter, and it is unnecessary for news workers to assume that readers or viewers require an extensive background to appreciate the story (Sacco 1995).

Crime occurs all the time, especially in large urban areas where newspapers and TV stations are located. Hence, there is an unlimited supply of available crime stories from which to choose. However, crime stories must fit in with all the other news, so the demand for crime stories varies depending on other noncrime stories. Depending on the size of the news "hole," crime coverage may be expanded or contracted in compensatory fashion. Crime stories are the news hole fillers because crime stories are constant, everything else is variable (Sacco 1995).

News Sources

When crimes are committed, the normal way they come to the public's attention is by private citizens reporting them to police. So, how does the news media find out about crime? What is their source of information? Hypothetically, the news media could discover crime from any of the following sources: private citizens, the police, district attorneys, public or private defense attorneys, judges, correctional practitioners, parole board members, criminologists, published data describing criminal events and crime trends, crime victims, and other possible sources.

As it turns out, the overwhelming majority of information obtained by the news media comes from one source, the police. According to Sacco:

> . . .the relationships that link the police to news agencies serve law enforcement as well as media interests. The police role as the dominant gatekeeper means that crime news is often police news and that the advancement of a police perspective on crime and its solution is facilitated. It has been argued that this results in the adoption of an uncritical posture with respect to the police view of crime and the measures necessary to control it. More generally, the frame of reference offered by a government bureaucracy or other recognized authority with respect to crime problems may only infrequently be called into question and, as a consequence, competing perspectives may become marginalized.

> (Sacco 1995)

As most people in the criminal justice system know, the police "take" on a criminal event may sometimes be accurate, sometimes not. Prosecuting and defense attorneys dedicate their entire careers to debating the veracity of police depictions of crime. The point is this: if news agencies accept police descriptions of crime events, they get only one version of the criminal event.

Further, news accounts of crime events based on police descriptions rarely, if ever, provide any historical, social or economic perspective surrounding the crime. With this type of background information, different understandings of the crime event usually emerge. Often, the crime victim is implicated in complex but involved ways in the crime. Also, with this background information, different crime control strategies are suggested, such as safe houses for battered women, substance abuse treatment for both the perpetrator and the victim, a decent paying job for the perpetrator, and other considerations. With complete background information, it is difficult to maintain the simplistic dynamic of bad guy/helpless victim.

Nevertheless, gathering background information on crime events is problematic for the news industry. To obtain background information takes time (as most probation officers know so well when preparing a presentence report). News agencies set hourly deadlines that rarely permit the allocation of several days of work on the background of a single crime (unless it involves a well-known event or a prominent person).

The media and the police share an important feature of their work: the police confront criminal events each day; the media rely on and use discrete crime incidents each day. In this way, the relationship between law enforcement and the media is quite symbiotic.

Examples of Slanting the News

North Carolina Fire in Chicken Processing Plant

An example of how news reporting puts particular slants on events is the coverage of a fire in a chicken processing plant in North Carolina in 1991. Ninety people were working in the plant at the time, twenty-five died and fifty-six were injured. The plant sustained extensive damage and the community lost its largest employer. Survivors of the fire reported that exit doors had been either locked or blocked, severely hampering their escape from the fire. The locked doors were only the tip of the iceberg. The plant was more than 100 years old, had no working plantwide sprinkler system, no windows to provide alternative escape routes, and too few exit doors in critical areas. In its eleven years of operation, the plant had never been inspected by state safety inspectors. The state insurance oversight agency found the plant in violation of nine sections of the building code and six state laws.

A content analysis was done of ten newspapers, representing a cross section of national print media. Researchers then created content categories that measured important dimensions of the case, such as cause, harm, intent, responsibility, and sanctions. These categories were used to code the stories of the fire. The findings: of the ten newspapers, nine covered the plant fire. Of these, five ran the initial news of the fire on the front page. Over the course of the first week, the priority of the story faded as follow-up reports were placed further back in the paper.

The newspapers detailed the enormous harm from the plant fire and did not define the case simply as an industrial accident or the result of worker negligence.

The print media depicted corporate violence and did not seek to localize responsibility in terms of having bad luck (accident) or blaming the victims (the plant workers). Yet, the newspapers showed little consciousness that corporate violence might be seen as a criminal act. Newspaper accounts of the fire did not describe the workers' deaths as homicides and did not suggest that plant owners should or might be prosecuted as any other criminal. In other words, the media was not proactive, but reactive. Instead of describing the fire as a potential criminal offense, the news reports socially constructed the worker's deaths as a breakdown in government safety regulations (Wright, Cullen, Blankenship 1995).

Colorado's Summer of Violence

In the summer of 1993, the media participated with others to create a "summer of violence." As the media (both print and TV) portrayed it, young thugs and gang members were ravaging the streets of Denver, creating chaos and making threats of victimization to the entire populace. What was really going on was the governor was running for reelection. He met with the district attorneys and others in the law enforcement establishment. Between them, they "created" the summer of violence. The media, seeing an opportunity to improve ratings, was a willing participant in this fabrication. In fact, the level of violent youth crime in 1994 was less than the previous year, when no such public pronouncements were made. The results of this political, criminal justice, and media collaboration was a special legislative session that authorized the expenditure of many millions of dollars for more prisons, the governor was reelected, the relations between elected officials and criminal justice leaders were solidified; the media's role was confirmed, and violent crime by youth remained the same (Prendergast 1996).

New York City Crime Wave Against the Elderly

In the mid-1970s in New York City, there was an apparent wave of crime against the elderly. The local print and TV media ran numerous stories on crimes against the elderly and concluded that the city was in the midst of a crime wave. This reporting resulted in both heightened public perceptions of the risks of crime and an increase in public fear. This all happened in spite of the fact that police data indicated that the crime wave essentially had been a fabrication of the media (Fishman 1978, Durham 1995).

There is a Better Way

There are different ways to present crime to the public. A TV station in Austin, Texas has developed a unique approach that seems to be working. Starting in early 1996, Austin's ABC affiliate, KVUE-TV, has been trying to present crime news based on some established criteria that related to the general community's interest and was not geared exclusively to ratings and the economic bottom line.

The criteria were developed by Carole Kneeland, news director and Cathy McFeaters, executive producer of KVUE-TV. The criteria emerged after Kneeland and McFeaters listened to citizens in a series of community meetings on the quality and slant of news coverage. Citizens were almost unanimous in their feeling that news coverage overemphasized crime, particularly violent crime. After many months of listening, they incorporated the thoughts of citizens into five crime news selection criteria:

1. Does (community) action need to be taken?

2. Is there an immediate threat to (community or public) safety?

3. Is there a threat to children?

4. Does the crime have significant community impact?

5. Does the story lend itself to a crime-prevention effort?

A few weeks after adopting the criteria, several heinous crimes occurred. The other TV stations covered them, of course. In the words of Jeff Godlis, news director for K-EYE-TV, "When someone gets killed, that's news." But KVUE stuck to their new policy. None of the crime incidents met their criteria and none of the stories were aired. The results have been quite positive, even in the view of the chief of police, Elizabeth Watson. She states: "I think it's commendable for a major TV news station to really take a look at responsible reporting. Sensationalized reporting fuels fear. It makes people feel powerless." The ratings for KVUE-TV have not been damaged by covering crime with a more responsible community focus (Holley 1996).

Media distortion of crime is not helpful if the goal is to reduce prison use, and especially to reduce the racial disproportionateness inside of prisons. Citizens and other groups must organize to put pressure on local television networks to present crime that reflects the actual incidence of crime and balances crime stories with important local, national, and international news events.

On a more constructive vein, media can be an important aid in educating the public about the stability of crime in spite of the incredible increase in jail and prison use and correctional expenditures. This message would go a long way to help the general public understand how crime and prison use are not connected, how crime is a very complex social phenomenon and prison use is a result of arbitrary choices of public and elected officials acting in their own professional and political self-interests.

Impact of Media Distortions of Crime

The research literature on this topic is equivocal, that is, it is unclear how much of the public's fear of crime results from the presentation of crime by news agencies and how much is the result of talking with friends or neighbors about a crime event (Sacco 1995). However, distorted and exaggerated media depictions of crime influence the public's opinion about crime in general, and are major contributors to the public's fear of crime, especially violent crime, and place a reliance on established crime control techniques (more cops, more prisons).

Summary

According to Schlesinger and Tumber (1994), crime reporting is an especially appropriate domain for exploring contemporary problems in the public sphere. In so doing, crime reports provide a small window through which much larger and more urgent questions concerning the legitimation crisis of institutional authority in contemporary society may be viewed. Crime and crime reporting in recent years have aroused heated debates over the authority and independence of the police and criminal justice system, the political appropriation of crime by conservative law and order politics, and the racist and sexist assumptions that frame popular conceptions of the social order (Schlesinger and Tumber 1994).

Crime-related information should come from specialists who know about crime causation, crime trends, crime victimization, and other specialized crime topics. The sole reliance on police as the source of crime information must change. In the words of Gregg Barak:

> If we are ever to approach anything resembling rational crime control, then we need to think and talk about crime in terms other than alarmist outrage. By engaging the mass media, criminologists and others can interact in the social production of crime and justice representations that the public consumes daily as the prevailing ideologies. In doing so, the news making criminologists must attempt to consciously alter the public's perceptions and understandings of crime and justice. In confronting the prevailing myths, stereotypes, and biases concerning crime and justice in America, criminologists can interrupt the "smooth passage of regimes of truth," disrupt those forms of knowledge about crime which have assumed a self-evident quality.
>
> (Barak 1995)

Perhaps the best and most classical example of a criminologist successfully interjecting a "different view" into the popular culture was Edwin Sutherland's introduction in the 1940s of the concept of "white collar crime."

Chapter 4

Crime: Rates, Theories, Descriptions

Background: How Crime Policy Is Constructed

If this book were written only for practitioners in adult corrections, they might perceive that a chapter on crime was redundant. Probation officers and jail staff deal with crime and criminals on a daily basis. However, this book has other audiences, including state legislators and college students. The typical legislator thinks a lot about crime because crime is a popular topic on constituents' minds. However, many legislators' understanding of crime may come primarily from the 10 o'clock news and not from a scientific or from a broad knowledge base. This is also true for most students.

Even some people working in the criminal justice system may be uninformed about the causes of crime. Without a good understanding of the causes, remedies will be off the mark. The retiring chief of police of New York City issued his ideas on crime in the newspaper under the title: "How to Win the War Against Crime." His plan included five points: (1) delegate more decision-making power to precinct commanders, (2) provide a computerized system (ComStat) so police will have better data with which to solve crime problems, (3) make busts of all crimes, serious ones as well as minor ones, (4) do better detective work, develop and follow leads, and (5) increase wages for police (Bratton 1996).

Yet, in the opinion of this author, the New York City/Bratton crime plan is quite typical of how law enforcement officials view crime and how to "fight" it.

What is interesting is that there is not a word in this plan that relates to 100 years of crime theory. For example, from criminological theory, we know that antisocial attitudes are learned from people in their immediate family and social group(s). Crime values are formed at an early age and blossom in teenage years (peak age for males is 16.8 years). A procriminal lifestyle is a result of many different risk factors, such as antisocial attitudes and beliefs; procriminal associates; temperamental and personality factors conducive to criminal activity; a history of antisocial behavior; a family history of attitudes conducive to procriminal beliefs and values; low levels of affection, caring and cohesiveness in the family of origin; and low levels of personal achievement in education, vocation, or financial (employment) status. It is strange that a law enforcement veteran would not either know the crime literature or choose to ignore it in favor of narrow organizational interests.

By contrast, a criminologist's plan to fight crime would recommend assaulting (to continue to use warrior or warlike language) antisocial attitudes (by promoting prosocial activities such as healthy leisure time activities, and volunteer work); cutting ties with antisocial peers; fostering social bonding and intrafamily affection, encouraging commitment and involvement (turning off that TV and engaging in recreation with your kids!); and participating in extensive academic and vocational training (Andrews, Leschied and Hoge 1992, Andrews and Bonta 1994).

One significant difference between the chief of police of New York City and criminologists is that the chief of police has access to a bully pulpit. By contrast, criminologists talk to themselves at esoteric, low-visibility conferences a few times a year. Legislators assume that they should pay attention to those with bully pulpits and lots of "air time," that their opinions are valuable, almost to the exclusion of others. Crime and corrections' policy thus is shaped (this is but one way, there are others) in ways that are inconsistent with decades of aggregated knowledge about who commits crime and why.

Yet, carefully constructed and rigorously tested crime theories can and should guide correctional practice. However, when correctional theory is bad, it leads to mistakes in policy and practice. Theories of crime have supported the torture and killing of thousands of human beings who were entirely innocent of the alleged wrongdoings. "Witches" have been burned at the stake. Mental and moral "unfits" have been sterilized, institutionalized, and killed. Persons have been incarcerated for long periods based on ill-founded predictions of their future behavior. Such atrocities have been committed in the name of fighting crime and evil and have been rationalized by the theories of crime causation that were dominant at the time (Brown, Esbensen, Geis 1991).

An example of out-of-date or outmoded theory is Lombroso's concept (1870s) of physical attributes. He said that people with weird-shaped heads are more likely to be criminal than those with "normal" heads. Lombroso's motivation was not to demonize particular types of people, even though some people interpreted his findings in this manner. Today, demonization of criminals is a frequent media and political topic. Ideologically and financially motivated academicians working closely with conservative policy organizations describe criminals as "fatherless, Godless, and jobless, a national wolfpack of conditioned superpredators" (Shapiro 1996). Demonization of criminals paves the way for criminal justice and corrections' policy to continue to operate in a highly ideological manner and justifies more punitive corrections policies—without the benefit of criminological theory.

Nevertheless, bad theory can be based on faulty or inaccurate data, such as the theory generated between 1925 and 1950 based only on police reports. This exclusive reliance on police reports (and other theoretical and methodological mistakes) led social scientists to believe that only low-income people committed crimes. Further, bad theory also can be generated from small unrepresentative samples, or from theory that has not been vigorously tested and retested, debated, and criticized by professional peers.

The objective of this chapter is to describe macrolevel crime trends and microlevel descriptions of who commits crimes, at what ages, the role of race and social class, and some explanation (theories) of why some people commit crimes. Hopefully, with this broader understanding of crime, public and elected officials will be more thoughtful in their legislative, judicial, and administrative decisions when dealing with crime prevention or reduction.

The Big Picture: Crime in Abundance

The first important point is that there is a lot of crime in the United States of America. Whether one talks about crime from a legal, moral, social, or psychological perspective, there simply is a lot of it. Why the United States has more crime than similar first-world countries has not been fully explained. Canada's homicide rate is 2.8 per 100,000 (Statistics Canada 1992); the rate in the United States is 7.9 (Kalish 1988). To make matters worse, the United States' murder rate is increasing. In 1993, the number of murders was 23,271, up from 18,954 just four years earlier. The 1993 rate was 9.5 per 100,000 (Sourcebook 1994). There are more (749 in 1990) murders in Philadelphia, the "city of brotherly love," than in all of Canada (between 500 and 600) in a given year (Uniform Crime Report 1990, Currie 1985). Crime is a large-scale social phenomenon in this country.

The second important thing to understand about crime is that it changes all the time—but not much. Large-scale shifts in crime types or volume rarely occur. The minor fluctuations of crime types and volume published each year by the Federal Bureau of Investigation can be explained in large part by macroeconomic (massive shifts in jobs) or demographic changes (at-risk males increasing or decreasing in number). Crime statistics in the following charts illustrate these general points.

Crime Trends: 1973 to 1993

Crime trends over the last twenty years are the driving force behind the "get tough" movement of the 1980s and 1990s, or at least the general public was led to believe that they were (see Chapter 2). The implication, until very recently, was that crime was an irrepressible force, growing and becoming more threatening year after year. Given this depiction, the "only responsible" public policy was to increase jail and prison use and put a stop to (or at least dramatically curtail) the crime "monster." Chart 4.1 illustrates crime trends in the United States over the past twenty years.

CHART 4.1: Rates* of Crime as Reported by Police and Crime Victims: 1973 to 1993

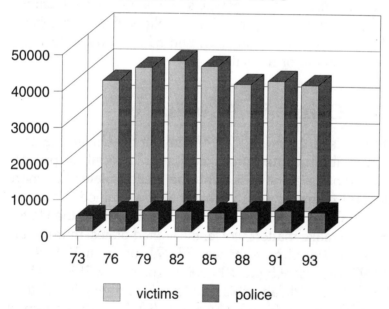

Sources: Police reports are from the Federal Bureau of Investigation, *Uniform Crime Reports*; crime victims' information is from Bureau of Justice Statistics, *Criminal Victimization Reports*.

The difference between the police reports (about 5,000 per 100,000) and crime victims' reports (about 36,000 per 100,000) is the gap between what crime victims actually experience and the amount of crime reported to police. Independent of the numeric differences between the two reports, the overall trends in both police and crime victim reports are quite similar. From 1973 to the early 1980s, both sources indicate an increase in crime. From the early 1980s to 1993, police reports show a decline, an increase, and another decline. During the same period, crime victims report a decline and then a general stabilization into the early 1990s, with select crimes decreasing slightly. Stepping back a bit from both police and victim reports, it is fair to say that neither group reports a dramatic increase nor decrease (crime victims show more of a decrease than police) in crime since 1979, certainly nothing comparable to the increase in crime reported by both police and victims during the 1970s.

When particular types of crime are examined, there are differences between police and crime victims' reports. Police reports show: (1) murder reached a peak in 1980 and then declined until 1985, and then increased somewhat after that, but never reached the 1980 level, (2) rape, aggravated assault, larceny/theft, and motor vehicle theft are higher than ever before (Uniform Crime Report 1995). By contrast, crime victims present a different picture, see Chart 4.2.

CHART 4.2: Criminal Victimizations: 1973 to 1991 (crimes reported by victims; number of crimes per 1,000s)

Year	Total Crimes	Violent Crimes	Personal Theft	Household Crimes
1973	35,661	5,350	14,970	15,340
1978	40,412	5,941	17,050	17,421
1983	37,001	5,903	14,657	16,440
1988	35,796	5,910	14,056	15,830
1991	34,730	6,424	12,533	15,774

Source: Bureau of Justice Statistics 1995. Note: Survey technique changes introduced in 1992 do not permit the use and comparison of more current victimization data.

Crime trends, as seen by crime victims, reveal the following: the overall rate of crime is fairly stable, violent crime is up somewhat, personal theft is down, and household crimes increased during the 1980s but returned to 1970s level by the early 1990s.

Crime in the United States is a persistent national problem. Both violent and property crimes are unacceptably high. Yet, as shown in Chapters 2 and 3, actual crime trends do not match the media and elected officials' portrayal of crime. Overall crime is not increasing by leaps and bounds.

Very recently, in a few areas of the country, the number of crimes reported to police actually decreased. This is the case in New York City in 1995. Policing practices have been shifting from traditional (two officers cruising in a squad car) to community policing (police assigned to one neighborhood with a more per-sonalized orientation to that neighborhood), which may account for a very small portion of the decline in reported crimes. However, the larger explanation for the decline in New York City is probably related to shifts in demography (fewer at-risk males) or an improvement of education and/or the job opportunities for at-risk males.

Crime: Does Age and Gender Matter?

Yes, age and gender matter. Crime is a young person's, more specifically, a young man's game. It takes a bit of physical ability to jump through windows to perform a burglary. It also takes a brazen attitude to steal a car. Usually, the older we get, the less physically agile and brazen we are. Also, young boys are given permission, sometimes encouragement, to take chances, to be daredevils, and challenge authority. Traditionally, young girls are more likely to have been given parental messages of conformity and docility (Hoffman-Bustamonte 1973). This research is more than twenty years old, but is still valid, in spite of some shifts in parenting values and styles toward a more egalitarian approach for young males and females (Brown, Esbenson, and Geis 1991). Chart 4.3 illustrates the rates of crime committed by white males and females by three age categories: teenage years (twelve-to-seventeen); young adult (eighteen-to-twenty) and adult (twenty-one years of age and older).

CHART 4.3: Crime Rate (per 100,000) by Age (whites only)

Sex	12 to 17	18 to 20	21 years +
Males	7,974	15,054	3,786
Females	2,124	1,138	264

Source: Hindelang 1981.

A Historical Perspective _____

(Adapted from *Managing Delinquency Programs that Work*, Barry Glick and Arnold Goldstein, editors, 1995.)

Once juvenile courts were established and empowered to protect the health and welfare of children, a system of voluntary childcare agencies flourished throughout the United States. These agencies were dedicated to dealing with the delinquents who were incapable of living at home. By 1925, the training school, a self-sufficient, large institution that housed delinquent juveniles between the ages of seven and twenty-one, was prominent throughout the South and Northeast. These facilities relied on rigid regimentation and corporal punishment to control acting-out and aggressive adolescent behaviors, and quickly developed into repositories for juveniles who could not be maintained in their homes and communities.

By 1940, the training school movement had developed a reputation for warehousing children. Many advocacy groups developed, including the American Law Institute, to monitor the growing failures of institutional placement for juveniles. During the early 1940s, child advocacy groups recommended that youth correction authorities be established throughout the United States. California, Massachusetts, Minnesota, Texas, and Wisconsin were the first states to heed the recommendation and form some sort of youth authority. By 1945, states such as New York had formalized their youth commissions into state agencies responsible for juvenile services and programs to prevent delinquency and promote positive youth development.

In summary, the juvenile justice system evolved from an informal structure supported by church people who provided services to the unwanted and destitute children of the country, to a multibillion dollar industry that employs thousands of people to provide services and implement programs for juvenile delinquents, some of whom have committed the most heinous of crimes.

_____

The older males and females get, the less crime they commit. Both males and females hit their prime crime years at about seventeen (males a few months younger than females), but both reduce their criminal activity dramatically as they become young adults. However, Chart 4.5 shows the prime crime years for commission of murder are between twenty and twenty-four years for males and females.

Some Young People Commit More Crimes Than Others

Yes, some young people do commit more crimes than others, which should be no surprise to anyone, especially parents who have obedient children and rambunctious ones in the same family. Chart 4.4 is based on a sample of 4,000 junior and senior high students, who self-reported any crimes committed, and these were verified by official crime records.

CHART 4.4: Distribution of Crimes Among Teenage Males in Percentages

Criminal Acts	White Males	African-American Males
No criminal activity	68	43
Had a record, but none recorded in last two years	8	12
One offense in last two years	11	18
Two offenses in last two years	5	9
Three or more offenses in last two years	8	18

Source: Hirschi 1969.

ACA Public Correctional Policy on Juvenile Justice

INTRODUCTION:

The correctional functions of the juvenile justice system (prevention, diversion, detention, probation, residential, and aftercare) must provide specialized care and rehabilitative programs for young offenders in our society consistent with protection of the public. These functions of the juvenile justice system, although sharing in general the same overall purpose as adult corrections, has significantly different processes, procedures, and objectives which require specialized services and programs.

POLICY STATEMENT:

Children and youth have distinct personal and developmental needs and must be kept separate and apart from adult offenders. The juvenile justice system must provide a continuum of services, programs, and facilities that ensures maximum opportunity for rehabilitation. Each of these alternatives should provide programs which include the principle of accountability for behavior. The best interest of the individual youth must be the primary concern and should be balanced with the protection of the public including victims and the maintenance of social order. To implement this policy, juvenile justice officials and agencies should:

A. Establish and maintain effective communication with all concerned with the juvenile justice system—executive, judicial, and legislative officials, prosecution and defense counsel, social service agencies, schools, police, and families—to achieve the fullest possible cooperation in making appropriate decisions in individual cases and in providing and using services and resources.

B. Provide the least restrictive appropriate range of community and residential programs and services to meet individual needs, including education, vocational training, recreation, religious opportunities, individual and family counseling, medical, dental, mental health, and other specialized programs and services such as substance abuse, AIDS counseling, and sexual offender treatment.

C. Use family and community as preferred resources and include families whenever possible, in the decision-making processes at all stages in the continuum of services.

D. Operate a juvenile classification system to identify and meet the program and supervision needs of the juvenile offender, while actively considering the public's need for protection.

E. Exclude from placement in a secure facility serving adjudicated delinquent youth those individuals accused or adjudicated for status offenses; i.e., offenses which are not criminal if committed by an adult.

F. Provide a range of nonsecure and secure short-term detention pending adjudication.

G. Ensure that secure pre-adjudication detention facilities are not used as a post-adjudication disposition alternative.

H. Provide planned transitional services for youth returning to community placement from residential care.

I. Establish written policies and procedures that will protect the rights and safety of the accused, the adjudicated, the victim, and the public in as balanced a manner as possible.

J. Establish procedures to safeguard the accuracy and use of juvenile records and support limitations on their use according to approved national standards, recognizing that the need to safeguard the privacy and rehabilitative goals of the juvenile should be balanced with concern for the protection of the public, including victims.

K. Implement evaluation and research procedures that will supply demographic, trends, and outcome information from which program effectiveness and systems operations can be measured.

This Public Correctional Policy was unanimously ratified by the American Correctional Association Delegate Assembly at the Congress of Correction in San Antonio, Texas, August 23, 1984. It was reviewed January 17, 1990, at the Winter Conference in Nashville, Tennessee, with no change. It was reviewed and amended at the Winter Conference in Miami, Florida, January 10, 1993.

A small number of white and African-American young people accounted for a large portion of crime committed. In a longitudinal study (looking at the same individuals over a time span of several years), Farrington discovered that only 6 percent of his sample had six or more convictions but these chronic offenders accounted for 49.1 percent of the total number of convictions (Farrington 1983).

Crime and Disadvantaged Position

CHART 4.5: Age, Sex, and Race of Murder Offenders, 1995

Age	Total	Sex			Race			
		Male	Female	Unknown	White	Black	Other	Unknown
Total	22,434	14,609	1,400	6,425	7,071	8,285	418	6,660
Percent distribution[1]	100.0	65.1	6.2	28.6	31.5	36.9	1.9	29.7
Under 18[2]	2,169	2,044	125	—	861	1,225	66	17
Under 22[2]	5,875	5,580	295	—	2,274	3,413	151	37
18 and over[2]	12,468	11,246	1,219	3	5,846	6,219	322	81
Infant (under 1)	—	—	—	—	—	—	—	—
1 to 4	—	—	—	—	—	—	—	—
5 to 8	—	—	—	—	—	—	—	—
9 to 12	29	25	4	—	12	17	—	—
13 to 16	1,268	1,182	86	—	492	723	40	13
17 to 19	2,875	2,749	126		1,117	1,675	69	14
20 to 24	3,555	3,329	226	—	1,398	2,067	73	17
25 to 29	2,017	1,812	204	1	939	995	69	14
30 to 34	1,573	1,345	228	—	794	716	50	13
35 to 39	1,136	966	170	—	612	480	36	8
40 to 44	813	690	121	2	496	291	20	6
45 to 49	501	425	76	—	295	189	13	4
50 to 54	305	263	42	—	184	113	5	3
55 to 59	199	175	24	—	122	68	7	2
60 to 64	134	120	14	—	80	47	4	3
65 to 69	91	86	5	—	60	29	1	1
70 to 74	64	54	10	—	44	19	1	—
75 and over	77	69	8	—	62	15	—	—
Unknown	7,797	1,319	56	6,422	364	841	30	6,562

[1] Because of rounding, may not add to total.
[2] Does not include unknown ages.

Source: Crime in U.S. 1995. *Uniform Crime Report.*

Happily, this very high rate of crime greatly diminishes as this age group becomes older, as shown in Chart 4.5. Those children who are raised by inexperienced and inattentive parents who use violence or the threat of violence to discipline their children, and who are exposed to passive violence (watching violence on TV) and active violence (getting hit by parents, siblings, relatives or peers), negative adult behavior modeling, poor quality of family life, failure in public schools, disruption and violence in neighborhoods and schools—are more apt to develop procriminal attitudes.

The crime connection can be understood best as a constellation of factors and not as a single-dimensional problem. For example, boys who were poor achievers in high school were more likely to become delinquent. Thus, school failure is an aspect of a larger constellation of adverse social conditions—constituting what the researchers call a disadvantaged position—that is inextricable from the overriding problem of racial and class inequality. The more these conditions combined in the youth's lives, the more they were at risk of becoming delinquent, in the first place, and of committing serious and repetitive crimes once delinquent (Currie 1985).

Crime and Social Class

Do poor people commit most crime? The answer is complicated and sometimes different depending on who is answering the question.

The starting point in this crime/social class discussion is understanding that there are three separate and very different methods of calculating, tabulating, and measuring crime. There are police reports, victims' reports, and self-reports. All three methods capture a slightly different piece of the crime puzzle. Police reports are more likely than victims' or self-reports to reflect street crimes, such as car theft, assaults, burglaries, and the like. Victims' reports list crimes that often are not reported to police such as intrafamilial crime, incest, and domestic violence. Self-reports, unlike police or victims' reports, show that at least for minor acts (such as shoplifting) during adolescent years, crime is widespread across all income groups. However, highly sophisticated embezzlement and white collar crime rarely, if ever, appear in any of the reports.

So, is crime a poor person's game? It may depend on which crime statistics one uses. Police reports clearly reflect the poor and working-class crimes; self-reports show a more universal distribution of crime, at least among young people; reports from crime victims will show theft offenses that individuals choose not to report to police. However, when one looks in courtrooms, jails, and prisons of America, criminals look very poor, and are overwhelmingly of a lower social class. Going beyond the surface appearances, a typical prison inmate has less than a high school degree, difficulty expressing himself or herself in English or any other language, and little or no formal skill training (National Center for Education Statistics 1994).

Research literature on the crime and social class link indicates that the statistical connection between the two is very weak and not at all convincing (Tittle *et al.* 1978, Thornsberry and Farnworth 1982). Andrews and Bonta confirmed these findings by constructing a multifaceted picture of risk factors associated with crime. Six major and three minor risk factors explained most crime. Lower-class origin was one of the minor risk factors (Andrews and Bonta 1994).

Social class is a factor to be considered. However, like race, social class is but one of several factors that must be incorporated into the explanation of crime.

The important point is this: identifying one factor as THE explanation of crime is incorrect and not the way to proceed. Crime and its remedies are multifaceted and complex. The temptation, however, is to reduce the crime discussion to uni-dimensional factors such as race or social class.

Explaining Crime: Why Do Certain People Commit Crimes and Others Not?

Criminological theory has been under development for about 200 years, starting with Italian social philosophers in the late eighteenth century. Today, the best explanations of crime causation come from a hybrid of theories. Some of these theories were developed almost sixty years ago, such as differential association theory; some began with social learning theory which originated in Russia (Pavlov *et al.*) and were refined by learning theorists and psychologists in the United States after World War II. With the advent of more sophisticated methods that allow for testing many variables simultaneously, integrated theories became popular. Integrated theories can incorporate many theoretical approaches using the most powerful predictive variable elements of each theory. This author advocates the integrated theory called the Psychology of Criminal Conduct (PCC) (Andrews and Bonta 1994).

Most of the theory used in the twentieth century in criminal justice and corrections was based on large-scale sociological notions of social class. These large-scale theories are also known as social structure theories of crime. The core thesis is that the lower the social class status, the more likely one was to be or become a juvenile delinquent or an adult criminal. Social class-based theories were generated in the early part of this century and used until very recently. The following list shows examples of macrosociological theories that shaped our criminal justice and correction's policy for decades (Empey 1978):

Sociological Theories of Crime: 1920 to 1970

Cultural Deviance Theory
Prime sponsors: Clifford R. Shaw and Henry D. McKay

Basic concept: They rejected the idea that criminal conduct is genetically inherited or can be traced to universal antisocial impulses. Instead, they theorized that criminal acts are learned beliefs that make crime an appropriate response to social conditions. Criminals are nothing more than social individuals who are behaving in accordance with the values and norms of their particular group.

Middle-class Subculture Theory

Prime Sponsors: Parsons, 1942; Davis, 1944; Coleman, 1961; Glaser, 1971.

Basic concept: Adolescence, especially for the middle class, is an ill-defined period in the life cycle in which peer relationships take on unusual significance. Because adolescents are segregated from the adult world, a youth subculture is created that is hedonistic and irresponsible, which leads to delinquency.

Strain Theory

Prime Sponsors: Albert K. Cohen, 1955; Richard A. Cloward and Lloyd E. Ohlin, 1960.

Basic concept: Human nature is socially (not biologically) determined. People feel morally obligated to conform to social rules and are sensitive to the expectations of others. Unlike cultural deviance theory, strain theory assumes that the social order is characterized by value consensus, not by conflict. Rather than being divided into competing class structures, lower as well as middle-class people share in the American dream and want to achieve it. Criminal behavior is generated from the lower classes out of frustration of their legitimate aspirations (not being able to achieve the American dream), not by immature fixations or pathological motives.

Symbolic Interactionist Theory

Prime Sponsor: George Herbert Mead, Edwin H. Sutherland, Donald R. Cressey, et al.

Basic concept: This is a social-psychological perspective on crime causation. Like other learning theories, symbolic interactionists believe that parental training is important and that broad cultural standards affect behavior. However, they do not believe that children are cast into a permanent mold by either set of forces. Instead, they theorize that human behavior reflects a changing concept of self. This perspective holds that human nature and social order are opposite sides of the same coin. Neither is permanent; both are plastic and subject to change.

Differential Association Theory

Prime Sponsors: Edwin H. Sutherland, 1939; Donald R. Cressey, 1955.

Basic concept: This is a variant of the symbolic interactionist theory. The principles are that criminal behavior is learned in interaction with other persons in a process of communication. The key part of learning criminal behavior occurs within intimate personal groups. This learning of criminal behavior includes learning techniques of committing crimes and also include the specific direction of motives, drives, rationalizations, and attitudes. These motives and drives are derived from viewing the legal code as favorable or unfavorable. A person becomes delinquent (or criminal, if adult) because of an excess of definitions favorable to the violation of law over definitions unfavorable to the violation of law. These differential associations may vary in frequency, duration, priority, and intensity.

Social Control Theory (also known as: Psychosocial Control Theory or Control Theory)

Prime Sponsors: Bordua, 1962; T. Hirschi, 1969

Basic concept: This is a variant of Freud's theory. The key elements of social control theory are attachment, commitment, involvement, and belief. Attachment refers to the ties of affection and respect between children and parents, teachers, and friends. A strong bond with all three will be a major deterrent to delinquency. Of the three, a strong bond with parents is the most essential. Commitment is a rational component, similar to Freud's ego. If children commit themselves to getting an education and dedicating themselves to long-term goals, they develop a stake in conformity and will not get involved in delinquent acts. Involvement assumes that "idle hands are the devil's workshop." Adolescents are either constructively busy or likely are involved in delinquent acts. The belief component of control theory assumes that some young people have a strong belief in the law and its assumptions, and some do not.

Labeling Theory

Prime Sponsors: Cooley, 1910 (est.); Tannenbaum, 1938;
Lemert, 1951; Becker, 1963, Erickson, 1964.

Basic concept: This is a variant of symbolic interactionist theory.
Labeling theory, however, is concerned mostly with the stig-
matizing effects of officials' reactions to offenders, than with
the processes of interaction that produce illegal behavior in
the first place. Labeling theorists assume that delinquents
and criminals are basically "normal people" but become
criminals due to the negative effects of labeling by teachers,
police, judges, and correctional authorities on them.

Radical Theory

Prime Sponsor: Quinney, 1974.

Basic concept: Crime is a product of a perpetual class struggle in
which the ruling segments of capitalist society, (1) define
what criminal behavior is, based on their particular self-interests, (2) create social conditions that make criminals out of
working class people; (3) then, devise legal machinery by
which to maintain control of these people. The rules and
practices that govern crime are the products of the inequities
and injustices of a capitalist social order.

Changing Theoretical Tides: 1975 to 1985

One of the basic problems with macrosociological theory was its inability to
explain why, on a given city street (or neighborhood in a small town), half a dozen
young men were delinquents who turned into adult criminals and two or three
young men from the same street attended college and went on to become middle-class professionals. These sociological theories focused on external factors
(race, age, social class) and were not grounded in what particular individuals did,
how particular individuals dealt with their parents and home environment, how
they were or were not physically abused by their parents, the amount of TV they
watched each day, and the role of TV in the home. For example, was TV used as
a surrogate parent or selectively watched for special programs?

Further, the bases or data sources for theory changed in the mid to late
1960s. From the 1930s up to the early 1970s, the national, state, and local crime
consciousness was shaped entirely by police reports of crime. Police reports of
crime only depicted street crimes, such as burglary, theft, assault, and the like.

White collar crimes rarely showed up in police reports. In the mid to late 1960s, social scientists began to get crime information from two new sources: crime victims (National Crime Survey) and criminals themselves (self-report studies).

From criminals in the self-report studies, we discovered that the vast majority of crime was committed by adolescents and young men. Another discovery was that most adolescents and young men committed delinquent acts. Crime was committed not just by low-income minority youth. Most of these delinquent acts were minor in nature, but violated social norms, nonetheless. This finding upset decades of crime theory that was based on social class assumptions. From crime victims, we discovered that many violent crimes, such as assault and rape, committed within families, were not reported to police. The extent and scale of delinquent and criminal acts was not revealed until years later when a few sophisticated longitudinal (analyzing the same sample of people over many years) and self-report studies were undertaken (Wolfgang and Ferracuti 1967; Elliott, Ageton, and Cantor 1979; Gottfredson and Hirschi 1995).

Integrated Theories of Why Individuals Commit Crime

By combining theories, you increase the explanatory power of single theories. Starting in the 1960s, integrated theory became the theoretical approach of choice. An early example of this type of theory integration was Cloward and Ohlin's delinquency and opportunity theory (1960). In their integrated theory, Cloward and Ohlin combined strain and social-learning theories.

In 1979, Elliott, Ageton, and Canter used social control theory to explain individual levels of attachment to conventional persons and commitment to conventional activities, with their belief in the validity of the moral order. Additionally, they contended that strain theory variables interact with these early social control factors and either strengthen or weaken the initial bonds. Finally, they stated that association with delinquent or conventional peers will affect the probability of involvement in delinquent behavior (Brown, Espensen, and Geis 1991).

From Integrated Theory to the Psychology of Criminal Conduct

Due to the use of much more sophisticated research methods (such as meta-analysis), the way we approach the examination of crime has changed from a large-scale, deductive approach to an inductive, individual approach. Summary statements can be generated from this new psychosocial approach, but are based on very empirically derived, carefully tested notions of why particular individuals have committed specific antisocial acts.

A few social scientists are quite angry over the fact that social class-based theories of crime had dominated the field for so long. In the words of Andrews and Bonta:

> Overall, the conclusion must be that the theoretical dominance of class of origin in mainstream sociological criminology was, from the beginning, not based on evidence. When the social psychology of criminological knowledge is finally written, the theoreticism of mainstream sociological criminology in regard to social class may well become one of the intellectual scandals of science (1994).

Psychology of Criminal Conduct

Andrews and Bonta and others in the "Ottawa School" have developed a new theory called the psychology of criminal conduct. The psychology of criminal conduct theory is new only in its name. In all other dimensions, it has been, like all other good, empirically derived theories, in the development stage for decades. The psychology of criminal conduct is a theory of criminal conduct based on the general psychology of human behavior. The antecedents to the psychology of criminal conduct included the following: (1) the radical behavioral perspective of B. F. Skinner, (2) the cognitive behavioral perspective of Albert Bandura, Walter Mischel, and Donald Miechenbaum, (3) the early work of symbolic interactionist George Herbert Mead, (4) the work of Sheldon and Eleanor Glueck during the 1940s, and (5) the psychosocial bonding perspective of Travis Hirschi in the late 1960s.

The psychology of criminal conduct is both a subfield of interdisciplinary criminology and a subfield of human psychology. In this sense, it is consistent with the recent development of integrated theories.

One of the primary objectives of the psychology of criminal conduct is to understand that people vary (differ) in the number, type, and variety of criminal acts in which they engage. This variation usually is both between individuals as well as within the same individual. The types of understanding sought by the psychology of criminal conduct are empirical, theoretical, and practical.

On the empirical level, the psychology of criminal conduct seeks knowledge of observable facts, and personal, situational and social variables associated (correlated) with criminal behavior. It also seeks to isolate the causes of criminal conduct based on biology, personality, attitudes and beliefs, aptitude and skill, learning history, family, peer relationships, broader social arrangements, and the immediate situation or action.

On the theoretical level, the authors are searching for general, rational, simple, emotionally pleasing, and an empirically accurate explanation of variation in criminal conduct that has predictive accuracy. The theory is adequate if it can accurately measure variation in criminal behavior and if it has the potential to actually influence criminal activity through deliberate interventions that focus on the causal variables suggested by the theory.

What are the Lessons from the Psychology of Criminal Conduct?

Perhaps the most important finding of the psychology of criminal conduct is that there are substantial individual differences in the criteria of criminal conduct. People differ in the frequency of their criminal activity and in the number, type, and variety of criminal acts in which they engage. Additionally, while accounting for a disproportionate amount of the total criminal activity, the more criminally active offenders do not tend to be specialists. The following list contains some of the correlates of criminal behavior. When the risk factors are sampled together using multiple correlation methods, the explanatory power reaches the 0.70 level. In social science terms, that is quite powerful.

Major Risk Factors for Criminal Conduct:

1. Antisocial/procriminal attitudes, values, beliefs and cognitive-emotional states

2. Procriminal associates and isolation from anticriminal others

3. Temperamental and personality factors conducive to criminal activity including psychopathy, weak socialization, impulsivity, restless aggressive behavior, egocentrism, below-average verbal intelligence, a taste for risk, and weak problem solving/self-regulation skills

4. History of antisocial behavior evident from a young age, in a variety of settings and involving a number and variety of different acts

5. Familial factors, in particular, low levels of affection, caring and cohesiveness; poor parental supervision and discipline practices; and outright neglect and abuse

6. Low levels of personal educational, vocational, or financial achievement and, in particular, unstable employment.

Minor Risk Factors for Criminal Conduct:

1. Lower-class origins

2. Personal distress; whether measured by social strain, anomie, or alienation variables or by clinical constructs of low self-esteem, anxiety, depression, and other factors

3. A host of biological/neuropsychological indicators

Does this list of risk factors have any policy implications for state and federal legislators, governors, judges, and the like? Yes, of course, programs and funding to support struggling families will improve all family members, especially the young and impressionable members. In-school and after-school programs that work with and support children and youth from families in which both parents are working or in single head of household families in which that parent is working also will be good short- and long-range social investments.

Do these findings have any meaning for probation officers, community corrections staff, parole board members, or parole officers? Certainly. This list is an excellent road map for correctional personnel. With the use of this road map, correctional staff can pinpoint much more accurately which type of resources need to be mobilized on behalf of offenders. However, correctional staff should not attempt to change the behavior of offenders without simultaneously reaching out to employment, substance abuse, mental health, and other specialists in the surrounding community. Also, correctional staff should not assume that all offenders have all of these problems. See Chapters 9-11 for help in deciding which offender needs which type of supervision and treatment.

Policy Implications

Policymakers can use this broader base of knowledge of crime to shape legislation which might lead to prevention of crime and more effective criminal sanctions and correctional programs. Also, this type of crime knowledge can be used to halt legislative proposals that are inconsistent with current understanding of crime causation. Boot camps (first- and second-generation ones, especially) are a prime example. Nothing in any crime theory would suggest that one to four months in a military-style boot camp would lead to a reduction in criminal activity. This is especially true if failure in boot camp will result in a prison sentence. Youthful offenders exposed to abusive language and extreme physical conditioning will try to conform to the short-term rigor of boot camp but will learn nothing new in terms of forming prosocial skills that will keep them out of trouble once they are released to the community. Abusive language and threats of violence are what most youthful offenders received from their parents, relatives, and siblings for years.

Abusive language, degrading disciplinary rituals, and a very rigid program structure typified first-generation boot camps. In 1996, some boot camps were maintaining the outward appearance of boot camps (because they closely correspond to what their legislative sponsors and others in the media and general public think prison inmates "deserve"), while simultaneously reprogramming the content of boot camps to conform to what the correctional intervention literature tells us about what actually works in reducing recidivism. These third- and fourth-generation boot camps have been shown to be more effective in recidivism reduction, but only if they build in what works. Some of the features of effective programming include the following: (1) carefully assessing both static and dynamic risk factors, (2) applying appropriate treatment services based on assessments, (3) basing high-treatment dosages each day on individualized needs of offenders, (4) paying attention to offenders' individualized styles of learning, (5) employing a meaningful set of positive reinforcers tailored to each offender on a frequent basis (Gendreau and Goggin 1996).

The American Correctional Association book on boot camps (1996) articulates the various program features of well-organized boot camps around the country. Unfortunately, there is little empirical information regarding the effectiveness of boot camps in reducing recidivism compared to matched samples of offenders not in boot camps. Presently, it is difficult to discuss this topic meaningfully because there are so many different types of boot camps in existence. Boot camps as a program model are not as important as how the program is structured, the qualifications of staff, and the other treatment features.

The current and emerging literature on effective correctional interventions indicate that most intense surveillance programs (boot camps, electronic or home monitoring, and residential programs) are no more effective in reducing recidivism than less intense surveillance. What is more effective in reducing recidivism is appropriate treatment for criminogenic needs. This topic is discussed more fully in Part II, the section for the practitioner. Getting tough, by itself, is not helpful and even may be counterproductive.

Summary

The development of criminological theory mirrors the development of knowledge, in general. We knew a lot less in the nineteenth century than we do today. We knew less as recently as fifteen years ago, than we do today. With this high rate of learning and theory improvement, the field of criminal justice should begin to improve and do so rather quickly. If this does not occur, it will be, in large part, because we as practitioners have not paid attention, have not done our homework, and have not kept up with the professional literature in our field. Nevertheless, others also must change their roles and professional activities.

Chapter 5

Drugs, Alcohol, and Prison Use

Background

Highly addictive (physically and/or psychologically) drugs are ravaging the lives of many citizens. Also, drugs are providing very lucrative incentives for an illicit drug industry, which, in turn, is creating a monumental problem for the criminal justice system. However, like prisoners in general, the criminal justice system and the policymakers who have an impact on the criminal justice system have difficulty in making important distinctions between nonaddictive and highly addictive drugs, drugs that are socially approved (almost encouraged), and those that are taboo. Often decision makers have difficulty selecting settings that are conducive to treatment such as community-based settings and those that are not, which includes most institutions. To a great extent, those making such distinctions are not rewarded by the media and the public.

Marijuana is a very popular drug for millions of Americans in spite of evidence that even moderate use can have adverse effects on psychomotor, cardiac, endocrine, and reproductive functions and sometimes lead to psychological dependence on it (Select Committee 1982). Of all the people charged and convicted of drug violations, 78 percent are for marijuana offenses. Strangely, marijuana, under most state criminal statutes, is dealt with almost as harshly as cocaine, a highly addictive drug. Both are classified under the same schedule 1 under federal law (Bureau of Justice Statistics 1988, and National Institute of Justice 1990).

ACA Public Correctional Policy on Offender's Substance Abuse

INTRODUCTION:

Substance abuse, and the criminal activity and human suffering associated with it, are a major problem in society. A substantial majority of offenders have documented substance abuse problems, and therefore, the impact has reached critical dimensions within correctional programs and facilities.

POLICY STATEMENT:

A comprehensive response to the substance abuse crisis must include coordinated local, state, national, and international plans and actions, along with a national commitment to provide substance abuse treatment to those who need such services. To support a comprehensive response, correctional agencies should:

A. Maintain an organizational climate that discourages substance abuse, including policies consistent with a drug-free workplace;

B. Advocate for and cooperate with interagency and community efforts to prevent substance abuse, and to interdict the supply of illegal substances;

C. Provide education and information sources to offenders that create awareness of chemical dependency and the need for treatment;

D. Identify offenders needing substance abuse services, and provide the range of treatment services needed to promote a lifestyle of recovery;

E. Maintain appropriately trained staff for the delivery of care, programs, and services;

F. Maintain professionally appropriate record keeping of the services and programs provided;

G. Evaluate the quality and effectiveness of services provided; and

H. Provide leadership and advocacy for legislative and public support to obtain the resources needed to meet the needs associated with substance abuse.

This Public Correctional Policy was ratified by the American Correctional Association Delegate Assembly at the Winter Conference in Portland, Oregon, January 22, 1992. It was reviewed and amended January 29, 1997, at the Winter Conference in Indianapolis, Indiana.

Impact of Drugs on the Criminal Justice System

The number of adults coming into the state and federal prison systems for drug-related crimes is astronomical. Chart 5.1 provides an indication of this impact.

CHART 5.1: Arrests for Drug Offenses and New Court Commitments to State Prisons for Drug-related Offenses 1980 to 1992

Year	Number of Arrests for Drug Offenses	Percent of Inmates Sent to Prison for Drug Offenses	Number of Inmates in Prison for Drug Offenses
1980	471,200	7	8,822
1983	583,500	9	15,596
1986*	742,700	16	33,140
1989	1,247,700	31	90,837
1992	980,700	31	101,961

* The federal antidrug campaign began in 1986.
Source: Bureau of Justice Statistics 1994.

This is a phenomenal rate of growth, which cannot be sustained by state prisons. Just as importantly, assuming that a significant number of these drug offenders are addicted to drugs, the prison is one of the least conducive settings for treatment of drugs. Prison staff do not have the specialized training and skills to get drug addicts to kick their habits. Ironically, many drug offenders are not addicted to drugs, do not need drug treatment, and do not constitute a threat to public safety.

The United States, after many years of trying and many billions of dollars expended, might benefit from other countries' experiences in coping with drug use. For example, many European countries have a much more permissive policy toward marijuana use. Once they changed their drug policy regarding marijuana, street crime did not increase, drug-related problems decreased somewhat, and the impact on the criminal justice system was a beneficial one (Treaster 1993).

Classification of Drug Offenders

Chart 5.2 draws important distinctions between different types of drug users. Public policymakers would do well to make similar distinctions (Clear 1988).

CHART 5.2: Commitment to Crime and Commitment to Drug Use

		Commitment to Crime	
		High	Low
Commitment to Drug Use	High	Predator	Addict
	Low	Seller	User

Chart 5.2 illustrates four distinct groups:

1. Individuals with a high commitment to both crime and drug use: predators

2. Individuals with a high commitment to drug use and a low commitment to crime: addicts

3. Individuals with a low commitment to drug use and a high commitment to crime: drug sellers

4. Individuals with a low commitment to both crime and drug use: recreational drug users

There are important public drug-policy implications of these distinctions.

Group one: predators. This group constitutes a threat to public safety and also is in need of treatment. Many in this group will need some form of incarceration, at least for a short period of time. They probably do not need to serve decades in prison as many now do, but they will need some cognitive and value changes to take on prosocial attitudes of behavior, and they will need drug treatment.

Group two: addicts. This group desperately needs drug treatment. Addicts should be placed in highly structured community-based treatment programs (see Chapter 6) and not in prison.

Group three: drug sellers. If the drug sold is a highly addictive drug, this presents a public safety and public health problem and authorities must deal with it. Drug sellers should be brought into the criminal justice system. However, drug treatment for the nondrug-using seller is inappropriate and a waste of taxpayers' time and money. The best approach for corrections to take with this group is to help them find another legitimate way to make money.

Group four: recreational drug users. They should never be placed in prison. This group is made up of nonaddicts. At least in their self-perceptions, they are not criminals and have not adopted antisocial lifestyles. The criminal justice system should purge itself of this type of person. If intervention is needed at all, the public and mental health systems are much better equipped to deal with this group than is the criminal justice system. If this policy shift occurs, some correctional funding also should be shifted to the appropriate public health or mental health agencies.

This drug-use typology suffers from category overlap like most typologies do. In other words, the distinctions among the four drug-use types are not perfect; there is much overlap among the four groups. A typology developed by John Martin includes five categories of drug users: (1) urban underclass users, (2) adolescent users, (3) recreational users, (4) medication users, and (5) adult addicts. As Martin says, "My substance user typology provides an extremely simplified summary of a complicated reality. Consequently, it is incomplete, inconsistent, and amenable to modification" (Martin 1990).

However, typologies can be helpful to policymakers, in that policymakers deal with large generalizations. For example, a drug control strategy for adolescent users will be substantively different from that for adult medication addicts. It is important that policymakers understand the idea of making general classification distinctions, and the reader should understand that policy implications are inherent in making these classifications.

Negative Impacts of the "War on Drugs"

In addition to causing major problems in the criminal justice system such as overwhelming urban court dockets (Martin 1989), the "war on drugs" is wreaking havoc on other dimensions of our lives. In the process of trying to control drugs, we are impinging on sacred constitutional principles. For example, federal law permits local law enforcement to seize the property of drug-using and drug-dealing suspects (not yet adjudicated). This practice violates the United States Constitution's provision of a presumption of innocence prior to a finding of guilt (Labaton 1993). The proceeds from the sales of seized properties have become an essential part of the daily operating funds of local law enforcement agencies (General Accounting Office 1992). Some economists and libertarian groups claim that the war on drugs is criminogenic, in other words, it leads to more crime, and legalization of drugs would result in a reduction of the monetary value of drugs. Accordingly, legalization would result in a reduction of street crime (especially robbery and burglary) associated with drug sales (Treaster 1993, Kopel 1994).

ACA Resolution on Drug-free Correctional Workforce

WHEREAS, the membership of the American Correctional Association (ACA) recognizes the importance of ensuring that the correctional workforce are capable of discharging their assigned duties and responsibilities as members of the criminal justice system;

WHEREAS, no large workforce can claim immunity to drug abuse by its employees;

WHEREAS, illegal drug use and addiction by staff of correctional institutions or community agencies can lead to significant health problems and serious security risks for staff, inmates, and the general public; and

WHEREAS, making every effort to ensure a safe and secure workplace is a responsibility of the correctional agencies and workforce;

THEREFORE, BE IT RESOLVED, That the American Correctional Association endorses a drug-free workplace and actively encourages all members to develop and implement those education, training, assistance, and control methods necessary to ensure that the correctional workplace is drug free.

This resolution was adopted by the American Correctional Association Board of Governors on January 10, 1993, at the Winter Conference in Miami, Florida. It was reviewed without change January 16, 1996, at the Winter Conference in Philadelphia, Pennsylvania.

Lessons for Corrections from the Substance Abuse Field

For reasons that remain somewhat mysterious, the term "drugs" usually means cocaine, heroin, and marijuana. Noticeably missing from this list is alcohol and tobacco. Tobacco, in spite of being a highly addictive substance and the cause of thousands of deaths from cancer, heart attacks, and other illnesses each year, is legal and hence not pertinent to this book. However, in 1996, the federal government decided to classify tobacco as a dangerous and addictive substance, which, of course, it is. Alcohol, the other legal substance, is a mind-altering substance, and many behaviors associated with alcohol use are life threatening, and some of these are classified as illegal. Alcohol addiction is much more of a problem for criminal offenders (as it is for the general public) than all other substances we classify as "drugs" combined. Hence, a section on alcohol is included in this chapter and appropriate alcohol assessment and treatment strategies are included in Chapter 9.

Alcohol

Approximately 18 million Americans have alcohol problems. Unfortunately, less than 15 percent of the 18 million are receiving treatment (Cooney, Zweben, and Fleming 1995). It behooves all of us, especially those working in the field of adult corrections, to know more about what works in this field.

The field of alcoholism has an extensive history and literature. Many adult offenders have alcohol problems. If there are theories or treatment strategies that have worked with alcoholics, some of those same approaches are bound to be helpful in the correctional intervention field. Relapse prevention is one example of an alcoholism treatment approach that has been successfully applied to the offender population (Maletsky 1991). Relapse prevention is a therapeutic approach which recognizes that addictive behavior is a process. It involves detailed assessments and reassessments at short (weekly, if needed) intervals and "take-home" assignments (see Chapter 10 for further information on treatment approaches).

Drugs

The majority of adult offenders have some type of drug problem. Drug testing in Dade County among felony defendants found 29 percent tested positive for cocaine only, 29 percent were positive for THC and cocaine, 5 percent were positive for THC, and 23 percent provided no urine specimen (Goldkamp and

Gottfredson 1988). Nationally, drug use patterns of jail inmates are illustrated in Chart 5.3.

CHART 5.3: Drug Use Among Adult Offenders in Percentage

	Ever Used	Regularly Use
Any drug	78	58
Cocaine or Crack	50	31
Heroin	18	11
LSD	19	6
PCP	14	5
Marijuana	71	48

Source: Bureau of Justice Statistics 1991, Drugs and Jail Inmates.

However, drug use is not restricted to criminals. When the general population was asked, "Have you had (any of the following substances) in the last twelve months," the responses were as follows: alcohol: 66.5 percent; marijuana: 9.0 percent; cocaine: 2.2 percent; crack: 0.5 percent; inhalants: 1.0 percent; hallucinogens: 1.2 percent; stimulants: 1.1 percent; PCP: 0.2 percent; heroin: 0.1 percent; anabolic steriods: 0.1 percent (U.S. Department of Health and Human Services 1993).

Former first lady Nancy Reagan suggested that the best way to deal with drugs is "just say no." This approach assumes that all drug users have the same history, physiology, genetic makeup, social learning, and conditioning. If that were the case, the "just say no" approach may hold some promise. However, this position ignores the great diversity of backgrounds, motivations, and differences among drug users.

Are Alcoholics "Sick" or Is Alcoholism a Learned Trait?

A popular misconception about alcohol and drugs is that those who have trouble controlling alcohol or drug use are suffering from an incurable disease. The disease model is a convenient categorization that meets the needs of many groups. According to Miller, people with alcohol problems like it because they get special status, recognition, and treatment. Nonalcoholics like the disease model because they can tell themselves they do not need to worry because they are not "diseased." The substance abuse treatment industry loves it because there is money to be made. The liquor industry loves it because under this theory, it is not alcohol that is the problem, but the person, the alcoholic (Miller 1994).

With this broad base of support, the disease model became the explanation of choice of most people concerned about substance abuse. For example, the disease model is the cornerstone of the Alcoholics Anonymous approach (Miller 1994); many hospitals and treatment programs base their entire treatment approach on recognizing and treating substance abuse as a disease. Placing all or most problem drinkers in a disease model program is an example of not matching the unique needs of the client with either the special skills of the therapist or the unique features of a particular treatment program.

Assembling the Alcohol Literature

About 1976, a group of clinicians and researchers (members of the group are identified in Hester and Miller 1995) began a comprehensive review of the causes of alcoholism and various treatment approaches. The first task of this group was identifying 600 articles on the topic of substance abuse treatment. The second task was reading the articles, which took the group six months. The third task was another six-month effort which resulted in a 110-page summary of the 600 articles.

The findings of this 110-page summary were that a very large number of treatment methods had been tried, a wealth of information existed that had immediate and practical application to the field of substance abuse treatment, and the body of literature demonstrated the value of systematic, cumulative, and programmatic research.

In 1986, the same group of clinicians and researchers refined their literature search to only those studies with proper control and comparison groups. With this new, narrow, and more demanding view of the literature, they discovered: a number of treatment methods were consistently supported by controlled scientific research; there is no single treatment approach for alcohol problems that is superior to all other methods; and virtually none of these identified and verified treatment methods were in common use in the United States (Hester and Miller 1995).

The third collaborative effort of this group was geared to matching clients to treatment approaches. The finding from this effort was that different people respond best to different approaches, which corresponds to the responsivity principle. In spite of this rather common-sense finding (different strokes for different folks), most treatment programs offered a relatively consistent program to all clients. Further, clients who failed to respond to "the program" were often blamed for the failure because they were "unmotivated" or "in denial."

The fourth effort of this group focused on the question of whether more "intensive" treatment programs would be superior in effectiveness to less intensive alternative programs. The group accepted only the results of controlled studies using random assignment or matching designs, a very high research standard. They found two dozen studies comparing longer with shorter treatment, residential and nonresidential, and more versus less intensive treatment approaches. None of the studies showed any advantage for the more intensive, longer, or residential approaches over less intensive and less expensive alternative programs (Hester and Miller 1995).

This last finding has important implications for the field of adult corrections and is consistent with other findings regarding length of stay and intensive supervision programs (Byrne 1990). Legislating longer prison sentences may gather more political support for elected officials and may momentarily reduce the general public's fear of crime. But longer stays in prison have not resulted in reducing the risk of recidivism upon release from prison (Wilkins 1967). To a certain extent, the "punishing smarter" or "smarter sentencing" movement of the 1980s (Intensive Supervision Programs, boot camps, and electronic monitoring) included longer community supervision and longer detention, jail, and prison sentences. None of the evaluation literature on "smarter" programs has shown less recidivism (Cullen, Wright, and Applegate 1996, Gendreau 1996).

Conceptual Models of Alcohol Problems

The review of the alcoholism literature covered the gamut of the different treatment approaches. Chart 5.4 summarizes the different conceptual models for dealing with alcoholism.

CHART 5.4: Conceptual Models of Alcohol Problems

Model	Causal Factors	Interventions
Moral	Personal responsibility; self control	Moral suasion, social and legal sanctions
Temperance	Alcohol	Exhortation, "just say no"control of supply
Spiritual	Spiritual deficit	Prayer, spiritual growth, AA
Dispositional disease	Irreversible constitutional abnormality of the individual	Identification of alcoholics, confrontation, lifelong abstention
Educational	Lack of knowledge and motivation	Education
Characterological	Personality traits, defense mechanisms	Psychotherapy
Conditioning	Classical and operant conditioning	Counter conditioning, extinction, altered contingencies
Social learning	Modeling, skills deficits	Skill training, appropriate behavioral models
Cognitive	Expectations, beliefs	Cognitive therapy, rational restructuring
General systems	Boundaries and rules, family dysfunction	Family therapy, transactional analysis

Source: Hester and Miller 1995.

According to the authors of Chart 5.4, some evidence exists to support each of these conceptual models. Each, likewise, can be shown to be limited in its ability to account for alcohol problems. No one of these models appears to be the whole truth, though each contains truth. No one of them is likely to be adequate in guiding efforts to intervene with and prevent alcohol problems (Hester and Miller 1995). See Chapter 10 for more information on particular treatment strategies for substance abusers.

Summary

Consistent with the theory of the psychology of criminal conduct, the individual is the unit of analysis—not society, not poverty, not self-esteem. Crime causation can be understood best by understanding the individual first and then building up (inductively) from there. The quality and character of the individual's peers (as well as parents, neighborhoods, and schools) are important, as probation and parole officers have known for decades. However, the individual is most important.

Adult offenders are not a special class of creatures any more than airline passengers or hospital patients. When honoring these individual differences, the quality of communication between staff and offenders will improve, the trust and rapport will increase, recidivism rates will decrease, and the field will begin to gain some broad scale respect with the general public and policymakers.

Responsivity, from the criminologists of the Ottawa School (Bonta, Andrews, *et al.*) and motivational interviewing from the alcohol specialists (Miller, *et al.*) are two critically important tools that are available to corrections practitioners now. If responsivity is used in tandem with the other two elements of the psychology of criminal conduct, risk and needs, then real progress can be made toward improving the overall efficacy of correctional intervention.

Until the entire country changes its posture on drug use, drug prevention, and control of drugs, it is likely that we will continue to pay enormous amounts of public money for a clearly unsuccessful effort to contain, control, or limit drug use.

Chapter 6

Race and Prison Use

Disproportionalness

The disproportionate number of African-Americans, Latinos, and Native-Americans in prison has been a controversial issue for some time. For example, one out of every three black men in his twenties is in jail or prison, or on probation or parole (Sentencing Project 1995). Since the mid-1980s prison-population explosion, ethnic and racial disproportionateness has become even more of a problem (Bureau of Justice Statistics 1994). Some prisons, such as the Lorton Prison in Virginia, several upstate prisons in New York, the Pelican Bay Prison in northern California, and most prisons in the South are overwhelmingly populated by ethnic and racial minority group members.

Admissions to prisons have increased for all ethnic groups, all ages, for males and lately for females, as well. While the growth in prison admissions of white prisoners was three times larger in 1986 than it was sixty years earlier, the growth of African-American prisoners was nine times larger over the same period (Bureau of Justice Statistics 1991).

In some geographic areas, in specific crime categories, and in very specific age groups, racial and ethnic minorities constitute a disproportionate share of the offender population (Elliott 1994). However, because a very small number of racial and ethnic minorities are frequent offenders, this should not justify a wide-scale policy leading to their disproportionate population growth in the juvenile and adult justice system. In terms of drug use, African-Americans use drugs at about the same rate as the rest of the population. They make up only 13 percent of the general population, but are 35 percent of those arrested for drug possession and 55 percent of those convicted for drug possession, and 74 percent of prison inmates doing time for drug possession (Wideman 1995). This constitutes a clear pattern of disproportionateness toward African-Americans as they move through the criminal justice system.

Increase in African-Americans in the Criminal Justice System

Chart 6.1 illustrates the increase in the proportion of African-Americans (primarily males, but a growing number of females) in prisons in America.

CHART 6.1: Proportion of African-Americans in Prison in the United States: 1926 to 1990

Year	1926	1930	1940	1950	1960	1970	1980	1990
Percent of Admissions to Prison	23	24	29	30	34	43	42	54

Source: Bureau of Justice Statistics 1991b, Tonry 1994.

In 1926, African-Americans were 10 percent of the general population; today they are about 13 percent. Even in 1926, African-Americans were in prison at double their representation in the general population. African-Americans today are overrepresented in prison about three-and-a-half times their number in the general population.

When the rate of incarceration is examined, the racial disproportionality becomes even more apparent. The rate of incarceration for white adults is about 210 per 100,000 general population. For adult African-Americans, the rate is a staggering 1,500 per 100,000 general population. This is seven times greater than for whites (Stern 1995). This is not fair, and it should not continue. Legislators, judges, prosecutors, corrections officials, and others should consider ways to reduce the number and proportion of African-Americans in America's prisons and jails.

The same general finding is applicable to Mexican-Americans, other Latino populations, and Native-American Indians. The difficulty in speaking about the Latino populations is that the United States Census Bureau and the state prison statistics have not separated Latino populations from the majority populations. This is being done now, but there is no historical data to show long-term trends and changes.

A Case Example: California Versus South Africa

To gain some cross-cultural and comparative perspective on criminal justice practices in the United States, the racial makeup of the corrections system in California is compared to that of South Africa. Elliott Currie, a renowned criminologist at the University of California at Berkley, has written books that offer excellent examples of how much there is to learn from cross-cultural comparisons: *Confronting Crime* (1985) and *Reckoning* (1993).

The general populations of California and South Africa are quite comparable, 36 million in California and 33 million in South Africa. Chart 6.2 compares crimes reported to police in both California and in South Africa.

CHART 6.2: Crime in California and South Africa: 1983 and the 1990s

Number of Crimes Reported in:

	California		South Africa	
	1983	**1990**	**1983**	**1990**
Murder	2,639	3,553	8,573	20,135
Rape	12,093	12,688	15,342	24,812
Robbery	85,826	112,208	38,229	79,927
Assault	93,933	182,602	121,716	137,800

Sources: Terblanche 1995; Bureau of Justice Statistics 1983, 1992.

There are some interesting similarities and differences in reported crimes. The number of rapes in California and in South Africa was very similar in 1983, but doubled in South Africa by 1992 and stayed the same in California in 1990. However, there were more differences than similarities between the two jurisdictions. Robberies in South Africa were much less than in California in both time periods, in spite of a doubling of robberies in South Africa between 1983 and 1992. The number of assaults in 1983 was less in California than in South Africa, but much more in California in the 1990s. Murders were much more frequent in South Africa than in California in both time periods. In general, with the exception of assault, California's crime pattern has been quite stable. By contrast, crime in South Africa is on a dramatic rise.

Prison use is often seen as a response to crime, or a means to contain or reduce crime. Chart 6.3 illustrates incarceration in California and South Africa.

CHART 6.3: Use of Incarceration in California and South Africa: 1980 to 1993

	California		South Africa	
	1980	**1993**	**1980**	**1993**
Adult Prison Population*	54,000	189,249*	100,677	111,798
Incarceration Rate*	236	590*	423	361
Percent African-Americans and Blacks in Prison	36	38	74	70
Percent Hispanics	25	29	Not applicable	Not applicable
Percent Coloured**	Not applicable	Not applicable	22	25
Percent White	36	31	4	3.8

*South Africa's prisons include less serious offenders, offenders awaiting trial, and violent and nonviolent sentenced offenders. To make a valid comparison between California and South Africa, California's local jail population and the state prison populations were combined. Sources: Terblanche 1995, Blue Ribbon Commission 1990.

**Coloured is a genetic mixture of black and white.

In 1980, the number of adults incarcerated and the rate of incarceration in California was about half that of South Africa. Thirteen years later, in 1993, South Africa's prison population was about the same. Due to general population growth in South Africa between 1980 and 1993, the rate of incarceration declined by 15 percent. By stark contrast, California's total adult incarcerated population almost quadrupled between 1980 and 1993, and California's rate of incarceration more than doubled.

The racial divisions inside of South Africa can be seen by the high percentage of African and Coloured (genetic mixture of black and white) people incarcerated. The proportions of each group remained stable between the two time periods. By contrast, the racial composition of California's prisons was anything but stable. Chart 6.4 illustrates the shifts in racial and ethnic populations in California over the last fifteen years.

CHART 6.4: Incarceration Rate of Racial and Ethnic Groups in California's Prisons (by percentage: 1981 to 1991 based on the general population)

Racial or ethnic group	1981	1991
African-Americans	36 percent, rate: 2,200	36.9 percent rate: 6,000
Whites	36 percent, rate: 200 per 100,000	30 percent rate: 450 per 100,000
Hispanics	25 percent rate: 550 per 100,000	30 percent rate: 1,200 per 100,000
Asian, Native-Americans, Other	2 percent rate: 100 per 100,000	5 percent rate: 450 per 100,000

Sources: Blue Ribbon Commission 1990 and Bureau of Justice Statistics 1991b.

The racial and ethnic disproportionality in South Africa's prisons is a sad comment on the former racist policies of that country. However, the trend in South Africa shows a decline in the rate of overall prison use while maintaining the same racial proportions inside that country's prisons.

In California, the picture is quite different. The racial disproportionalness in 1981 in California also illustrated a pattern of higher prison use for racial and ethnic minorities than represented in the general population of the state. Yet, California's use of prison for racial and ethnic groups increased dramatically between the 1980s and 1990s.

African-Americans made up 7.5 percent of the general population of California in both 1981 and 1991. The proportion of African-Americans in California's prisons also remained constant between 1981 and 1991, about 36 to 37 percent. However, due to the massive increase in prison use in California in the last 15 years, the rate of incarceration for African-Americans went from 2,200 per 100,000 in the 20-49 age group to an astounding 6,000 per 100,000 in that age group. The same pattern of increase also occurs with the other (Hispanic, Asian, and Native-American) minority ethnic groups.

What is to be made of this comparison? Prison use in South Africa is declining, despite an increase in crime. Yet, prison use in California has almost quadrupled in spite of a reasonably stable crime situation. Prison use is not related to crime in South Africa nor in California. As prison use in California increases, the racial and ethnic disproportionality in prison becomes more acute. Increases (California) and decreases (South Africa) in prison use are results of public policy changes made at the top levels of government, primarily in the legislative branch (Blue Ribbon Commission 1990; Terblanche 1995, Bureau of Justice Statistics 1986, 1994, 1995).

If prison use is a reflection of our justice system, our sense of fairness, and general societal values, as Alexis de Tocqueville eloquently stated about 150 years ago, then our society is not very fair, not very just, and our use of prisons must be fundamentally reexamined.

Racial Politics

There is also a need for more racial and ethnic minorities in positions of power and authority. This is by no means a cure-all for disproportionate handling of racial and ethnic minorities in the criminal justice system, but it is a necessary step, among many others, that is needed. Chart 6.5 illustrates the number of racial minorities and women placed on the federal bench by presidential term. At least at the federal level, appointments to the federal bench appear to be heavily influenced by political ideology. It would be preferable to make political appointments based on competencies, skills, and substantive issues, not on political connections, political "correctness," or individuals' surface utility for political appearances.

CHART 6.5: Federal Court Appointments by Recent Presidents

President	Number of people placed	Percent of women	Percent of minorities
Clinton	182	32	29
Bush	192	19	10
Reagan	378	8	6
Carter	258	16	22
Ford	65	2	9
Nixon	227	0	4

Source: Ted Gest 1996.

Policy Implications

The policy implications are quite evident and profound. African-Americans and other racial and ethnic minorities should be treated fairly and equitably. This should be the policy at all levels of the system, but especially at arrest. If this happened, then the other components of the system (charge setting, plea negotiating, writing of presentence reports) could be held to a fair and equitable standard. As it is now, racial disproportionality occurs at all points in the system.

The Triangle: Collaboration Among Practitioners, Policymakers, and the Research/Academic Community

The Triangle: Research, Policy, and Practice

The field of corrections, as any other human service, can be changed in three ways. Policy-level decisions can alter practice through changes in the law and increases or decreases in the level of public financial support. Practitioners can change the practice of corrections by starting pilot projects, or changing workloads from undifferentiated to ones differentiated by risk level, or changing supervision strategies and other tactics. Researchers can conduct carefully constructed (experimental or quasi-experimental designs) program evaluations, and publish the results, and disseminate them through training seminars and in professional journals to practitioners and policymakers. The objective would be to get the benefits of research to policymakers, and by so doing, alter the practice of corrections. Typically, all three operate at all times and have an impact on the field in subtle but very uncoordinated ways.

The Problem: Huge Gaps of Communication and Trust

Practitioners, researchers, and policymakers do not talk to each other much. If and when they do talk, there are suspicions about motives and credibility.

Oftentimes, this suspicion can be eliminated by the parties meeting each other socially or in workshops. The following depictions of practitioners, policymakers, researchers, and academicians are generalizations. They are summarizations of this author's observations in legislative hearings, in community corrections programs, and in college classrooms. They may offend individuals who do not think or act in the ways described. The intent is to enlighten and inform, not to offend.

Practitioners

Typically, practitioners focus on the here and now. This means probation or parole officers trying to manage very large caseloads (100 - 200), a correctional officer working in a cell block with 100 men designed for half that many, or a community corrections case manager with 25 or more high-risk offenders. With a large caseload of offenders, it is not easy to allocate time to read criminology articles or to meet with state legislators on pending legislation. Also, because practitioners are overwhelmed with the daily crush of offenders, they either envy academicians whom they view as having much free time, are cynical about policymakers whom they view as grandstanding and superficial, and view both academicians and policymakers as "out of the loop" of the daily demands of correctional practice. Too often, practitioners get into routines that inhibit their learning new ways of doing things or different ways of approaching a problem. In terms of making changes in the daily routines of correctional practice, they are suspicious and wary of both academicians and policymakers.

Policymakers

Elected officials usually operate on very short time frames. The longest time frame is the next election—typically a year or so in the future. When they analyze correctional problems, they do so within this short time frame and political context. Also, elected officials, as a rule, do not have a very in-depth understanding of how things work in the criminal justice system and the corrections' system, in particular. On occasion, they participate in discussions about corrections policy, but when they do, it is with other high-level policymakers and rarely with practitioners or researchers. As a result, they remain uninformed about the daily work demands of practitioners and the practitioners' view of how the system is functioning.

Often a corrections chief or chief judge will gloss over difficult or complex matters (how the inmates feel about double bunking, the rate of noncompliance of restitution payments among probationers, the escape rate of residential community corrections clients) and offer glib descriptions of what is going on in the field. This tends to keep the elected official only superficially informed. Elected officials rarely have the time to read any complex or lengthy reports, which also tends to keep them uninformed of what is best for policy. Many state legislators do not have the staff to read reports and provide summaries for them of technical reports. Elected officials think that researchers and academicians are "out of the loop" and do not know what is happening in the field or offer advice that is politically unacceptable. So, they do not have, nor do they create, opportunities to bridge the gaps with practitioners and researchers or academicians.

Researchers and Academicians

Researchers and academicians usually view their world in a small, tight circle. They write, conduct research, and teach within the research and academic community. When they venture out, away from the campus, they usually go to academic or professional meetings with the same type of people from other parts of the country. There is no professional reward system for researchers and academicians to reach out to correctional practitioners or policymakers. Also, the daily work environment for researchers and academicians is one of slow, tedious, careful scholarship—almost the opposite of both a correctional practitioner and policymaker. The mission of a researcher is to understand, to better explain, to reveal, to demythologize. This orientation is quite unique and does not match the other two groups.

ACA Public Correctional Policy on Research and Evaluation

INTRODUCTION:

Research and evaluation, and the use of the findings that result from such efforts, are essential to informed correctional policy, program development and decision making.

POLICY STATEMENT:

Correctional agencies have a continuing responsibility to promote, initiate, sponsor, and participate in correctional research and evaluation efforts, both external and internal, in order to expand knowledge about offender behavior and enhance the effectiveness and efficiency of programs and services. To encourage and support these research and evaluation efforts, correctional agencies should:

A. Establish clearly defined procedures for data collection and analysis that ensure the accuracy, consistency, integrity, and impartiality of correctional research projects;

B. Conduct regular and systematic evaluation of correctional management, programs, and procedures and implement necessary changes;

C. Review and monitor correctional research to ensure compliance with professional standards, including those relating to confidentiality and the protection of human rights;

D. Prohibit the use of offenders as experimental subjects in medical, psychological, pharmacological, and cosmetic research except when warranted and prescribed for the diagnosis or treatment of an individual's specific condition in accordance with current standards of health care;

E. Make available to others the information necessary for correctional research and evaluation, consistent with concerns for privacy, confidentiality, and security;

F. Involve and train appropriate correctional staff in the application of correctional research and evaluation findings; and

G. Encourage the dissemination of correctional research and evaluation findings.

This Public Correctional Policy was unanimously ratified by the American Correctional Association Delegate Assembly at the Congress of Correction in New Orleans, Louisiana, August 6, 1987. It was reviewed and reaffirmed January 22, 1992, at the Winter Conference in Portland, Oregon. It was reviewed without change January 29, 1997, at the Winter Conference in Indianapolis, Indiana.

There is another tremendous limitation to cooperation and coordination of information and decision making. That limitation is the structure and process of the juvenile and criminal justice system itself. The system is complex, multifaceted, competitive, turf-oriented, and very adversarial. Other human services such as education, mental health, and physical health are not nearly as complex as either the juvenile or the adult criminal justice system. Given this organizational complexity, we must work harder to break down structural barriers that inhibit communication, cooperation, and collaboration across the lines of correctional practitioner, researcher, and policymaker.

A Functional Analysis

Chart 7.1 illustrates the division of labor and respective responsibilities needed to address particular events or issues. If viewed proactively, these events constitute opportunities for collaboration among the three groups in question.

CHART 7.1: Three Perspectives on Every Issue

Event or Issue	Policymaker	Practitioner	Researcher
New legislation, criminal statute revisions	Allocate sufficient time to read the literature that relates to proposed legislation, analyze cost implications, establish performance goals, attend meetings with practitioners and researchers	Read proposed legislation and related literature on proposed legislation, attend meetings with legislators to discuss legislation, offer opinions about system impact of proposed legislation	Conduct literature review of proposed legislation, synthesize and interpret literature for practitioners and policymakers, attend meetings with practitioners and policymakers
New program development, pilot program testing	Read related literature on new programs, attend meetings with other policymakers and practitioners on the expectations and problems of implementation	Read related literature on new programs, inform others of the system impact of new programs, assist other practitioners in implementation and avoiding problems associated with new programs, attend meetings	Conduct literature review of related programs, prepare reports on this literature and present it to practitioners and policymakers, anticipate implementation problems
Publication of research findings	Read the research findings, attend meetings to listen to research findings, discuss systems implications of findings	Read the research findings, attend meetings to listen to research findings, discuss systems implications of findings	Write up research findings, prepare written material for policymakers and practitioners, conduct meetings to interpret and discuss the findings
Constructing research designs for correctional programs	Attend meetings to discuss performance and outcome measures; represent the public's interests, wishes and fears	Attend meetings, provide input about the system impact of research project and performance and critique and revise outcome measures	Develop research design, present design to practitioners and policymakers, revise design in relation to the issue raised by others
Orientation for new district attorneys, judges, legislators, governors	Attend new orientation meetings, read literature provided, visit correctional sites	Attend orientation sessions, provide information on correctional programs, host visits to correctional sites	Attend orientation sessions, provide performance information on existing and upcoming programs
Monitoring ongoing correctional programs	Read reports of ongoing programs, attend meetings to discuss program performance, present statewide perspective on correctional funding	Maintain MIS with current, reliable information, prepare reports for policymakers and researchers, attend meetings to explain ongoing operations	Obtain performance information from practitioners, prepare performance reports, conduct meetings, and interpret information for practitioners and policymakers

Chart 7.1 demonstrates a very different way of approaching correctional policy and practice. This approach requires a significant dedication of time and effort on the part of all three sets of actors. Is this possible? Is it overly optimistic? The answer to those questions depends on the level of commitment to excellence in corrections. If that commitment is "normal," the time allocated to this type of collaboration will be minimal. However, the rate of growth of correctional populations is forcing correctional issues to an ever higher public priority. The policy choice is to either deal with the issues proactively, anticipate problems and have a plan in place to handle problems, or wait until the problems occur and then address them in a crisis mode.

Institutionalize Collaboration

To implement this type of comprehensive collaboration, the following suggestions offer ways to institutionalize improvements in communication and coordination among the three groups.

Judges and Attorneys (prosecutors and defense): Incorporate these principles and practices into in-service training and legal education credits. Collaborate with state legislators on pending legislation. Attend workshops with researchers discussing correctional program performance reports, and go to meetings with practitioners to discuss correctional operations. These options should be given as much value as existing legal education credits.

New Legislators: The legislative leadership needs to take the initiative here. Require new legislators to participate in training sessions and workshops to learn from practitioners and researchers about correctional program operations and effectiveness. Some states already have established orientation programs for new legislators, but most do not have special programs focused on correctional issues and problems. The leadership also must require legislators to collaborate with practitioners and researchers on prospective legislation. A way to accomplish this is to have a standing committee that reviews prospective corrections-related legislation. The legislative committee then becomes the forum for the three groups to meet and discuss policy and operational issues.

Correctional Practitioners: Practitioners should take the initiative and meet with local church groups, attend Kiwanis and Rotary Club luncheons, and become active in other community groups. Practitioners also can testify at legislative hearings and attempt to hold elected officials accountable for their public statements on crime, crime prevention, and correctional intervention. Correctional practitioners have a moral, intellectual, and professional obligation to stay abreast of the development of knowledge related to causes and correlates of criminal behavior.

If that reason is not sufficiently compelling, then the success rate of our clients, the criminal offenders, should be the reason. Professional standards should be revised, and the points made in Chart 7.1 should be incorporated into personnel policies. Attending meetings and collaborating with policymakers and researchers should "count" as much as other in-service training credits, formal education, or other personnel enhancement criteria. Once these ideas are incorporated into personnel policy, then this type of collaborative effort will pay off in terms of higher wages, career advancement, and higher positions of authority.

Researchers and Academicians: The faculty of most colleges and universities operate on tenure. Tenure is gained through professional efforts, such as good teaching evaluations, research accomplished, publications in academic journals, and other activities. These collaborative efforts would fall under the residual category of "other activities." Academic deans and others at the policy level must take the lead here. They need to change the tenure criteria to include the types of collaboration described. This proposed change is not significantly different from any other outside research effort with a private foundation or a public funding agency.

Purposeful Collaboration

There are ways of creating or instigating collaboration. A student internship program can bring at least two of the three sets of actors together, namely researchers and practitioners. Such a program was established in Boulder, Colorado in 1990. A faculty member at the university serves as the academic sponsor and oversees the internship program from the university perspective. A local, private community corrections program provides the correctional setting. Undergraduate students are the student interns. They are required to take prerequisite courses in criminal justice in preparation for the actual internship placement. They, then, are placed in the community corrections programs doing entry-level work (line staff and security) and observation. They write progress reports and student papers and receive academic credit for their efforts. Graduate students provide ongoing support, training, and critiques for the student interns.

Another noteworthy collaborative effort was the Standardized Offender Assessment Program in Colorado. The program, enacted into law by the 1991 legislature, is administered by the State Office of Probation Services. The

Standardized Offender Assessment Program is a statewide process for uniformly assessing offender risk and prescribing levels of substance abuse treatment. It was developed by a committee composed of legislators, criminal justice representatives from state agencies such as corrections, the judicial branch, alcohol and drug professionals, and the division of criminal justice, professionals from local human service and corrections agencies, and researchers and academicians from state agencies as well as colleges and universities. The most impressive thing about the program is the amount and extent of collaboration among the different sets of actors. Thus far, the Standardized Offender Assessment Program is proving hugely successful in providing multiple and consistent measures of offenders' overall orientation to criminal behavior and substance abuse (Fogg and Bogue 1996).

Examples of the Changing Role of Researchers and Academicians and Some Suggestions for More Change

There is an abundance of knowledge about what works in the field of adult corrections, and this body of knowledge is expanding quickly. The challenge is how to bridge the gap between that body of knowledge and misinformed public policy, such as: more prisons lead to less crime.

The role of academicians and criminal justice researchers must change. These groups must reach out to other groups who need the knowledge that they possess. For example, this author would strongly recommend that this group take the initiative to communicate with the top leaders in the executive, legislative, and judicial branches of government. Further, this group should find a legislative sponsor and testify at legislative hearings. Also, this group should make presentations to the annual meetings of the International Community Corrections Association, the American Probation and Parole Association, the American Correctional Association, and other correctional groups. The members of these practitioner groups need information from current literature and program evaluations.

A few pioneers have done that in the past (Stuart Adams and Ted Palmer, both premier corrections' researchers who established their professional reputations in California in the 1960s and 1970s) and a growing number, but still very few in number, are beginning to attend practitioner conferences. The most recent example is the series of "What Works" conferences sponsored by the International Community Corrections Association (ICCA) that was attended by many well-known researchers and academicians.

One example of the changing role of researchers and academicians is Delbert Elliott, a dedicated criminologist who performed his traditional research and teaching roles for more than two decades. His research was conducted all over the country but his home base was the Institute for Behavioral Science in Boulder, Colorado. In 1993, Dr. Elliott began to reach out to new audiences. He met with the governor a few times. He testified in front of several state legislative committees. He met privately with a small group of members of the United States Congress. He worked with executive and legislative branch people on public policy papers on juvenile delinquency and violence (his area of expertise). His change of role from "ivory tower man" to "criminal justice policy advisor" has had a very positive impact. Many of the ideas that he has been discussing in academia for many years are now being integrated into public policy.

Other examples of researchers and academicians reaching out beyond their own areas of expertise are James Bonta, Donald Andrews, Paul Gendreau and others from the "Ottawa School" who have been sharing their ideas with the National Institute of Corrections, the American Probation and Parole Association, "What Works" conferences, and many specialized workshops around the country. William Miller from the University of New Mexico, a national leader in alcohol and drug treatment research, has been the catalyst in getting current research findings into the hands and heads of practitioners. Elliott Currie, professor of criminology and writer/researcher at the University of California at Berkeley, has broken traditional academic boundaries with his publications and his work with public policy officials in California and other states.

Researchers and others who know the correctional-intervention literature best are in a unique position to have a significant impact on how corrections does its work and how policymakers decide which program to support and which to cut. The particular types of people in the policy arena who should be targeted by researchers include governors, staff who work for the governor, state legislators, and staff who draft legislation for legislators, print and TV journalists with a special interest in criminal justice policy, and judges on the criminal bench.

Summary

Better coordination and cooperation among correctional practitioners, policymakers, researchers, and academicians will improve overall correctional performance. To achieve this coordination and cooperation, all these sets of actors should change their behavior. Organizational incentives and special projects can help bring about this type of collaborative effort. The benefits are many if it can be accomplished. We know what will happen if we do not do this by simply looking back on the last disastrous decade in the field of corrections.

Chapter 8

Developing a New Agenda for Corrections

There have been many calls for a new corrections' agenda (Gottfredson and McConville 1987; Edna McConnell Clark Foundation 1982, National Council on Crime and Delinquency 1987). This is another such call. The difference this time is that crowding in all components of corrections, institutions and community, has never been more acute; correctional expenditures have reached new highs at the very time that governmental revenues are decreasing; yet the field of corrections has advanced its tools, methods, and theories more in the last ten years than in the previous sixty years.

The intersection of these three factors offers the field of corrections a rare opportunity to make unprecedented changes. It will require courageous leadership, a unified vision of what is possible, and an unwavering determination to change. This sounds like an impossible dream, but this author has met people in the field who have these qualities and clearly are capable of this caliber of leadership. So, there is hope.

A Call to Reduce Prison Use

The new correctional agenda should include the following items:

- Literally hundreds of thousands of adults now incarcerated in state prisons could safely be released to some form of community supervision. This is possible IF we, (1) use current theory (Chapter 4) to guide our actions, (2) carefully assess risk when offenders come into the system (Chapter 9), (3) conduct a comprehensive needs assessment at program intake (Chapter 10); then, (4) followup the needs assessment with the delivery of appropriate treatment services, and (5) change criminal statutes that require low- and medium-risk offenders to be sentenced to jail or prison (Petersilia 1995, Campaign for an Effective Crime Policy 1992).

- Once low-risk and some moderate-risk offenders are released to more appropriate community corrections programs, state prisons and many local jails will have enough bed space to adequately house violent, dangerous, and repeat offenders. Both the rate of incarceration as well as the level of institutional crowding can be reduced significantly.

- Given the history of disproportionate handling of racial and ethnic minorities within the criminal justice system, a systematic reduction of their numbers in prison should occur to reduce the racial disproportionality of prison populations. As low-risk offenders are moved out of prisons, parole preference should be given to low- and moderate-risk racial and ethnic minorities.

- Halt all current plans to build additional prisons.

- Shift the funds that are scheduled for more prison construction to areas that can reduce the current offenders' risk for recidivism and prevent younger people from entering the criminal justice system (see Chapters 10 and 13).

- Require state legislators to find adequate amounts for construction and especially operating money for a minimum of twenty years in the future for every prison bed needed as a result of any bill that they propose.

- Clean up the community corrections system (see Chapter 13). Moving low- and medium-risk offenders out of jails and prisons without a corresponding effort to improve community corrections is simply repeating the policy mistake of the deinstitutionalization of the mentally ill in the 1960s. Community corrections must reserve their staff and resources for medium- and higher-risk offenders, and not waste time and staff on low-risk offenders.

Based on estimates from Bonta and Motiuk's work (1985, 1987, 1990, 1992) and this author's direct observations and analyses of jail and prison populations in many local communities and states, it appears reasonable to reduce prison admissions by one-third. A one-third reduction in prison admissions would accomplish six objectives:

- reduce institutional crowding

- reduce stress, suicides, alcoholism, and other health problems among prison staff

- reduce lawsuits related to crowding

- reduce inmate-on-inmate assaults

- reduce inmate-on-staff assaults

- halt the need for new prison construction

Is this general shift in corrections' policy possible? If the best risk/needs assessment instruments are used in making classification and release decisions and state and federal criminal statutes are changed, this shift is possible. Public safety need not be compromised. Whether this agenda will be approved by elected officials depends on implementing changes, previously discussed, in the political arena, the media, and in correctional practice (see Chapters 9-13). Later in this chapter, we present several states' efforts to reduce prison use.

ACA Public Correctional Policy on Use of Appropriate Sanctions and Controls

INTRODUCTION:

In developing, selecting and administering sanctions and punishments, decision-makers must balance concern for individual dignity, public safety and maintenance of social order. Correctional programs and facilities are a costly and limited resource; the most restrictive are generally the most expensive. Therefore, it is good public policy to use these resources wisely and economically.

POLICY STATEMENT:

The sanctions and controls imposed by courts and administered by corrections should be the least restrictive consistent with public and individual safety and maintenance of social order. Selection of the least restrictive sanctions and punishments in specific cases inherently require balancing several important objectives—

individual dignity, fiscal responsibility and effective correctional operations. To meet these objectives, correctional agencies should:

A. Advocate to all branches of government—executive, legislative and judicial—and to the public at large, the development and appropriate use of the least restrictive sanctions, punishments, programs and facilities;

B. Recommend the use of the least restrictive appropriate dispositions in judicial decisions;

C. Classify persons under correctional jurisdiction to the least restrictive appropriate programs and facilities; and

D. Employ only the level of regulation and control necessary for the safe and efficient operation of programs, services and facilities.

This Public Correctional Policy was unanimously ratified by the American Correctional Association Delegate Assembly, at the Winter Conference in Denver, Colorado, January 12, 1984. It was reviewed August 15, 1990, at the Congress of Correction in San Diego, California, with no change. It was reviewed January 18, 1995, at the Winter Conference in Dallas, Texas, with no change.

Examples of Efforts to Reduce Prison Use

Is it possible to restrict prison use through a more refined classification system and a narrowing of the criminal justice net? Not only is it possible, but several localities already have done it. Some of these efforts succeeded, some succeeded and then were overturned by legislative changes or by administrative decision making, and some are still in the works.

Juveniles in Massachusetts

One attempt to reduce prison use was the deinstitutionalization of juvenile offenders in Massachusetts in 1971. The state director of juvenile services, Jerome Miller, closed all the state prisons for youthful offenders. Instead of state prisons, youthful offenders were placed in local public and private residential and nonresidential programs, and a very small number were placed in higher-security programs or facilities in neighboring states.

This radical change in correctional policy ended in January 1973, when political pressures forced Miller to resign. The controversy surrounding both the substance and the process of change stimulated a national debate about the effectiveness of incarceration of juvenile offenders. Several evaluations of the short- and long-term effects of removing juveniles from institutions found that they posed no greater risk to the community when they were kept in nonsecure settings. A secondary benefit was the reduced cost, due to the closure of state correctional institutions (Clear and Cole 1986).

However, change is never easy or quick. The staffs of the juvenile institutions in Massachusetts were not happy to see their jobs at risk. They fought successfully to maintain their jobs—in spite of having little to do. The state was required to pay them full-time salaries based on their union contracts and the state's civil service system. Part of the staff and political reaction to the confrontative manner in which change was implemented resulted in the reinstitutionalization of a few (about 200) juvenile offenders. In the long run, in the opinion of this author, the effort was well worth it. Instead of 2,000 youthful offenders locked up in institutions receiving nothing more than heavy doses of social control, today there is a much more appropriate balance with a small number of difficult offenders inside institutions and the vast majority in a variety of community programs.

The lesson of Massachusetts is this: most juvenile offenders are served better in community programs than inside of correctional institutions. Not only is this possible, it is better for the young offenders, a cost saving for taxpayers as a result of operating fewer correctional institutions (assuming the personnel issues can be worked out), and the transfer of institutional cost savings to more effective programming.

Delaware: A Statewide Classification System

In 1987, a continuum of sanctions was approved by the state legislature and adopted by the courts in Delaware. The sanctions range from level one, unsupervised probation, to level five, incarceration. The principle inherent in the sanctions system was to sentence offenders to the least restrictive and least costly sanction commensurate with the seriousness of the offense. Earlier, this author suggested a uniform classification system for all offenders. Delaware's statewide sanctions system approximates a uniform classification and placement system. (What this author is advocating is matching the principle of the least-restrictive setting to the level of risk and not to the seriousness of the offense. The seriousness of an offense is an inaccurate and imprecise measure of risk.)

The Delaware sanctioning system went into effect in 1990. Some of the special features of the new system included: (1) increased certainty of punishment, a core principle of deterrence theory, (2) a reduction of the statutory maximum sentences for most crimes, and (3) early release from incarceration and community supervision for some offenders. The legislative plan was to halt the construction of new prisons by releasing low-risk offenders from prison, and increasing prison stays for dangerous and violent offenders.

The early results of implementing the new sanctions system were quite promising. New prison construction was avoided. The greatest amount of growth in the correctional system was in the lower risk/security levels. Judges were very supportive of nonincarcerative sanctions and wanted expansion of level-four programs, as alternatives to incarceration. More than 65 percent of halfway house clients and 79 percent of home confinement clients succeeded. Most failures in level three and four programs were due to program violations, not new crimes committed (Sentac 1991, Castle 1991). Despite these changes, since the early 1990s, Delaware has seen an increase in the rate of incarceration, due to mandatory sentencing laws and other statutory changes (Reback 1993).

Minnesota: Reducing Prison Use Through Sentencing Reform

Minnesota has been a national leader in prison and sentencing reform for more than two decades. In 1973, Minnesota enacted a comprehensive prison diversion—community corrections program. The legislature provided state funds to local community corrections boards and programs to divert nonviolent felons from placement into the state prison system. For all nonviolent felons that fit the state criteria, the state subsidized the cost to house them locally; if the local jurisdiction decided to send this same type of offender to prison, the cost of incarcerating those offenders would be deducted from the state subsidy.

After several years of operation, it was determined that the goal of diverting felons from prison was not being met (Knapp 1976). Local board members and service providers were "creaming," in other words, selecting low-risk felony offenders who would have succeeded anyway. These low-risk offenders were not prison diversion candidates. A different strategy to reduce prison use was required.

In 1978, a state sentencing guidelines commission was established. The purpose of the State Sentencing Guidelines Commission was quite similar to the 1973 legislation, namely, use prison less, or, at least, very sparingly. The State Sentencing Guidelines law specifically stated that the state would attempt to use existing prison space and not create demands for more space. The State Sentencing Guidelines Commission began operations in 1980. Its primary tool was a two-dimensional sentencing grid that called for incarceration for serious, repeat, violent offenders and community sanctions for lesser offenders.

The early reports of the impact of the new sentencing grid were very positive. Between 1980 and 1987, the rate of incarceration in Minnesota held quite steady (rate in 1980: 49/100,000; rate in 1986: 58/100,000). This was a period when prison use was increasing 8 to 12 percent per year in most of the rest of the country. The State Sentencing Guidelines Commission's third year report stated, "There was a 73 percent increase in imprisonment for offenders convicted of high-severity crimes with low criminal histories. There was a 72 percent reduction in imprisonment of those convicted of low-severity crimes with moderate to high criminal histories" (Minnesota State Sentencing Guidelines Commission 1984). This was exactly the goal: use prisons for violent and dangerous offenders and not for property offenders.

However, starting in the late 1980s, prison populations began to climb. By 1992, the state's prisons were full, even though the state's rate of incarceration was still only one-fourth of the nation's rate. Three factors were behind the increase in prison use. They included: (1) a substantial growth in felony convictions; 1981 - 5,500; 1991 - 9,161, (2) increased rates of revocation in probation and parole, and (3) major increases in sentencing severity adopted by the legislature and the State Sentencing Guidelines Commission.

The State Sentencing Guidelines Commission was set up, in part, to be insulated from the hot tempered "get tough on crime" arena of the media and the legislature. In the late 1980s and early 1990s, the State Sentencing Guidelines Commission was drawn into the full glare of the public debate and capitulated under media and political pressure. The legislature encouraged and supported the "get tough" sentencing laws of 1989 and 1992.

The conclusion is that not even Minnesota could sustain substantial reform (Frase 1993). The political script of "get tough on crime and criminals" is too seductive for public and elected officials to ignore. However, from 1980 to 1988, Minnesota demonstrated that if the political and media rhetoric could be contained, prison use could be curtailed without a significant loss of public safety.

The State of Washington

Washington State, following Minnesota's lead, passed sentencing guidelines legislation in 1981 and implemented it in 1984. Between 1984 and 1988, the legislature deferred changes in the state's sentencing laws to the sentencing guideline commissioners. Also, during this period, the state had a surplus of prison beds, due to an expansive construction period in the early to mid 1980s. During the last half of the 1980s, Washington rented out prison beds to various states and the federal government. If the Washington story ended here, it would be a "success story," describing how prison use could be reduced without increasing crime, and possibly reducing correctional expenditures.

However, starting in 1987, the political winds began to shift. Pressures began to mount to change the sentencing guidelines to increase penalties for drug offenders. A major actor in this move was the chief prosecutor from King County (Seattle).

In 1988 and 1989, political pressure was mobilized to increase prison sentences for sex offenders. Also in 1989, a legislator proposed that penalties for burglary be increased. The legislature passed all of the bills (even though the burglary bill was vetoed by the governor; the veto was overruled by the legislature) which resulted in an increased demand for prison beds.

In 1993 and 1994, groups of crime victims and prosecutors, with the help of a local conservative think tank, organized citizen initiatives to the state constitution. Both of these efforts succeeded. The targets of the two citizen initiatives were "three strikes" (repeat offenders) and offenders who used weapons in the commission of their crimes. Once again, the demand for prisons increased (Lieb 1993, Boerner 1995). The reform effort (1982 to 1988) was implemented, but like Minnesota, the "get tough" crowd torpedoed the effort with highly visible emotional pleas.

Reducing Prison Use in Finland

Between 1976 and 1992, the rate of incarceration in Finland was reduced by 40 percent. This decrease in prison use was brought about by the following measures: (1) statutory changes which reduced penalties for theft and drunk driving, (2) a lowering of the minimum time served in prison before eligibility for parole, and (3) increases in the use of suspended sentences. Chart 8.1 illustrates the specific impact of these changes.

CHART 8.1: Prison Admissions, Population, and Median Sentences in Finland, 1976 and 1992

	1976	1992
Total number of prisoners	5,706	3,511
Incarceration rate/100,000	118	70
Number of prison admissions	13,457	9,851
Months in prison, average	5.1	3.6*
Sentences to intermediate confinement	65%**	41%**
Suspended sentences	35%**	59%**

*1992 figures were unavailable; 3.6 months was the 1991 figure, which was the most current available.

**The confinement and suspended sentence data were for years 1971 and 1991.

Source: Tornudd 1993.

The numbers in Chart 8.1 are unlike anything in the United States—ever. According to Finnish officials, these changes would not have been possible without an almost unanimous determination, participation, and acceptance by top governmental officials, policy analysts, and criminologists. The Finnish experience convincingly demonstrates that the level of prison use is a result of deliberate policy choices, not the result of criminal acts, what inmates do after their release from prison, extent of poverty, or other such factors.

Summary of Sentencing Guidelines Legislation

The passage of sentencing guidelines legislation has been an effective tool in reducing prison use for select offenders. However, without widespread public and political support, sentencing guidelines, sentencing grids, and sentencing commissions are unable to maintain their organizational independence and stay removed from the "get tough" political rhetoric.

Classification of Offenders

The field of corrections should get out of the business of accepting, handling, treating, incarcerating, or supervising low-risk offenders. The definition of a low-risk offender is a person who has committed a minor offense, has little or no criminal history, and is, on any objective risk scale, at a low risk for recidivism. A more detailed discussion of risk is presented in Chapter 9.

Low-risk offenders can supervise themselves or can be watched, monitored, or cosponsored in the community by friends, family, or volunteers. There is absolutely no need to house low-risk offenders in jail, prison, or residential community treatment centers. As a matter of fact, when low-risk offenders are placed in highly structured, intensely supervised correctional settings such as jails, prisons, or residential programs, they get worse, not better (Bonta 1991).

Basically, there are two subsets of low-risk offenders: those who have treatment needs and those who do not. For those who do not, there is all the more reason for corrections to keep them out of their system. For those who have treatment needs, corrections should help them find the appropriate services in the host community. Existing human service agencies are much better equipped especially with specialized staff training to handle treatment needs than are probation agencies or the staff at local jails.

Correctional practitioners must take the lead on this issue. The practitioners on the front-end of the criminal justice system, police, prosecutors, probation officers in the investigation units, and judges, have little professional or organizational self-interest to screen out low-risk offenders. A low-risk offender to a prosecuting attorney is simply an offender who can increase the district attorney office's conviction rate and, hence, represents an asset. To a correctional staffer, a low-risk offender means a larger caseload, more paperwork, and if he or she is placed inappropriately in an intensely supervised program, puts that person at great risk for revocation (program failure). So, the burden of proof will be on the corrections practitioners to make the case for a change in policy regarding the low-risk offender.

The precise proportion of low-risk offenders in jails, prisons, and residential programs is unknown because assessments using objective risk assessments have not yet been conducted. Assessing for risk should go beyond the use of first- and second-generation risk assessment (see Chapter 9). Risk assessment must include measures of criminogenic needs (see Chapter 10). Some work has been done in select areas and components of the system to indicate that the number of low-risk offenders in the corrections system is significant. An analysis of the jail population in Connecticut in 1991 indicated that up to 40 percent could be considered for release to less intensely supervised community programs (Justice Education Center 1991). Bonta and Motiuk administered the Level of Supervision Inventory (LSI) risk/needs assessment instrument to an incarcerated population and discovered many low-risk offenders who could be safely released to the community (Bonta and Motiuk 1990, Bonta 1991).

A Uniform Classification System for All Offenders

After traveling to many local, state, and federal jurisdictions, one thing is clear: people have their own notion about who is a risk to the community and who is not. The second thing that is clear is that all people have their own idea about why a particular offender constitutes such a risk. This is particularly true when a standardized risk and needs assessment instrument is not used.

What seems logical and reasonable is to have one instrument used by all practitioners on all offenders. In this manner, all practitioners would be classifying offenders on the same basis, from the same theoretical assumptions, and for the same purpose (to reduce risk to commit crimes and risk for recidivism). Inter- and intra-jurisdictional decision making would be greatly enhanced with a common assessment language. Debates based on subjective notions of risk would be replaced with discussions of validity and reliability of information. Judges would be informed much better about which sentencing option to pick based on measurable risk and outcome (performance) factors. Probation officers preparing sentencing recommendations for judges would similarly be well served with the use of a uniform classification instrument. The same principle would apply to parole agents and parole board members.

Chapter 9 includes a discussion on how to assess for risk; Chapter 10 presents how to assess for criminogenic needs (those particular needs that lead or contribute to criminal activities), and Chapter 12 is a discussion of responsivity. The classification instrument of choice is the Level of Supervision Inventory (LSI). A more detailed discussion of the elements and use of the Level of Supervision Inventory is included in Chapters 9 through 11.

More Community Involvement

In the absence of a populist movement (like the one in South Africa in the early 1990s), public and elected officials, and, increasingly, narrow special interests (crime victims, prison correctional officers, local prosecutors, upwardly mobile politicians, construction companies, financial institutions), shape the use and scale of criminal sanctions. To develop a more balanced corrections system, a system that matches correctional settings with risk and need levels of individual offenders, a broader array of people should get involved in shaping correctional policy.

There is a need to get the general citizenry involved in revising and rethinking the use of criminal sanctions in the United States. Focus groups are a recent innovation in matching lay citizens with public and elected officials. Focus groups are carefully selected samples of people who meet to become informed about a particular substantive area, and after some basic education has occurred, they formulate opinions with the aid of a facilitator. Focus groups, unlike polling surveys, offer hope that the concerns of lay citizens can be communicated directly to public and elected officials without the distortions of special interest groups (Schoen 1995).

ACA Public Correctional Policy on Classification

INTRODUCTION:

Classification is a continuing process basic to identifying and matching offender needs to correctional resources. This continuing process involves all phases of correctional management.

POLICY STATEMENT:

Classification should balance the public's need for protection, the needs of offenders, and the efficient and effective operation of the correctional system. In developing and administering its classification system, a correctional agency should:

A. Develop written classification policies that establish criteria specifying different levels of security, supervision, and program involvement; establish procedures for documenting and reviewing all classification decisions and actions; describe the appeal process to be used by individuals subject to classification; and specify the time frames for monitoring and reclassifying cases;

B. Develop the appropriate range of resources and services to meet the identified control and program needs of the population served;

C. Base classification decisions on rational assessment of objective and valid information, including background material (criminal history, nature of offense, social history, educational needs, medical/mental health needs, etc.), as well as information regarding the individual's current situation, adjustment, and program achievement;

D. Train all personnel in the classification process and require specialized training for those directly involved in classification functions;

E. Use the classification process to assign individuals to different levels of control on the basis of valid criteria regarding risk (to self and others) and individual needs, matching these characteristics with appropriate security, level of supervision, and program services;

F. Involve the individual directly in the classification process;

G. Assign appropriately trained staff to monitor individual classification plans for progress made and reclassification needs;

H. Objectively validate the classification process and instruments, assess on a planned basis the degree to which results meet written goals, and, as needed, refine the process and instruments; and

I. Provide for regular dissemination of classification information to all levels of correctional staff and to involve decision-makers outside of corrections as an aid in the planning, management, and operation of the correctional agency.

This Public Correctional Policy was unanimously ratified by the American Correctional Association Delegate Assembly, at the Congress of Correction in San Antonio, Texas, August 23, 1984. It was reviewed January 17, 1990, at the Winter Conference in Nashville, Tennessee, with no change. It was reviewed January 18, 1995, at the Winter Conference in Dallas, Texas, with no change.

Section 2: Practice

This section of the book is written primarily for practitioners working in the field of corrections (primarily adult, but not exclusively). These are the professionals who have the responsibility to classify, assess, supervise, and assist juvenile and adult offenders under their jurisdiction. If this task is done with care and knowledge, offenders can move from procriminal to prosocial lifestyles. If that can be accomplished, people's lives can be turned around, less harm to crime victims will result, failure on probation and parole can be reduced—all types of good things can happen.

If the knowledge in this section of the book is ignored, failure while under community supervision (probation, parole, or community corrections) will continue to be high (20 to 30 percent for low-risk offenders; as high as 70 percent for high-risk offenders). When an offender fails, he or she is usually assigned the blame for that failure. Much of the blame rests with the offender, but when failure rates remain high year after year, the entire field of adult corrections becomes suspect.

Happily, there are many promising new theories and practices that can remove both the offenders and the correctional practitioners from this failure/blame dead-end road. The most promising new theory is the Psychology of Criminal Conduct (Andrews and Bonta 1994). Innovative practices include standardized assessment of risk and criminogenic needs, a proliferation of specialized assessment instruments for treatment needs, Motivational Interviewing (Miller and Rollnick 1991), Stages of Change (Prochaska and DiClemente 1982, Miller and Rollnick 1991, DiClemente 1991) and FRAMES, a reiterative process designed to resolve offender ambivalence and optimize motivation for change (Miller and Sanchez 1993). With a solid, empirically tested theory, accurate methods of assessing risk and criminogenic needs now are available. With an accurate assessment of risk, correctional placement decisions are facilitated greatly. The investigations division of every probation department in the country now can put this knowledge to use in their sentencing recommendations to judges. The uses are many and all are critically important.

This author hopes that policymakers also will read this portion of the book. Many policymakers are totally uninformed about what works in adult corrections and some of the same policymakers sponsor bills to lengthen prison sentences and require mandatory prison terms for particular crimes. For violent and predatory offenders, prison is the only responsible place to house them. There is little debate about that. However, violent and predatory offenders make up a very small fraction of all offenders. The debate should be about what we expect violent offenders to accomplish while they are in prison. The position of this book is that violent offenders, inside of prison, or in a community corrections program, should learn to treat other people and other people's property with respect, to become productive, law-abiding citizens. If agreement can be reached on that objective, then length of time in prison can be set with that objective in mind. Without agreement on that objective, length of time in prison becomes a bidding war between policymakers who can publicly inflict more punishment on the offender by means of longer and longer prison stays.

The same is true of all other types of offenders. Without knowledge of what works in correctional intervention, placement mistakes are made even with low-risk property offenders. Most state prisons, now housing over a million adults, are housing, feeding, clothing, and providing expensive medical care for literally hundreds of thousands of low-risk offenders. In the view of this author, this is extremely expensive policy, a policy that puts other important human services such a K-12 education at risk, and does nothing to change the behavior of these low-risk offenders. A good case can be made that placing low-risk offenders in prison is actually criminogenic (results in more, not less crime).

For the benefit of practitioners and policymakers, this second section of the book is dedicated to policymakers who want to learn about what works in adult corrections and to correctional practitioners who are committed to higher and higher standards of correctional service.

Chapter 9

Risk Assessment:
Making Critical Decisions

Prosecutors, judges, and probation officers making sentencing recommendations often commit three types of mistakes in deciding who needs incarceration, who can be safely released from jail prior to trial, and who should be released from prison on parole: (1) low-risk offenders are placed in (or not released from) high-security institutions or settings; (2) high-risk offenders are placed in low-security (probation) settings; and (3) on program intake, medium- to high-risk offenders are not accurately assessed and matched to appropriate levels of surveillance and treatment services.

If it is possible to reduce these three types of mistakes, society will be safer with high-risk offenders placed in more secure settings. Additionally, correctional costs can be reduced because incarceration is unnecessary and counterproductive for low-risk offenders. If these things occur, correctional practitioners will gain in professional stature as placement and classification decisions improve, and correctional policy will become more rational as elected officials develop more trust in decision making of correctional practitioners.

History of Risk Assessment in Corrections

Offender-risk tools have evolved and developed in a few different directions since the first Burgess validation study in 1928. After the federal courts recognized prison inmates' rights to due process hearings and notices (*Mempa v. Rhay* 1967) and O'Leary and colleagues developed the Salient Factor Score instrument for federal parole officials in 1973, correctional practitioners were forced to be more thoughtful about their placement and classification decisions. This, in turn, puts pressure on researchers to develop better risk assessment instruments.

The first effort to objectively assess risk for adult offenders on a statewide basis was in Wisconsin. Christopher Baird and others at the Wisconsin Department of Corrections developed a system of risk and needs assessment for adult offenders during the late 1970s.

The most important feature of these early years was the use of objective (actuarial) information and large samples (hundreds of offenders). The validity of those early risk-assessment instruments was increased greatly when researchers created quasi-experimental designs in which experimental groups that had received a particular type of intervention or treatment were compared to control groups that received the "normal" placement or sanction. Practitioners were learning from the successes and failures of many thousands of offenders. This is in stark contrast to people trying to make a decision on one offender based on their experience and "gut feelings." After two decades of research and development, the "bottom line" is that use of objective risk scales greatly improves professional judgment and prediction.

Political forces, professional practitioner pressures, and legal challenges propelled criminal justice researchers to speed up the development of better, more accurate, more user-friendly risk assessment instruments during this period. Some of the best work in risk assessment for criminal offenders was done by Canadians in the early to mid-1980s. James Bonta, Donald Andrews, Donald Hoge, Laurence Motiuk, Paul Gendreau, and others used meta-analysis, which is a synthesis of the findings of hundreds of research studies. They isolated the key issues and variables to build theory and refine a risk/needs assessment instrument called the Level of Supervision Inventory-Revised (LSI-R).

The Paradox of Assessing Risk

In spite of the fact that researchers, practitioners, and the general public view youthful and adult offenders as separate entities, the principles regarding offender risk, need, and responsivity (treatment matching) apply to both juvenile and adult offenders (Loeber and Stouthamer-Loeber 1987, Simourd and Andrews 1994, Gendreau 1996). Offender-recidivism risk stems from many factors. Higher-risk offenders generally have patterns of criminal behavior that began earlier and are more versatile and stable (durable) than other offenders. Paradoxically, however, a considerable amount of recent offender-rehabilitation research indicates that greater public safety returns (reductions in recidivism) are obtained through intervening with higher-risk offenders rather than lower-risk offenders. Given these findings, a corrections policy that screens or engages in a triage for offenders at risk is likely to have considerable merit.

Analysis of the Content of Risk Assessments

From the correctional practitioner's perspective, the reason to use formal risk and classification systems is to provide greater validity, structure, and consistency to the assessment and decision-making processes. From the system's perspective, the reasons to use objective classification instruments are to obtain a more efficient allocation of limited correctional resources by targeting and applying the most intensive and intrusive interventions for the most serious and chronic offenders (Weibush, Baird, Krisberg, Onek 1994).

Predictors of Future Misbehavior

The following factors have consistently emerged as valid predictors of future misbehavior:

1. Age at first adjudication

2. Prior criminal behavior (arrests, convictions, incarcerations)

3. Extent and history of drug use

4. Extent and history of alcohol use

5. Education

6. Employment

7. Family, marital status, and situation

8. Companions, peers, friends, social network

9. Emotional stability, history of psychological problems

10. Attitudes and beliefs regarding crime

Not all ten factors play an equal role in the future success or failure of a given offender. Factors one and two (age and prior criminal behavior) are static; they cannot change. The other factors are dynamic (it is possible to change them). Each factor has a different weight or impact on recidivism.

A Suggested Triage Approach

Acknowledging the crush of humanity that impinges on local jails, state prisons, probation and parole caseloads each day, a suggested triage approach is offered. The rationale for this approach is quick identification of two groups: low-risk and extremely high-risk offenders.

All (or at least most) would agree that a person convicted for the first time for check fraud is a low-risk offender. The appropriate place on the correctional continuum for this low-risk offender would be either unsupervised probation or a simple fine with restitution to the victim. No reasonable person would advocate jail or prison time for this offense and offender. Similarly, all would agree that a third-time pedophile is a very high-risk offender and should be locked up.

Hence, the moral, legal, and corrections debate is not about the two extreme ends—the very low-risk and extremely high-risk offenders. The debate is over how to determine the risk to the community of the moderate-risk offenders and the repeat offenders with high criminogenic needs (see Chapter 10) in the middle of the correctional continuum. If they are repeat violent offenders, there is little debate that most or all will be sentenced to jail or prison. If they are repeat non-violent property or drug offenders (who constitute the overwhelming majority of this medium-risk group), depending on many factors, they may be eligible for some type of highly structured community program.

Low-risk Offenders:

Offenders with little if any prior criminal record, a reasonable amount of prosocial attachment (a stable job or marital relationship) and few dynamic risk factors (antisocial values, procriminal associates, cognitive social and vocational deficits, substance abuse), in general, present a very low risk for recidivism.

Findings from numerous studies (Bonta and Motiuk 1987, 1990) support the notion that with low-risk offenders, public safety is best served by placing them in very low-surveillance correctional settings, such as minimal supervision, probation through mail-in or phone-in caseloads, day fines, administrative supervision, and the like. Most low-risk offenders are apt to correct their behavior on their own. Consequently, with low-risk offenders, less intrusive interventions tend to result in lower levels of recidivism.

A significant implication for corrections is that once offenders are reliably assessed as low risk, they can be moved from expensive incarcerated or residential settings to sanction conditions in the community that are less restrictive, less costly, and do not expose the individual offenders to the criminogenic needs (previously mentioned dynamic risk factors) of higher-risk offenders. Further, once low-risk offenders are moved to no or low-supervision settings, probation and parole staff can reduce caseload size and concentrate on medium- to higher-risk offenders.

Very High-risk Offenders:

The next triage decision is whether the risk level of the offender is so excessive that consideration of community placement should be ruled out. To adequately make this determination, both static (such as prior convictions) and dynamic (for example, use of alcohol) factors need to be reviewed impartially. Simply reviewing the cumulative static elements of an older (age more than thirty-five) offender's case would preclude ever detecting any significant positive or prosocial developments. With offenders who score high on a simple static risk scale (discussed later in this chapter), some consideration of their recent employment history and marital attachment is warranted to minimize false positive classifications that predict failure. Offenders thus delineated as truly high risk for subsequent new offenses are the best candidates for secure jail and prison settings. Movement into a less secure setting for this population only should be considered when either their behavior demonstrates real shifts in dynamic risk factors or their sentence nears completion and common sense mandates reintegration steps.

After triaging the lowest- and highest-risk populations, the remaining offenders should represent the population with the greatest potential for community corrections and intermediate sanctions programs. This is supported by the treatment-matching literature, which shows that adhering to matching criteria for treatment produces significant increases in successful outcomes for the middle 60 percent portion of the population, but not for either portion at the extreme ends (Bonta and Motiuk 1985, 1987, 1990, 1992).

The Gap: Identification of Treatment Needs and Available Treatment Resources

Differential offender assessment that integrates risk and treatment needs is referred to as third-generation risk measurement. To be effective, this type of offender assessment requires more than reliable and valid instruments. Good assessments require well-trained practitioners, firm administrative commitment, and ongoing quality assurance support. Different risk assessment models or systems exist (in places such as Colorado; Vermont; and Washington County, Minnesota), but the decision to establish an assessment system only should be undertaken after careful budget, human resource development, and information system considerations have been made. Often a project of this scope is managed best through a series of stages, beginning with a pilot phase.

Differential offender assessment, particularly if the assessment recommends a proscriptive treatment level, can be a double-edged sword. While such an assessment can be very useful for identifying individual and aggregate levels of treatment need, it also can be initially frustrating and vexing to clearly measure the discrepancy between treatment needs of offenders and adequate and available treatment resources. This system assessment occurs automatically (particularly when a systemwide Management Information System is operational) in the form of gap analysis when proscriptive recommendations are recorded along with the actual treatments received. Practitioners often wonder, why bother with differential assessment when adequate treatment matching resources are unavailable.

Risk Assessment Instruments: Generational Change and Development

Today, objective or actuarial assessment of offenders specifically for risk for recidivism is prevalent, though not necessarily well heralded nor well understood throughout the corrections field. Institutional corrections (detention for juveniles, jail and prison for adults) has many decades of history of classification for risk, but this is for intra-institutional placement only and does not apply to community life. Probation, parole, and other facets of community corrections have a less-extensive history of assessment. In the broader field of community corrections, there are now three generations of risk-prediction tools (Bonta 1996).

First generation. First-generation risk assessments are subjective clinical assessments or professional judgment calls. Not burdened by any actuarial devices, this approach was only as good as the individual practitioner and, consequently, resulted (and continues to result) in tremendous variance, dubious equity, and unreliable judgment criteria. The result of this very subjective, consensus-driven classification and risk-assessment system was that oftentimes low-risk offenders would be incarcerated and incarcerated for longer periods of time than needed for societal protection, and high-risk offenders would be released at the earliest opportunity because they were uncooperative, had a "bad attitude," did not possess critical skills for the institution, and were "bad" influences on other inmates. Moderate-risk offenders were released early or on time if they were docile, nonaggressive, and did not possess skills that the institution needed.

Second generation. Second-generation risk assessments entail a predetermined set of items or questions forming a scale. If the individual offender scores high on the scale (depending on how many risk predictors are scored), there is an established probability range for individuals with that or a similar score, to reoffend. Consistent with the adage that the best predictor of future behavior is past behavior, these types of risk tools rely heavily upon "static" items or risk-factor predictors. Two examples of such risk predictors are first arrested under age fourteen and more than three prior convictions. These are important risk predictors but are impossible to change. These types of tools are essentially actuarial devices similar to those that health and life insurance companies use for establishing predictive levels of health risk, and they can be equally effective when appropriately applied in corrections.

Second-generation or static offender-risk prediction scales have significant utility as well as limitations. Risk scales, often as not, can be administered or scored with little or no face-to-face interview time. In terms of predicting future criminal behavior, they provide classifications, such as low, medium, and high risk, that consistently predict better than both chance and officer judgment (first-generation risk assessment). Furthermore, since severity of presenting offense generally is found to be inversely related to risk for recidivism, these actuarial devices far outpredict sole consideration of the instant offense category. Instant offense category is what the media, most elected officials, and, consequently, the general public use to assess risk. Use of a second-generation risk scale provides a facile approach to getting a richer and more meaningful empirical picture of an individual offender, or, in aggregate, an offender population's risk levels.

While second-generation risk scales provide a decided improvement in prediction over chance and subjective decision making within the justice system, they also are fallible in both reliability and validity. They are best limited to predicting risk for general recidivism, not for a specific category or level of severity of new offense; and they are not clinically relevant. Their fallibility calls for quality assurance and confirmation from additional sources. There often is confusion between the probability of nonspecific, general recidivism and severity of offense risk, but these are two distinctly different features of risk to public safety. Finally, a limitation of second-generation assessments is that they tend not to be very helpful when it comes to diagnosing and guiding the best change process for individual offenders.

Third generation. This type of risk assessment incorporates second-generation risk factors as well as particular types of offender-treatable "needs" as a subset of risk factors. These treatable needs often are referred to as dynamic risk factors (see Chapter 10 for details). Research over the past several decades shows that some offender needs, in the areas of substance abuse, criminal peer associates, social and vocational cognitive deficits, are related to criminal behavior considerably more than others, such as self-esteem or depression. Hence, the best third-generation instruments incorporate only those treatment needs that empirically have been proven to be significantly related to recidivism.

Third-generation risk instruments allow practitioners to measure dynamic risk factors and better illuminate where and how the change process might be enhanced for a particular offender. Offender-assessment data derived from well-integrated risk/need tools organizes and profiles populations according to various "criminogenic" need areas, as well as risk levels. Multiple scales are used so that the assessment can differentiate which need areas are the most urgent and, in so doing, establish case-management priorities, which, in turn, are most likely to result in real reductions in criminal behavior.

As with any instrument or tool, third-generation assessment instruments have limitations and drawbacks. Third-generation assessments require face-to-face interview contact, ongoing staff time for interviewing, scoring, and filing (if not automated), as well as initial training time.

For many correctional agencies, there is little investment in obtaining clinically relevant information. Their mission is overwhelmingly custodial, and it is difficult to say what returns they might obtain from initiating this form of offender assessment. This is true particularly if these agencies do not follow up assessments with appropriate treatment services. Conversely, those corrections' agencies committed to fostering behavioral change will realize more positive results.

Those agencies that are striving to effect some prosocial changes in their correctional populations often already engage in practices aligned with either first- or second-generation assessments. In these situations, they routinely meet face-to-face with offenders to gather information for the PSI report, establish case plans, or to better supervise the case. Given this already established staff commitment to assessment, careful consideration of third-generation tools is warranted. In these cases, applying structured or semi-structured interviews (third-generation tools) often may result in obtaining the same desirable case information, but in a more systematic fashion—one that results in scales and profiles that are comparable among offenders and for the same offender over time. Chart 9.1 illustrates the differences among the three generations of risk assessment.

CHART 9.1: Differences Among Three Generations of Risk-assessment Instruments

Generation	Special Characteristics	Problems	Purpose
First **example:** **officer** **judgments**	Unstructured interview, general information collection, quite subjective	Inter-rater reliability is very low	Make general recommendations for intervention
Second **example:** **salient factor** **score**	Objective, empirical information, mostly historical information, such as criminal history	Provides little direction for treatment	Empirically derived estimates of the probability of delinquent/criminal behavior
Third **examples:** **LSI, CMC,** **Community.** **Risk-needs** **Management** **Scale**	Risk prediction is only one feature; delivery of appropriate treatment services to manage risk is another; treatment must be "matched" to each offender; criminogenic needs are dynamic	Identified needs do not predict criminal behavior; needs require reexamination	Make decisions about the degree of freedom; criminogenic needs are targets for correctional intervention and provide treatment goals for correctional staff

A Premier Example of a Third-generation Assessment Instrument: The Level of Supervision Inventory (LSI-R)

For an assessment instrument to be useful in the field of corrections, correctional staff must be able to use it correctly. The correctional staff includes a wide range of people with various levels of formal education and specialized training. The people working in residential treatment programs for juveniles often have graduate degrees in the social sciences. Prison staffs typically have high school diplomas. Given this, whatever assessment instrument is used must be understood and easy to use by a wide range of people. The LSI, unlike other classification instruments (such as the Minnesota Multi Phasic Inventory, MMPI), can be used by staff generalists who do not need specialized degrees. A few days of training is sufficient to prepare correctional staff to use the LSI competently.

The LSI-R is theory (social-learning) based. Social-learning theory provides a guide to practitioners in their daily classification, placement, and treatment decisions. The LSI-R has a fifty-four item standardized interview schedule. A 0-1 format is used to score each item with a check indicating a risk or need. The total number of checked items provides a total score; the higher the score, the greater the risk of criminal behavior.

In addition to each item, the LSI-R has various subcomponents. Each major subcomponent has a series of subscales: criminal history has ten subscales, education and employment has ten subscales, financial has two subscales, marital/family has four subscales, accommodations has three subscales, leisure/recreation has two subscales, companions has four subscales, drugs/alcohol has nine subscales, emotional/personality has five subscales, and attitudes has five subscales. These subcomponents serve to identify, assess, and prioritize criminogenic needs.

Dynamic and static items are interspersed throughout the LSI-R's ten subscales. Thirteen of the most dynamic risk factors, found in the subscales, have a simple rating scale (zero to three) attached to them to enhance inter-rater reliability. The protocol for scoring these thirteen subscales is to first rate the scale according to the anchors in the scoring guide and then to score the item according to the rating. A score of zero or one counts as a "hit" indicating a need for action or intervention; a score of two or three does not count. In general, a rating of zero indicates little if any prosocial reinforcement, a rating of one indicates some prosocial reinforcement, but an inadequate amount, a two is adequate, and a three is optimum.

By subsequently adding up the total score of the thirteen items' ratings, the practitioner can derive a measure of "protective" factors that is inversely related to the individual's risk factors (high score = low risk; low score = high risk). This summarization of "protective" factors ranges from zero to thirty-nine. Time one (at program intake) and time two (at set points during the program or at program termination) comparisons become a useful index for how an offender is progressing, or in the aggregate, how an overall caseload is progressing. The validity and reliability of the LSI-R have been tested and found to be sound (Bonta and Motiuk 1985, Andrews 1982, Andrews et al. 1983).

The research and development work associated with the LSI led to the next phase of assessment, the responsivity or the matching principle (discussed in more detail in Chapter 11). Matching involves identifying the unique learning style and other characteristics of the offender and providing the levels of surveillance and types of treatment consistent with those offender characteristics. An example might be helpful. For an illiterate offender, it does no good to hand him or her a book to read on alcohol dependency. Conversely, if the individual has a college degree, it may be counterproductive to place him or her in a group counseling session with illiterate high school dropouts. DiClementi, Marlatt, and Miller are some of the leaders of this very important matching principle.

The Timing of Assessments

Initially, for efficiency and implementation ease, short actuarial screening tools should be considered. After screening, use more in-depth assessment to match offenders with appropriate treatment resources. Chart 9.2 illustrates the types of information needed at various stages of the criminal justice system and the suggested risk-assessment instrument for that stage.

CHART 9.2: Information Needed at Various Stages in the Criminal Justice System and Risk-assessment Instruments for Each Stage

Criminal Justice Stage	Key Bits of Information	Risk Assessment Instrument
At arrest	Danger to self and others	Arrest standards
At jail booking	Community ties, determine the probability of returning to court, and risk to community	VERA scale, Colorado Criminal History Score
In community on bond	Special needs: mental health, substance abuse	Social Support Questionnaire, ADS, DAST, SUHM
At presentence	Summary of all risk and criminogenic needs	LSI + specialized needs; SUHM, DAST, ADS
At correctional setting	Responsivity, matching	CMC, LSI, Community Risk/Needs Management Scale plus specialized needs, SUHM, DAS

These risk-assessment instruments are only suggestions. Before putting these suggestions into practice, criminal justice actors need to be informed about the uses and validity of each instrument. Practitioners and others need to discuss the merits and limits of each. A consensus about these instruments will take time but is essential if the risk-level of an offender is to be matched with his or her appropriate correctional setting.

An example of a statewide program, which required several criminal justice agencies coming to a consensus (which is an accomplishment in its own right) to assess risk of offenders, is the Colorado Standardized Offender Assessment Program (CSOAP). The state legislature authorized its creation, and it is coordinated by the Office of Probation Services. Colorado Standardized Offender Assessment Program initially screens all offenders at presentence for substance abuse. In this first phase of assessment, two instruments are used: the Alcohol Dependence Scale (ADS) and the Drug Abuse Screening Test (DAST).

Offenders who need substance-abuse assistance at the initial screening are given a secondary differential assessment. The instruments used in this second phase are the Adult Substance Use Survey (ASUS) and the Substance Use History Matrix (SUHM). The third and final phase of assessment is the administration of the Level of Supervision Inventory (LSI-R) which assesses for risk and criminogenic needs. As a result of these three phases of assessment, a level of service on a surveillance/treatment continuum is determined for all offenders. The delineations of this continuum are as follows: (1) no treatment, (2) drug and alcohol education and/or increased urine testing, (3) weekly outpatient treatment, (4) intensive outpatient treatment, (5) intensive residential treatment, (6) therapeutic community, (7) assessment for psychopathy. From this point, judges and the attorneys can make major placement decisions.

Organizational Implications of Risk Assessment

A third-generation differential offender assessment may require more staff time initially, and, in the long run, certainly will require more staff skills and commitment. A well-designed assessment will incorporate self-report, official record, and collateral contact information whenever possible to obtain greater convergent validity. The assessment also will rely on multiple scales, some self-administered and some derived through interviews conducted by trained staff. The total time required typically ranges between forty-five and ninety minutes per assessment, not including the background check.

Initially, this may appear excessive. However, consideration of current investigation practices in probation, intake assessments in well-organized treatment agencies, or diagnostic and reception units in prisons often reveal that forty-five to ninety minutes is more the norm than the exception. The time to obtain information does not appear to be the critical issue; it is the method, or how this information is gathered and with which standardized assessment instrument, that varies. Methods such as those recommended in this section tend to be more efficacious than less formalized (first-generation) approaches. They, however, do require more staff skill.

The burden of substituting one method for another comes in the transition, the training, and learning curve that normalizes and reinforces a new level of performance. Systemwide projects, such as changing assessment policy and practice, are fraught with design and implementation pitfalls. See Chapter 13 for suggestions for improving organizational performance and creating organizational climates more conducive to change.

Suggestions for changing from the use of first- or second-generation to third-generation assessments include the following:

1. Develop a detailed flowchart of the current corrections system, highlighting the chronological movements of offenders, and the order of process functions and event cycles within those functions. Identify the critical and optimal points where conducting either screening or a differential assessment could be entertained, or, where assessment information might be valuable.

2. Form an interdepartmental committee to survey current assessment practice, tools, and related outcomes in different parts of the country. After critically analyzing the results of both the literature review and the survey, familiarize decision makers with whatever emerges as "best practice."

3. Collect the various options that derive from "best practice" and present them to focus groups consisting of vertical (administrator to supervisor) and horizontal (line staff to security staff) slices throughout the corrections system. Process results and highlight consensus areas for decision makers to select an approach or combination of approaches for piloting (field testing).

4. Pilot test whatever approaches are decided upon across a variety of agencies, but on a small and manageable scale. Include researchers throughout the process.

5. Secure outside pilot and demonstration grant funding (federal, private foundation, or university) based on the preliminary but existing track records. This will enable local practitioners to gain financial support for future benchmarking. They then will be funded from outside sources to carry new technology and practice elsewhere with reciprocating results.

By using assessment of risk, and matching of criminogenic needs and responsivity, valuable correctional resources can be used much more efficiently. Probation officers can reconfigure their caseloads so that low-risk, low-needs offenders can be placed on postcard or phone-in supervision. A paraprofessional, clerical worker, or volunteer can keep track of large numbers of low-risk, low-needs offenders with minimal risk to public safety. High-risk, high-needs community clients can be placed in residential or nonresidential programs or on intensive caseloads. The client-to-staff ratio can be reduced to match the supervision needs of high-risk clients. When high-risk clients get the supervision and treatment they need, recidivism is reduced significantly (Cullen, Wright, Applegate 1993; Eisenberg 1990; Wisconsin Department of Health 1989; Dickey and Wagner 1990).

System Accountability and Evaluation

An important consideration regarding offender-assessment instrumentation relates to accountability. The statement, "If you can't measure it, you can't manage it" has become axiomatic for business today. A similar principle applies when considering outcomes from the expanding array of alternative community corrections programs—if you do not have relevant measures of the populations entering community corrections programs, subsequent measures of the populations leaving these programs do not mean much. Legitimate corrections accountability occurs through three steps: establishing good measures of the population entering the program, applying the same measures of the population leaving the system, and performing outcome measures at some follow-up point, typically one-to-three years later.

Standardizing the offender assessment within a correctional system facilitates obtaining these measures, especially where one program or facility may serve multiple jurisdictions with varying correctional populations, such as probationers, diversion clients, intensive parolees, and others. In addition, establishing a standardized offender assessment is likely to improve data collection, achieve better assessment quality assurance practices, and provide more opportunities for interagency training.

Summary

The implications of the risk, needs, and responsivity principles for correctional institutions are quite profound. Low-risk offenders in jail and prison can be given early release or placed in community programs in lieu of incarceration. The proportion of low-risk offenders who are incarcerated will vary from community to community and state to state, depending on social conditions, sentencing policy, and state criminal statutes.

In the late 1990s, with the use of more sophisticated, third-generation risk, needs, and responsivity matching instruments, it is possible to identify and isolate violent and high-risk offenders at the point of sentencing (at the time of arrest, if we are so inclined) and use jails and prisons for these types of offenders exclusively. Nonviolent, moderate- to high-risk offenders can be placed in residential or nonresidential community programs. Correctional intervention with low-risk offenders should be minimal.

Chapter 10

Identifying and Meeting the Treatment Needs of Offenders

Introduction

Daily newspaper articles trumpet the wonders of prison inmates cutting weeds along public roads. Prison inmates are chained together and a watchful white man sits on a horse supervising the inmates (Staples 1995). Inmates in other prisons are lifting ten- to fifteen-pound sledge hammers pulverizing rocks for no apparent reason other than some opportunistic legislators think that inmates who pulverize rocks while in prison will commit fewer crimes once released (*Seattle Post-Intelligencer* 1995).

This is a retro-corrections period. In the early nineteenth century, the Auburn, New York school of corrections thought that hard, physical labor conducted in total silence was the best way to "cure" criminals (Clear and Cole 1986, Roberts 1997). The idea was not successful and did not last long. Pounding rocks for no apparent reason and chaining prisoners together while they work also will have no measurable impact on post-release rates of crime. In spite of the hard evidence against retro-correctional practices, time will tell whether they will become mainstream correctional practice.

This chapter is about rehabilitation of criminal offenders, which many people contend is a waste of time. The conventional "wisdom," as measured by public opinion polls, documents widespread support for both the death penalty and "three strikes and you're out" legislation. However, when opinion polls present hypothetical case examples instead of asking highly abstract general questions, it turns out (see Chapter 2) that the public is quite supportive of rehabilitation and treatment for adjudicated offenders.

This is nothing new. Twenty years ago, academicians and corrections practitioners had this same debate (Martinson 1974). By the early to mid-1980s, the academic portion of the debate was just about over, and the "winners" were the advocates for treatment, over the "nothing works" group (Gendreau 1979; Blumstein, Cohen, Martin, Torry, 1983).

In spite of the emerging agreement among academicians, researchers, and a significant number of correctional practitioners, most public and elected officials still are advocating a punishment, deterrence, incapacitation approach. Hence, there is a significant gap between public policy, which is overwhelmingly punitive, and what correctional insiders and researchers know, which clearly favors rehabilitation.

For example, we know that offenders who receive appropriate treatment services while under correctional supervision have lower rates of reoffending (recidivism) than those who receive punishment or supervision only (Lipsey 1990, Andrews 1994). Also, offenders who receive a more severe or longer punishment than a matched sample of offenders receiving a less severe punishment, have a higher rate of reoffending (Andrews 1994). These two bits of information alone should settle the punishment/treatment debate. Nevertheless, the debate is fueled by and for political and institutional self-interest, which has nothing to do with the efficacy of rehabilitative treatment services for criminal offenders.

The specific topics that this chapter addresses are as follows: (1) If significant proportions or the majority of offenders are unemployed, have problems with alcohol and drugs, and have little or no money at the point of arrest, is it not reasonable to require all of them to receive some form of employment counseling, job training, and job placement, substance abuse treatment, and money management training? (2) What methods and tools are available to figure out which offender needs which type of rehabilitative treatment service? (3) If an accurate assessment of treatment needs is conducted at an early stage of criminal justice processing and this assessment is followed by appropriate treatment, what is the expected outcome?

The first assumption that must be understood and accepted is: not all offenders are alike, so they should not be treated as a homogeneous group. Requiring all offenders to participate in generalized treatment services, assuming one size fits all, is not helpful and even may be harmful (Andrews and Bonta 1994). Many offenders, when forced to conform to a general program, as opposed to one that is tailored to their unique treatment needs, react negatively and exploit the opportunities for procriminal values and behavior modeling. The task today is to identify the specific treatment needs unique to each offender and provide treatment services that address only those needs.

Remember, criminogenic needs of criminal offenders are a subset of risk factors, and if not addressed, the offenders' risk for recidivism becomes greater; these needs are dynamic and, therefore, subject to change. Out of a whole constellation of needs, only criminogenic (those leading to or contributing to pro-criminal behavior) needs are important to identify and address. Criminogenic needs should be identified quickly, a plan of action to address these needs should be worked out with the offender almost as quickly, and the offender, working with correctional staff and other service providers in the community, should engage in a program in which he or she learns new prosocial attitudes, beliefs, and behaviors. This chapter provides justification for this position and shows specific tools and techniques practitioners can use to carry out this task.

A Personal Tale

About twenty years ago, this author was the director of a higher education program for prison inmates. The program was sponsored by a private liberal arts college in Denver and conducted out of the Colorado State Prison in Canon City. One of the student/inmates, Kenny, was doing time for murder. By the time this author met him, Kenny had served almost ten years and had a good institutional (prison) record. In the higher education program, he proved himself capable of completing a bachelors' degree within the two-year time frame of the project.

Kenny was released from prison about halfway through the two-year project and lived in a minimum-security work camp in a Denver suburb. Not surprisingly, he acted out in minor ways, but continued his college work. This author's approach to Kenny and the other student/inmates was that our program should provide a strong social support team, that the program staff should help create a sense of group solidarity among the twenty student/inmates, and use the promise of a four-year college degree as the critical link between prison life and a successful integration into community life.

To make a long story short, about seven months after Kenny was released from prison, he fled the state, was discovered by interstate parole and law enforcement officials in a motel room in a nearby state, and instead of giving himself up to the authorities, he killed himself.

The purpose of this unfortunate tale is to reveal the critical mistake that this author made as a corrections professional. The mistake was this: the theory used was flawed and because of it, he made mistakes regarding Kenny's supervision and treatment needs. He was operating on an oversimplified notion of crime causation, thinking globally, and holding onto social strain theory assumptions (see Chapter 4), and missed the identification of Kenny's criminogenic needs and a case management plan to address his needs. He needed to learn a new set of prosocial attitudes, beliefs, and social skills that fit the outside world, not the prison inmate code.

Hence, the goal for this chapter is both professional and personal. This author wants to impart some knowledge that corrections professionals can use to make accurate and effective treatment decisions and minimize the possibility of error, especially errors such as the one that he made.

Making Critically Important Distinctions about Individuals' Needs

For any competent medical practitioner, the first task is to figure out who needs which type of treatment. In corrections, the question is which inmate needs substance abuse treatment and which one needs job training, and so on. More specifically, if someone needs substance abuse treatment, what particular substance is the problem? How tenacious is the addiction? Is the offender ready to address the addiction? Does the addiction render the offender dysfunctional on the job, at home, or in other settings? If offenders can be convinced to change their behavior, which technique best matches their style of learning (Hester and Miller 1995)?

The same line of reasoning applies to employment-related problems. If the offender has an employment problem, what is the nature of that problem? Does the offender have any marketable skills? If there are any marketable skills, are these his or her skills of choice? In other words, does the offender want to continue working in this general area or is he or she interested in a different area? If so, does the offender know how to find or develop new skills? How much does it cost to be trained in a new skill area? Are there public funds available to subsidize learning new skills? If marketable skills are not a problem, oftentimes on-the-job behavior is a problem. Misuse of alcohol or drugs or an inability to articulate ideas and feelings can hinder job performance (Azrin and Besalel 1982).

All of these issues must be identified at program intake. If any of these types of issues are missed at program intake, the prospect of helping the offender move to a prosocial, noncriminal lifestyle is greatly diminished. A number of needs assessment instruments have been developed which can help identify the unique (criminogenic) needs of offenders.

Examples of Needs Assessment Instruments

The screened pages provide a list of needs assessment instruments. These instruments have been used with offenders with very good results. For a more complete listing and description of assessment instruments related to substance abuse, see Hester and Miller (1995).

Taking the Measure of Needs Assessment

Alcohol Dependence Scale: This is a single-scale screening tool for alcohol abuse and dependence. There are twenty-five multiple choice items for an offender to respond to in this self-administered tool. This screening tool requires about five minutes for the offender to complete and less than a minute for a staff person to score. This is a useful tool for efficiently screening offenders for significant alcohol problems.

Drug Abuse Screening Test: This is a single-scale screening tool for drug abuse and dependence. The offender can respond to twenty yes/no items in this self-administered tool, which takes about two-to-three minutes of the offender's time to complete and less than a minute for a staff person to score. This is a useful tool for efficiently screening offenders for drug problems.

University of Rhode Island Change Assessment (URICA): The URICA instrument is used to assess a person's readiness for change using the Stages of Change Model (Prochaska and DiClemente 1982) adopted by the National Institute of Medicine. The stages of change are precontemplator, contemplator, determination, action, and maintenance. The URICA instrument has thirty-two items and is self-administered. It takes about seven minutes for the offender to complete and about two minutes for a staff person to score.

Risk Supervision Inventory (RSI): The Risk Supervision Inventory was designed to determine the level of risk (for recidivism) and provide a profile of criminogenic needs. This is a two-stage tool that initially requires twenty-to-thirty minutes for the offender to self-administer and complete. The second stage entails a staff-guided interview of approximately eight-to-ten minutes.

Stage of Change Readiness and Treatment Eagerness Scale (SOCRATES): The SOCRATES instrument is designed to assess readiness for change in alcohol and other forms of drug abuse. SOCRATES 5-A is a tool for alcohol assessment; SOCRATES-D is a tool for assessing non-alcoholic drugs. SOCRATES has forty items and is self-administered. It takes about seven minutes for offenders to complete and about two minutes for a staff person to score.

The Social Support Questionnaire (SSQ): The Social Support Questionnaire is a twenty-seven item, two-tiered assessment for perceived social support. Offenders identify who is likely to provide them support in differing social contexts. It is self-administered, and requires about thirty-to-forty minutes to complete.

The Social Support Network (SSN): The assessment tool is a network diagram that the offender initially draws up in collaboration with a staff person that identifies four network areas of social support. There are an abundance of specialized tests for different types of crimonogenic needs.

Level of Supervision Inventory (LSI)-revised: The Level of Supervision Inventory-revised is a comprehensive instrument to gauge general risk related to criminal behavior. It is the primary assessment instrument recommended by this author to assess for risk and need at various points in the criminal justice procedure. For a more complete description see Chapter 9.

Adult Substance Use Survey (ASUS): This is a sixty-item, self-administered instrument with seven subscales. The subscales include involvement, disruption, social behavior, emotional behavior, defensiveness, and motivation. The Adult Substance Use Survey takes about five-to-ten minutes for the offender to complete and less than one minute for a staff person to score.

Substance Use History Matrix (SUHM): The Substance Use History Matrix is a staff-conducted structured interview. Completion of this test generates a criminogenic need score for substance abuse, a recommended level of treatment; the level of treatment actually received by the offender is compared to the the offender's need. It allows for an override (the ability of the staff person to ignore the course of action recommended by the rationale provided by this test).

Situational Confidence Questionnaire (SCQ): The Situational Confidence Questionnaire is a thirty-item self-administered tool for assessing an offender's self-efficacy relative to eight different areas associated with recidivism or relapse. The eight areas include unpleasant emotions or frustrations, physical discomfort, social problems at work, social tension, pleasant emotions, positive social situations, urges and temptations, and taking control. The instrument takes about five-to-seven minutes for offenders to complete and less than two minutes for a staff person to score. This tool can be used for screening offenders for relapse prevention, but it also is useful for determining treatment and education priorities.

Boston University Stress Exam: This is a 230-item, self-administered assessment for stress. There are fifteen subscales, seven of which represent various life-stress areas, such as financial management or family; seven other subscales depict stress symptoms, such as muscular, immune systems; and the remaining subscale measures coping skills. This instrument takes about thirty-to-forty minutes for the offender to complete and about five minutes for a staff person to score.

Client Assessment of Treatment (CAT): The Client Assessment of Treatment is self-administered after program completion. Ideally, this should be given to groups of offenders so that it can be completed anonymously. There are eighteen items in the instrument assessing clients' satisfaction with various program features. Its results can provide an important component of a database and be reported out to supervising agencies at fixed intervals.

Wisconsin Risk, Needs, Client Management Classification System: This classification system is an attempt to develop differential treatment models for different groups of clients. The goals, approaches, and techniques delineated do not constitute an exhaustive list, but attempt to provide a general framework of treatment recommendations to consider with each group.

Other instruments: Other instruments are available to assess more specialized problems or situations. Some include: Hares Checklist for Psychopathy, Domestic Violence Behavioral Checklist, Alcohol Positive Outcome Expectancy Test, Cocaine Positive Outcome Expectancy Test, Marijuana Positive Outcome Expectancy Test, The Relapse Strategy Test, and Motivational Inventory. Corrections professionals should learn about the existence of these assessment instruments and receive training in the appropriate uses of the instruments, and then, hopefully, use them consistently with offenders.

Identifying Criminogenic Needs

According to Andrews (1989), published research reports show the following list of criminogenic needs are important in reducing the risk of recidivism. If these criminogenic needs are not identified at program entry, it is quite unlikely that staff will address them during the program. Once these needs are identified at program intake, they need to be dealt with while the offender is in the correctional program (preferably with help from other community-treatment providers). The box displays specific criminogenic needs of individual offenders that are predictive of antisocial, procriminal behavior.

Criminogenic Needs of Individual Offenders

1. Antisocial attitudes

2. Antisocial feelings

3. Antisocial peer associations

4. Familial affection is poor or lacking and communication is problematic

5. Familial monitoring and supervision are (or have been) problematic

6. Child neglect and abuse are prevalent (or have been)

7. Identification/association with procriminal role models

8. Little self-control, self-management, and few problem-solving skills

9. Lying, stealing, and being aggressive are common

10. Chemical dependencies

11. Preponderance of personal, interpersonal, and other rewards for criminal activities

12. Chronically psychiatrically troubled offenders cannot cope with everyday life and revert to procriminal lifestyles

13. Offenders are unable to carefully distinguish and recognize risky situations and, hence, do not have an alternative, prosocial plan available

14. Offenders are unable to overcome the personal and circumstantial barriers to client motivation and other background stressors (Andrews and Bonta 1994)

Unless these types of criminogenic needs are identified and this is done so early on in the criminal justice process (and ideally, early on in the offender's life), effective treatment is quite unlikely. If these criminogenic needs remain unidentified, there will be little or no match between the offender's unique treatment needs and whatever treatment services are offered.

Developing an Offender-treatment Plan

The next task is the development of an offender-treatment plan. The identified criminogenic needs of offenders become the treatment goals, which are incorporated into a treatment or case plan. If correctional intervention is working, offenders can change quickly and often. A good case management/treatment plan should be dynamic and be able to document, track, and monitor any and all changes by offenders, by staff working with offenders, and by other agencies supervising or treating offenders. Case planning provides the direction and a detailed map for the changes that the offender understands and agrees to and that will be initiated, facilitated, and monitored by the program staff.

There are many standardized treatment plans, case planning techniques, or case management formats. No attempt is made to include all of them here. One, called FRAMES, is discussed later in this chapter. Another is the Substance Abuse Question Inventory (SAQI), developed by Todd Clear (1980). Both provide simple but compelling decision-making technologies for case analysis and prioritization.

A popular classification tool used during the 1980s was the Case Management Classification System (CMC) developed by Chris Baird and others in Wisconsin in the late 1970s and early 1980s. The tool was developed for probation and parole officers to quickly understand an offender's problems and needs, to anticipate impediments to resolving problems, and to develop a case management plan. Today the CMC is well established in many probation and parole agencies around the country.

However, there are a few problems with its use. The Case Management Classification system does not sufficiently flag high-priority criminogenic need areas, does not sufficiently delve into substance abuse, and has not been vigorously tested regarding risk prediction. On a hopeful note, a recent test of the Case Management Classification's predictive validity for its risk and needs scales found them both to be predictive of failure on probation (Bonta 1996).

Another good, well-tested risk/needs case classification and case management tool is the LSI-R (Level of Supervision Inventory) instrument (see Chapters 9 and 11). The beauty of the LSI-R includes the following: (1) it is based on social learning theory, (2) it is highly accurate in terms of using static variables to classify for risk, (3) it isolates dynamic criminogenic need variables and targets them for treatment, and (4) there are subscales for all the criminogenic need variables. One of four delineations can be made on each of the subscales, providing an opportunity to create a baseline of information for case monitoring and client and program evaluation (Bonta and Motiuk 1985).

Program Strategies for Effective Treatment

Previous chapters presented suggestions to develop and operate an effective community corrections program. Paul Gendreau identified the following program characteristics, associated with significant reductions of recidivism among offender participants.

1. The services are intensive and are based on differential association and social learning conceptualizations of criminal behavior. Intensive services should occupy 40 to 70 percent of the offender's time while in a program and should be three-to-nine months in duration. The offender behavioral programs are based on operant conditioning, which means reinforcement. Reinforcement refers to the strengthening or increasing of a behavior so that it will continue to be performed in the future. Provide positive reinforcers (a weekend pass, a reduction of reporting requirements) on a contingency basis (quid pro quo: I'll do X if you do Y). Positive reinforcers may be tangible (money), activities (shopping, sports, TV) or social (special attention, praise, approval). Negative reinforcers (no weekend pass, an increase in surveillance requirements) also work but should be used sparingly and only when therapeutically necessary.

2. The programs are behavioral, primarily of the cognitive and modeling type, and target the criminogenic

(continued on next page)

Program Strategies for Effective Treatment (continued)

needs of high-risk offenders. Treatment is more effective when it is matched with the offender's risk level.

3. Program services should adhere to the responsivity principle (see Chapter 11), that is, they are delivered in a way that facilitates the learning of new prosocial skills by the offenders. Responsivity incorporates the matching principle, which involves three dimensions:

    • Match the treatment approach with the learning style and personality of the offender

    • Match the characteristics of the offender with those of the therapist, clinician, or correctional worker

    • Match the skills of the therapist with the type of program

4. Program contingencies (either positive or negative changes) are enforced in a firm, fair manner, with positive reinforcers used more frequently than punishment by at least four to one. Internal control, such as drug testing, is used very judiciously (not as a general policy) to detect possible antisocial activities.

5. Therapeutic integrity is vital. Therapists relate to offenders in interpersonally sensitive and constructive ways and are trained and supervised appropriately. Staff must have special skills and training to be effective. (See Chapter 13 for a discussion of staff competencies.)

6. Program structure and activities reach out to the offenders' real-world social network and disrupt the delinquency (or criminal) network by placing offenders in situations where prosocial activities predominate.

Until we learn more in our field, which we will if we keep up the pace of the last few years, these six successful program characteristics should be placed in a prominent location over the desks of all correctional managers and clinicians and read daily. In addition to these six success elements, relapse-prevention strategies and a sustained advocacy and brokerage of community services on behalf of offenders also contribute to overall program success (Gendreau 1996).

Just as important as learning and knowing what has been successful, we also need to know what has not worked. Programs that did not reduce offender recidivism used:

- Traditional psychodynamic and nondirective/client-centered therapies

- Sociological strategies that were based on subcultural and labeling perspectives on crime

- "Punishing smarter" programs or those that centered on punishment/sanctions, such as boot camps, drug testing, electronic monitoring, restitution, and shock incarceration

- Any program, including behavioral ones, that targeted low-risk offenders or noncriminogenic needs or did not focus on the multiple causes of offending (Gendreau 1996)

Several techniques have been used, tested, and have proven effective with substance abusers, people with addictions, sex offenders, and others with behavioral problems. Some of these techniques are beginning to be employed with criminal offenders. The preliminary information available is that they are useful techniques that can assist offenders in making needed changes.

Motivational Interviewing

A technique, which has emerged from the alcohol field, that has great potential for use in the adult corrections arena is motivational interviewing (MI). In the words of its creators, William R. Miller and Stephen Rollnick, "Motivational Interviewing is an approach designed to help clients build commitment and reach a decision to change. Motivational Interviewing draws on strategies from client-centered counseling, cognitive therapy, systems theory, and the social psychology of persuasion. The appearance of a motivational interviewing session is quite client-centered; yet, the counselor maintains a strong sense of purpose and direction, and actively chooses the right moment to intervene in incisive ways. In this sense, it combines elements of directive and nondirective approaches. It can be integrated with a broad range of strategies, and also can be used to prepare a motivational foundation for other approaches, such as participating in behavioral training or cognitive therapy, attending Twelve-Step groups, and taking medication."

The theoretical basis for Motivational Interviewing lies in two broad areas. It draws heavily on the construct of "ambivalence" and the conflict between indulgence and restraint in addictive behaviors. Failure to change a behavior that is causing problems is a phenomenon that extends well beyond addiction; the immobilizing effects of ambivalence can be seen in many spheres. A more general conceptual base is found in theory and research on "self-regulation" (Miller 1991).

Motivation, as understood and used in the alcoholism field, is yet another element that could be put to good use in the adult corrections field. Addiction specialists do not view motivation as a personality problem, or something static that is genetically fixed. Instead, they view motivation as dynamic. Motivation, in the addiction specialist's view, is a state of readiness or eagerness to change. In the course of studying motivation, researchers discovered that most people change on their own, without the assistance of specialists. However, whether people change on their own or change with the help of a specialist, they seem to pass through a similar pattern or stages of change.

Stages of Change

Offenders (and nonoffenders alike) typically go through distinct stages before and during behavioral changes. Prochaska and DiClemente (1982) identified five stages of change; Miller and Rollnick added one more. Chart 10.1 illustrates six stages of change.

These six stages of change can be put to use in the adult corrections field. Offenders attempting to change their attitudes, values, and beliefs go through the same or similar stages of change. An attentive correctional practitioner can use these stages of change to assess more accurately what stage the offender is in, provide appropriate support, and intervene at appropriate times, as offenders attempt to modify their behaviors.

CHART 10.1: Motivational Stages of Change and Therapist's Tasks

Client Stage	Therapist's Motivational Tasks
Precontemplation: do not recognize a problem. Behavior: reluctance, rebellion, resignation, and rationalization	Raise doubt; increase the client's perception of risks and problems with current behavior
Contemplation: a paradoxical, ambivalent stage, thinking about change but not yet committed to it	Tip the balance; evoke reasons to change and risks of not changing; strengthen the client's self-efficacy for change of current behavior
Determination: decide to take appropriate steps to stop the problem and make a commitment to action	Help the client to decide on the best course of action to take in seeking change
Action: make a public commitment to do something, get external confirmation of the plan, seek support	Help the client to take steps toward change
Maintenance: a three- to six-month stage, build new patterns of behavior	Help the client to identify and use strategies to prevent relapse
Relapse: return to negative behavior	Help the client to renew to process of contemplation, determination, and action without becoming stuck or demoralized because of relapse

Source: DiClemente 1991 and Miller and Rollnick 1991.

FRAMES: An Aid for Working with Offenders

Another technique used to insure that offender dynamics are not overlooked is called FRAMES (Miller and Sanchez 1993). FRAMES is an acronym for a reiterative process designed to resolve offender ambivalence and optimize motivation for change. FRAMES is particularly helpful in brief therapies and motivational interviewing. The FRAMES components are the following:

Feedback: Provide clients impartial feedback

Responsibility: Emphasize clients as decision makers

Advice: Give simple advice, with warm regard

Menu: Offer range of options

Empathy: Show empathetic understanding

Self-efficacy: Reinforce clients' self-efficacy

Source: Miller and Sanchez 1993

Using the principles of FRAMES during case planning will create a solid working relationship between the offender and the correctional worker. Given these points, it is critical that practitioners learn and cultivate skills to work with the offender's energy for change. While this energy, at least initially, may not coincide perfectly with the criminogenic needs that staff has prioritized, it should not be dismissed. Ultimately, a balancing dialog is necessary between staff and offenders. Once a comprehensive and accurate assessment of treatment needs has been conducted and a treatment or case plan has been completed, the next task is to provide the service(s) specific to each offender.

Delivering the Goods: Providing Appropriate Treatment

In the 1970s and early 1980s, the conventional wisdom was to provide treatment services with "in-house" staff, who were a part of the community corrections' agency. From what we know today, it is better to have existing community agencies provide specialized treatment services to offenders than to provide these services "in-house." The reason is simple: when the community corrections agency has good, functional agreements with collateral agencies (mental health, substance abuse treatment, money management, and job-related agencies) and offenders can move easily and quickly from the criminal justice jurisdiction to these collateral agencies, it broadens the community support network for offenders and teaches them to rely on existing agencies and not on corrections resources (which are, hopefully, less permanent in their lives than other human services).

Also, using existing, noncorrectional community resources provides more opportunities for prosocial modeling for offenders. Evaluation results show that using community resources is a more effective way to approach the delivery of treatment services to offenders (English, Chadwick, and Pullen 1994).

Cognitive-behavioral Approaches

Cognitive skill deficits (such as poor self-regulation skills, an inability to think consequentially, or an inability to take another person's perspective) are fairly endemic to most corrections populations. These deficits often impede progress in a structured corrections environment or result in limited gains that translate into short-term compliance. To correct these skill deficits, interventions of substantial intensity, duration, and integrity are required. Cognitive behavioral programs are a way of helping offenders that has proven very effective (Kendall and Hollon 1979, Garrett 1985, Gottschalk 1987, Gordon and Arbuthot 1987, Lipsey 1989,

Izzo and Ross 1990, Andrews and Zinger 1990, and Palmer 1996). Andrews and Bonta recognize the special features of a cognitive-behavioral approach:

> With a behavioral approach, there is no reason to believe that any one set of events will always function as reinforcers for all persons all the time. Thus, it is important that one who is going to influence behavior (of offenders) through reinforcement has a wide variety of potential reinforcers at hand. The characteristics of a high-quality relationship (between correctional practitioner and offender) constitute just such a collection of reinforcers. Sometimes simply eye contact and statements that show you are listening will be sufficient; at other times, there must be emphatic expressions of support and agreement. Sometimes more concrete events, such as a shared movie or a shopping trip, will be the reinforcers.
>
> (Andrews and Bonta 1994)

Cognitive behavioral approaches are sometimes referred to as skill training. However, skill training does not necessarily mean how to put a radio in a car or fix a leak in the bathroom sink. Cognitive behavioral skills training refers to a more generic mental process, a cognitive skill and an approach to solve particular problems. Usually, cognitive behavioral approaches entail highly prescriptive tasks offering specific directions, instructions, and assignments. Hence, cognitive behavioral approaches teach coping behaviors through instruction, modeling, directed practice, and feedback (Miller and Rollnick 1991).

Unlike psychosocial or psychodynamic interventions, cognitive behavioral approaches involve highly structured, routinized, and often repetitive techniques to engage offenders in meaningful skill development that translates to increased self-efficacy, lifestyle balance, and prosocial reinforcement. Skill training must be individually relevant, challenging but attainable, and rewarding to be generalizable. All of this requires competent and trained staff with effective communication skills, assertive case management, and flexible and innovative means for reinforcing offender participation (Com Corr Coop 1995).

Peer Associates: Disrupting and Replacing

Types of peer associations and social networks have long been identified as key elements in the development and maintenance of criminal behavior. More recently, social support also has been identified as one of the most significant determinants of successful treatment outcomes (Havassy et al. 1991). As with all criminogenic needs, the first step is assessment. Correctional practitioners must conduct formal assessments of the social support network of each offender soon after a program intake. Measures for prevalence of prosocial or procriminal, sober or active addicts should be obtained with the use of standardized assessment instruments such as the social support questionnaire. These assessment measures will serve as a guide in case planning and setting individual objectives.

Attending Alcoholics Anonymous and Narcotics Anonymous (which are not treatment programs but can be effective social or peer support programs), volunteering with human service programs, or working with community volunteers and mentors are all productive activities that can provide alternatives to association with procriminal peers. Corrections staff must be proactive in this arena (Read 1996). Offenders are not likely to break ties with old procriminal associates and reach out to prosocial peers without encouragement from the staff.

Employment Assistance

Employment is a big problem for most adjudicated offenders. For a variety of reasons, many, if not most offenders, have poor job histories, few marketable skills, and poor work habits. Many offenders lack the vocational and cognitive skills to advance beyond unemployment or minimum-wage jobs. A concentrated employment assistance program is a key element toward promoting better job skills, which, in turn, will provide a good foundation for future individual success. A good job program involves state-of-the-art career planning, teaching employment-seeking skills, offering on-the-job training, and helping an individual achieve career advancement in a chosen occupational field.

The first step is assessment. Any third-generation assessment instrument (see Chapter 9) will collect general information about work history and marketable skills. If there is a need for improvement, more specific assessment is advised. There are three general areas that need exploration: (1) basic educational competencies (reading, writing, and performing mathematical operations), (2) occupational skills and interests, and (3) attitudes and beliefs regarding work.

Basic educational competencies and occupational interests can be assessed with the use of any of the three following tools:

- the Comprehensive Adult Student Assessment System (CASAS), which is designed to determine literacy skills

- the Test of Adult Basic Education (TABE), which assesses the level of basic education skills

- *Career Anchors.* This is a guided workbook that helps adults identify the basic components of their preferred career. It also analyzes their present job to see if it meets an individual's job satisfaction and salary needs. The best part of career anchors is that it assists in planning future career moves using certain insights (Schein 1990).

Occupational interests and skills can be determined more precisely with the aid of specialists at the local vocational-technical school, post-secondary schools that emphasize work-related training. They exist in or near most urban areas in the United States. Most vocational-technical schools already have established tests and specially trained staff to administer vocational interest tests. If there is a charge for this service, it is minimal or based on the individual's ability to pay. Occupational interest tests can be very helpful in choosing general career areas within which a person can specialize.

Vocational-technical schools also are helpful in providing basic education, General Education Development test preparation and testing, and they offer a wide range of specialized training curricula such as electronics, car repair, computer repair, air-conditioning certification, hair cutting and styling, and others. It behooves community corrections staff to have good working arrangements and referral agreements established with the local vocational-technical school.

Work attitudes and beliefs are an important part of improving employment. Two types of approaches have proven effective. One is modeling, where the offender directly observes another person demonstrating a behavior that he or she can benefit from imitating. The other is cognitive-behavioral training, wherein an attempt is made to change the offender's cognitions, attitudes, values, and expectations that maintain antisocial behavior. Techniques used to bring about attitudinal change are problem solving, reasoning, self-control, and self-instructional training.

Even with all the steps outlined, correctional staff will find it difficult to "solve" the employment needs of offenders under their jurisdiction. Private employers hold the key to jobs, and correctional staff must reach out to private employers to gain better access to jobs.

One suggestion is to view private employers as any other community resource. Community corrections practitioners have some experience working with lay citizens in the context of advisory boards. Using this approach, correctional staff can organize a private employer advisory board, call it a private industry council (PIC). (Private Industry Councils have been used effectively under U.S. Department of Labor auspices). Private Industry Councils can assist offenders in their attempts to find employment that is a notch or two more challenging and rewarding than entry-level minimum-wage jobs. A Private Industry Council could be a clearinghouse for jobs, a forum to discuss and resolve job performance issues, an aid in job preparation and training, and a career advancement strategy. Private Industry Councils also could assist correctional managers in establishing better organizational goals, objectives, and strategies for the community corrections agency itself.

Another strategy is a Job Finder's Club. Job Finder's Clubs were initially developed by Azrin and Besalel in 1980 and have been implemented by the Safer Foundation in Chicago. The basic elements of a Job Finder's Club include the following:

1. Unemployed offenders will be actively involved in the job search process.

2. Offenders need training and support in how to contact prospective employers by phone or in person.

3. Role playing is an effective technique to prepare for job interviews.

4. Training, role playing, and making telephone inquiries are more effective in a group context than in an individual context.

5. Once a job has been obtained, offenders need assistance in maintaining good work habits, resolving conflicts on the job, being punctual, and working effectively with a co-worker (Azrin and Besalel 1982).

Success at work, both in terms of getting a decent job and keeping it, is an essential element to community corrections. Employment must be understood as a multidimensional problem and approached accordingly.

Substance Abuse Treatment Strategies

The majority of offenders have some level of a problem with alcohol, drugs, or both. How effectively we deal with substance-abusing offenders greatly determines the overall success of correctional intervention. Clinicians and researchers conducted literature reviews and analyzed the program effectiveness (Hester and Miller 1995) of different approaches to the treatment of alcoholics. This section summarizes their findings.

Brief Intervention

Brief intervention has one of the largest literature bases, and currently the literature is most positive toward this approach. Within one-to-three sessions, the goal is to trigger a decision and commitment to change. There are six elements in effective brief interventions: (1) feedback, (2) responsibility, (3) advice, (4) menu of alternative strategies for changing problem behaviors, (5) empathy, and (6) self-efficacy. A cornerstone of brief intervention is a belief that the problem drinker has the ability to carry out or succeed in making necessary changes (Bien, Miller, and Tonigan 1993, Hester and Miller 1995).

Broad-spectrum Skill Training

Broad-spectrum treatment approaches place primary focus not on alcohol consumption per se but on other life problem areas, often functionally related to drinking and relapse. According to this approach, drinking problems arise or continue because the individual lacks important coping skills for sober living. The idea is to teach such coping skills to problem drinkers. The literature supports particular types of broad-spectrum training, such as social skills training and community reinforcement, but is not supportive of other approaches, such as stress management strategies and systematic desensitization (Miller and Hester 1980).

Marital/Family Therapy

Relationship therapies seek to promote sobriety by improving the quality of family and/or marital relationships. The focus is on teaching communication skills and increasing the level of positive reinforcement within relationships. The literature indicates that most marital and family therapies have shown promise (O'Farrell 1993).

Cognitive-behavioral Treatment

Cognitive-behavioral approaches include a wide variety of treatment strategies. Some are behavioral contracting; using self-help manuals, cognitive therapy, behavioral self-control training, relapse prevention, functional analyses, and self-monitoring, and BAC (blood/alcohol content) discrimination training. The general idea is to alter the beliefs and thinking patterns presumed to underlie problem drinking. The literature is mixed but generally supportive of this approach (Kendall and Hollon 1979, Garrett 1985, Gottschalk 1987, Gordon and Arbuthot 1987, Lipsey 1989, Izzo and Ross 1990, Andrews and Zinger 1990, and Palmer 1996).

Aversion Therapies

Aversion therapies seek to develop in the client, via classical Pavlovian conditioning strategies, a conditioned negative response to the sight, smell, taste, and even the thought of alcohol. Aversion therapies have not been exhaustively evaluated. The small but existing literature reveals mixed findings using this approach (Rimmele, Howard, and Hilfrink 1995).

Antidipsotropic Medications

Antidipsotropic agents are medications that induce illness only if one drinks alcohol. Antabuse is one such agent that is used frequently with adult offenders by probation and parole officers. The efficacy of these agents in the literature is a mix, about equal between positive and negative outcomes. The obstacle with this approach is medication compliance. When medication compliance is up, so are the results (Fuller 1995).

Psychotropic Medications

Psychotropic medications are intended to diminish drinking by alleviating related symptomatology. Antipsychotic and psychedelic agents are thought to facilitate treatment. Lithium and other antidepressants are thought to diminish drinking directly. Such medications may impact beneficially on concomitant problems, and except in the case of addictive drugs, there is no reason to withhold them in treating dually diagnosed individuals. Research has indicated mixed results with psychotropic medications (Hester and Miller 1995).

Psychotherapies

Controlled studies of group or individual psychotherapy for alcohol problems have yielded negative findings with remarkable consistency. The only exception to this general trend is client-centered therapy, based on the writing of Carl Rogers (1959) (Bien, Miller, and Tonigan 1993, Hester and Miller 1995).

Confrontational Approaches

Confrontational counseling styles have enjoyed particular popularity in United States alcoholism treatment. Yet, confrontational approaches have failed to yield a single positive outcome study (Annis 1983, Sannible 1988, Andrews *et al.* 1990, Gendreau 1996).

"Standard" Treatment Components

This is an ubiquitous grouping. Within this "standard" treatment group is milieu therapy, which suggests that recovery is aided by taking the client to a special place where healing occurs (the Betty Ford clinic is such a place); general counseling; educational lectures and films; and Alcoholics Anonymous (AA). There is little support in the literature for these standard approaches. As stated earlier, Alcoholics Anonymous and Narcotics Anonymous (NA) sometimes are quite helpful as a social or peer support network; however, they should not be viewed as treatment programs (Brandsma, Maultsby, and Welsh 1980 and Hester and Miller 1995).

Other Approaches

Acupuncture, exercise, hypnosis, and sensory deprivation are examples of other approaches. There is some positive support for acupuncture, exercise, and sensory deprivation; no support is available for hypnosis as a treatment for alcohol (Murphy 1986, Bullock 1987, Cooper 1988, and Hester and Miller 1995).

As was stated earlier, the treatment approaches such as AA, confrontational approaches, psychotherapy, and the use of antabuse, have the least amount of support in the research literature. The programs that have the most support are brief intervention and cognitive behavioral approaches.

A Suggested Eight-step Format for Substance Abusing Offenders

A suggested approach for practitioners dealing with substance abusers in correctional settings is outlined below. View these suggestions as a general set of guidelines, not something set in concrete that applies to all substance abusers all the time (Com Corr Coop 1995). Justification for each of the steps can be found in Hester and Miller's book, *Handbook of Alcoholism Treatment Approaches* (1995), and Miller and Rollnick's book, *Motivational Interviewing* (1991).

Duration of treatment: Three months generally is accepted as the minimum length of involvement for producing positive outcomes. As the severity of the substance abuse problem increases, the minimum length of time needed for treatment becomes longer.

Behavioral leverage: Various forms of contingency contracting, in which both positive and negative reinforcements are used, increase treatment effectiveness with offenders. Specifically, such approaches promote prosocial behavioral changes.

Repeated assessments and staged delivery of needed services: Treatment strategies which work best are malleable and cover a wide range of approaches that allow for various levels of treatment and supervision intensity. Differential assessments should be conducted with the use of standardized instruments (discussed earlier in this chapter). The goal is to capture the type, history, and severity of substance abuse unique to each offender. Because no single treatment approach is effective for all substance abusers, applying the matching principle is strongly advised. Match the offender with the appropriate type of treatment, programming, and therapist. Matching requires sensitivity to the offender's progress in treatment, the changing nature of his or her needs, the competencies and deficiencies of the offender, his or her motivation (stages of change) level, and the degree of risk to the community he or she presents.

Continuity of care: Research shows that after a person leaves a residential treatment program, additional social and peer support is needed for maintenance of improvements. This ongoing support can be realized by linking the offender to a 12-step program, other self-help groups, or offender alumni groups which can be a part of the corrections program.

Treatment integrity: Substance abuse programs must have integrity. This means that the program must be rigorously and continuously evaluated to ensure case manager efficacy. Additionally, staff development and specialized training, regular reviews of offender case files, and formal management information systems are essential elements of treatment integrity. Management information systems can format appropriate data elements, facilitate case manager information gathering and information retrieval, and organize information for case management reports.

Linkages with other services: Substance abusers have multiple needs and problems. Linkage and coordination of services with other programs in the community are essential to strengthen the offender's overall treatment experience. Substance abuse programs should go about this the same way that previously described offender employment programs do.

Treatment approaches: Although no single treatment approach to substance abuse has emerged as the clear choice, research has found that strategies which are behavioral interventions are most supported in controlled outcome studies (Keane 1984, Guydish 1987, Monti 1990, and Heather 1990). Examples of these types of interventions are cognitive-behavioral and contingency management (a form of performance contracting to achieve very specific behavioral objectives).

Relapse prevention: Unfortunately, many substance abusers get on the "wagon," off the "wagon," and back on again. "Off the wagon" is referred to in the literature as relapse. Relapse prevention is a therapeutic approach which recognizes that addictive behavior is a process. Relapse prevention involves detailed assessments and reassessments at short (weekly, if needed) intervals and "take-home" assignments for offenders. The assessments include demographic information, descriptions of drinking patterns and related problems, identification of high-risk (for substance abuse) situations, and self-efficacy ratings. The "take-home" assignments involve self-monitoring, autobiographical sketches, completion of standardized tests (Inventory of Drinking Situations), a craving diary, a written log of coping instructions, anger episodes, and other components (Marlatt 1978, Allsop and Saunders 1991, Miller and Rollnick 1991, Hester and Miller 1995). Employing this eight-stage programming with substance-abusing offenders will greatly improve offender performance and reduce the rate of relapse (Com Corr Coop 1995).

Mental Health

In general, the recommended approach for mental health services is approximately the same as that for resolving employment problems, previously described. Use existing mental health services; do not duplicate services. It is expensive to purchase specialized mental health staff. Even if the money were available and mental health specialists provided service inside the correctional program, this is not a recommended option because offenders are denied a chance to learn where mental health services are and how to access them.

Occasionally, mental health services do not exist, either because of remote geographical location or because of the lack of competency or willingness of mental health care workers. In these cases, specialized mental health services must be contracted out to private therapists. Prior to any outside referral, correctional staff can administer standardized assessments that can provide general indications of mental health treatment needs. Some of these previously described assessment instruments that may be used include the Social Support Questionnaire and the Situational Confidence Questionnaire.

More severely mentally disordered offenders with histories of both psychiatric and criminal justice involvement may respond best to a monitored, low-stress sheltered workshop environment (Fairweather et al. 1969). For these types of offenders, firm but fair use of authority, anticriminal modeling and problem solving efforts that focus on criminogenic needs are generally effective when offered in an interpersonal, facilitative, and enthusiastic manner (Andrews, Bonta, and Hoge 1990).

What We Can Expect If We Do It Right

There is a high degree of cynicism among many elected officials regarding the rehabilitation for criminal offenders. A few legislators want to believe that rehabilitation programs work, but do not see much evidence that they do. The majority of legislators have little or no hope that rehabilitation works. Because of this belief and many political "opportunities" offered by the "get tough" scenario, they support new bills to lengthen prison sentences.

However, empirical evidence is building that documents the growing success of carefully crafted rehabilitation programs. Charts 10. 2 and 10.3 are from James Bonta's work. Their implications for treatment and its effects are quite profound. Some explanation and definition of terms is necessary to understand the full relevance of Chart 10.2. Often, the term "treatment" is used so broadly that it hardly has any meaning. By contrast, Bonta separated programs based on what actually occurred in them. Criminal sanctions were judicially imposed sanctions, such as community service programs, shock probation, and boot camp. Inappropriate programs were correctional programs that had no apparent merit. Appropriate programs were correctional programs that had merit.

CHART 10.2: Effect of Type of Treatment on Recidivism

Type of Offender and Setting	Criminal Sanctions	Inappropriate Treatment	Appropriate Treatment
Overall Results	-.07	-.06	+.30
Juvenile Offenders	-.06	-.07	+.29
Adult Offenders	-.12	-.03	+.34
Community Setting	-.05	-.04	+.35
Correctional Institution, Residential Setting	-.14	-.15	+.20

Source: Bonta 1991.

The study compared the results of 154 correctional programs. The statistic used to make comparisons is called the phi. Phi coefficients can range from -1 to +1. They can be interpreted in the same way as the more widely known Pearson correlation coefficient. A phi value of -1 means that every time you have a program, it will automatically increase recidivism by 100 percent. A phi of +1 means every program will bring a 100 percent reduction in recidivism. On the top row, for criminal sanctions, the phi score is -.07. This means that criminal sanctions were associated with a mild increase in recidivism. For inappropriate programs the phi is -.06, also a mild increase in recidivism, and for appropriate programs, a phi of +.30. When a phi of +.30 is translated into percentages, it means a 50 percent reduction in the recidivism rate. The same pattern of results exists when comparing juvenile and adult offenders.

The correctional setting factors are also important. When offenders are placed in correctional institutions or residential settings and given criminal sanctions or inappropriate programs, the results are higher rates of recidivism than similar programs that were conducted in (nonresidential) community programs. These programs appear more harmful when they are conducted within jails, prisons, or residential settings.

Appropriate programs were moderately effective when conducted inside of correctional institutions, but not as effective as when the same programs were conducted in the community. The combination of appropriate programs in nonresidential community settings have the most powerful effect in reducing recidivism when they are delivered in a community setting.

The implications for community corrections are this: programs in the community are ideally suited (if everything else is in place) for optimum treatment intervention. Placing an offender in a residential community center, by itself, with no appropriate treatment program, can be more harmful than helpful. Residential settings only should be used when offenders require this level of intense supervision (namely for high-risk offenders) and only when appropriate treatment programs are administered.

Chart 10.3 illustrates the importance of the relationship between the level of the (treatment) service and the risk level of offenders. When there is a match between treatment and risk, good results occur.

CHART 10.3: Risk Level and Treatment (By Percentage of Recidivism)

Study	Offender's Risk Level	Minimal Service	Intensive Service
O'Donnell, *et al.*, 1971	Low High	16 78	22 56
Baird 1979	Low High	3 37	10 18
Andrews and Kiessling 1980	Low High	12 58	17 31
Andrews and Friesen 1987	Low High	12 92	29 25

Source: Bonta 1991.

Looking at all the studies in Chart 10.3, when low-risk offenders received minimal treatment service, their recidivism rate was lower than when they received intensive supervision. For example, when low-risk offenders received minimal treatment service, their recidivism rate was 16 percent. When they were given intense treatment services, their recidivism rate increased to 22 percent. When high-risk offenders were given minimal treatment, their recidivism rate was 78 percent. With intensive levels of treatment, high-risk offenders failed at a lower rate of 56 percent.

The policy implication for judges and parole board members is clear: they should stop placing low-risk offenders in intense supervision or intense treatment programs. Low-risk offenders do not need this level of intense programming; they just get worse, not better! Conversely, high-risk offenders need a lot of assistance, a lot of supervision, and usually a lot of treatment services. However, when and if high-risk offenders get the "corrrections" they need, significant improvements can be realized (Bonta 1991).

Summary

The best summary of this chapter comes from Donald Andrews, a professor of criminology at Carleton University and a psychologist with many years of experience working in the corrections field on the principles related to an effective reduction of recidivism for criminal offenders. He said:

> Official punishment (in other words, punishment sanctioned by the state) without the introduction of correctional treatment services does not work. Providing correctional treatment services that are inconsistent with the principles of risk, need, and responsivity does not work. What works is the delivery of clinically and psychologically appropriate correctional treatment service, under a variety of setting (probation, jail, and others) conditions that may be established by the criminal sanction. The delivery of appropriate correctional treatment service is dependent on assessments that are sensitive to risk, need, and responsivity (1994).

The summary point is this: do it right and rates of recidivism will decline significantly. Do it right and the use of jails and prisons can be reduced significantly. Ignore these points and state legislators will continue to lengthen prison sentences, continue to build more prisons, and force legislative budget committees to shift public funds from education to prisons.

Chapter 11

Responsivity: Tailoring Treatment and Supervision to the Unique Characteristics of Each Offender

If people outside of prison are not alike, why do we continue to treat people inside of prison as if they were a single homogeneous group? If we differentiate prison inmates at all, we use offense of conviction (murderer, burglar, rapist). Unfortunately, offense of conviction reveals very little about the inmate's risk for recidivism, treatment needs, or any unique learning or motivational attributes. We know this to be true from the literature on variability of crimes committed among offenders (Hindelang 1981, Andrews and Bonta 1994). Focusing on offense of conviction is a focus on the severity of the offense, not the offender. Variables such as age, gender, and race are more powerful predictors of prospective criminal activity than offense of conviction (Andrews and Bonta 1994).

As the field of adult corrections becomes more electronically sophisticated, and more high tech gadgets are added to the correctional arsenal, old operating assumptions have not been challenged. For example, many, if not most, community-based offenders are now routinely required to take the drug antabuse, have periodic urinanalysis tests, pay for the electronic monitoring device, and attend Alcoholics Anonymous (AA) or Narcotics Anonymous (NA) meetings.

There is a critical mistake with this approach. Not all offenders are alcohol or drug addicts. Some are moderate drinkers; some do not drink at all. Requiring all offenders to attend AA meetings ignores the individual differences among the offender population. Further, offenders not only differ on the basis of their criminogenic needs (see Chapter 10) but also differ greatly in their styles of learning or conversely, their ability to resist change. Figuring out the styles and methods of learning unique to each offender is the focus of this chapter.

The Development of Responsivity

Matching offender or client characteristics with the helping or counseling style of staff members is not new. Freud (1953) warned psychodynamic therapists that their highly verbal, evocative, relationship-dependent and insight-oriented therapy was inappropriate for individuals with poor verbal ability and/or with cases displaying narcissistic and/or psychotic disorders. Freud stated that some degree of experienced discomfort and an ability to enter into an emotional relationship with the therapist were crucial to success. Further, he added that without immediate social support for both treatment and personal change, the chances of successful treatment were miniscule (Andrews and Bonta 1994).

The Gluecks (Sheldon and Eleanor) challenged conventional social science outlooks in the 1940s and 1950s by directing their energies and research toward the individual. They did not ignore low-income status nor the general social and economic conditions of the neighborhood, but insisted that individual differences had more explanatory power regarding delinquent or criminal acts than social class or other large-scale conceptualizations of human behavior. In the words of the Gluecks: "The varieties of the physical, mental, and social history of different persons must determine, in large measure, the way in which they will be influenced by social disorganization, culture conflict and the growing-pains of the city" (Glueck and Glueck 1950).

Ted Palmer, seasoned veteran of correctional intervention techniques and research related to the effectiveness of correctional intervention, started his work more than forty years ago in California. As early as 1965, Palmer began publishing articles entitled, "Types of treaters and types of juvenile offenders," in 1967, "Personality characteristics and professional orientations of five groups of community treatment project workers: A preliminary report on differences among treaters," and in 1973, "Matching worker and client in corrections." Many years ago, Palmer obviously saw the validity of matching the unique helping styles of correctional workers with the unique learning styles and motivations of correctional clients.

The I-Level Classification system was developed and used in California with youthful offenders starting in the 1960s. I-Level is a classification system that categorizes offenders into a limited number of groups based on the unique personal qualities of each individual. Case management decisions then are made based on the category in which the offender fits. I-Level recommendations regarding differential treatment have high face validity and considerable clinical appeal (Harris 1988).

The Wisconsin Risk Assessment Scale includes considerations of risk and need, and is useful for case management strategies (see Chapter 9). In a study of parolees in Texas, parolees placed in the community under the Case Management Classification (CMC) system, which is a part of the Wisconsin's classification system, showed Case Management Classification intervention to be the most effective condition in reducing recidivism among medium- and high-risk offenders—after a six-month follow-up period. No impact was seen with low-risk offenders. The study authors (Lerner, Arling, and Baird 1985) attributed this success to matching the level and type of intervention to offender-risk level, as opposed to normal parole supervision where these types of distinctions and differences are ignored.

Responsivity Defined

The responsivity principle is rooted in the notion that there can be potent interactions between the characteristics of individuals and their settings or situations (Gendreau and Ross 1979 and 1981). Responsivity, as described by James Bonta, is as follows. There may be two offenders who need alcohol treatment, but many ways of providing alcohol treatment. Treatment can be in a group session, by individual therapy, or simply by giving the client a book to read. Clients differ. If the client is very intelligent and self-motivated, bibliotherapy may be all that is needed. For somebody who is shy and withdrawn, placing this client into a group program may be ineffective because it is inhibiting (Bonta 1991).

Donald Andrews' thoughts on responsivity also reflect the principle of matching unique styles and features of the "helper" with the unique learning styles and features of the offender. According to Andrews, styles of communication may be very important in the context of corrections, and particularly in interaction with a particular type of offender. Interpersonally anxious offenders do not respond well to highly confrontational and critical interpersonal exchanges, while the less anxious offender can respond as long as there is the background condition of caring and respect. The less verbally gifted and cognitively immature offender will not pick up on highly verbal and analytic approaches to interpersonal influence. Similarly, the less empathic, less interpersonally sensitive offender may not be expected to respond to subtle cues and suggestions. Generally, in fact, it is best for communication to be concrete and direct (Andrews 1994).

The responsivity principle suggests that behavior—criminal and noncriminal—is influenced by the outcomes of particular acts, signaled by the incentives and disincentives of the immediate situation of action. Further, behavior is influenced by the personally and interpersonally mediated sources of these signaled rewards and costs for criminal versus noncriminal action. Given this, the most empirically defensible and powerful theory of criminal activity is a broadly based social learning perspective that suggests how both self-control and interpersonal influences occur (Andrews and Bonta 1994).

According to Andrews and Bonta, the five dimensions of effective correctional supervision and counseling entail:

1. Relationship factors: relating in open, enthusiastic, caring ways

2. Authority: "firm but fair," distinguishing between rules and requests, monitoring, reinforcing compliance, not interpersonal domination or abuse

3. Anticriminal modeling and reinforcement: demonstrating and reinforcing vivid alternatives to procriminal styles of thinking, feeling, and acting

4. Concrete problem-solving: skill-building and removing obstacles toward increased reward levels for anticriminal behavior in settings such as home, school, and work

5. Advocacy and brokerage: as long as the receiving agency offers appropriate correctional service (Andrews and Bonta 1994)

The Matching Principle

The matching principle is of utmost importance in recognizing that offenders have unique treatment needs, their own learning style, and are at different stages of readiness to change (Hester and Miller 1995). Given this, it does no good to think globally and place, for example, all low-risk offenders in community service programs, or all high-risk offenders in AA or NA programs with frequent urinalysis checks. Matching can and should occur on several levels.

The principle of responsivity, according to Gendreau, simply states that treatment should be delivered in a manner that facilitates the learning of new prosocial skills by the offender. The three components of responsivity include: match the treatment approach with the learning style and personality of the offender; match the characteristics of the offender with those of the therapist; and match the skills of the therapist with the type of program (Gendreau 1994).

Some examples might be helpful. Offenders who prefer high degrees of structure or are impulsive are likely to function better in programs such as graduated token economies, which initially provide considerable external control with concrete rules for appropriate behavior. Offenders who are more anxious respond best to therapists exhibiting higher levels of interpersonal sensitivity. Therapists who have a concrete conceptual-level problem-solving style will function best in a program that is highly structured. Therapists who do not have such a style will function well in a self-directed, participatory organizational environment. Surveillance/self-control staff have great difficulties with offenders who are verbally hostile and defensive. Interpersonally anxious offenders do not respond well to highly confrontational and critical interpersonal exchanges. Relationship oriented (staffer uses nondirective, empathic messages) counseling is helpful with offenders who have above average empathy scores, but may increase criminal behavior of offenders with less empathic scores. Psychiatrically troubled offenders will perform better in low-pressure, sheltered-living environments (Bonta 1991, Palmer 1992, Gendreau 1994, Andrews 1994).

The implications of these findings for the field of corrections are clear: (1) carefully assess the unique learning styles and motivation levels of individual offenders, (2) know the special skills, counseling and supervision styles of your correctional staff, (3) match offenders and staff in ways that complement the learning, counseling and supervision of both, (4) when referring offenders to outside agencies, make sure the same type of careful matching of offenders to staff occurs. These matching efforts will pay large benefits in improvement of offender behavior.

Examples of Programs that Violate the Responsivity Principle

Research findings are now available indicating that correctional programs that violate responsivity principles have been quite unsuccessful in reducing recidivism among criminal offenders (Gendreau 1996, Palmer 1996).

Boot camps, electronic monitoring, home detention, and diversion programs are correctional settings, places, and contexts in which some positive or negative things can occur. It is possible to organize boot camps according to the principles of responsivity, but usually the desire to establish order, control, and discipline are given higher organizational priority.

Effective rehabilitative efforts involve workers who are interpersonally warm, tolerant, and flexible, yet sensitive to conventional rules and procedures. Practitioners of this type make use of the authority inherent in their position without engaging in interpersonal domination. They demonstrate in vivid ways their own

Program Features Inconsistent with Responsivity Principles

1. Group programs designed according to the principles of clinical sociology. These programs create intense group interactions without the leader of the group gaining control over the expression of antisocial sentiments

2. Programs designed according to the principles of deterrence (swift, sure, and severe punishment)

3. Programs designed according to the principles of labeling (reducing the impact of a negative label, avoiding negative labeling, diversion programs)

4. Yelling at people (boot camps)

5. Fear of punishment programs (Sacred Straight)

6. Radical nonintervention, doing nothing in the face of antisocial potential, especially for medium- to high-risk offenders

7. Community service orders

8. Restitution programs

9. Nondirective, client-centered counseling

10. Unstructured psychodynamic therapy

(Gendreau 1996, Palmer 1996)

anticriminal/prosocial attitudes, values, and beliefs. They enthusiastically engage the offender in the process of increasing rewards for noncriminal behavior. They expose and make attractive concrete alternatives to procriminal attitudes and behavior. Alternative (prosocial) ways of thinking and doing are demonstrated through words and actions and explorations of the alternatives are encouraged through modeling, reinforcing, and offering concrete guidance (Andrews and Kiessling 1980, Andrews, Bonta, and Hoge 1990).

The following summary statements are from different sets of responsivity research.

1. In general, more mature offenders with highly developed interpersonal skills do better when matched with seasoned veterans who possess strong verbal and interpersonal skills and have plenty of professional experience.

2. Immature offenders with low-conceptual levels, low empathy, and antisocial characteristics do better when matched with less skilled, less experienced correctional workers, and workers with a more structured, authoritative approach.

3. Styles and modes of correctional treatment that are interpersonally and verbally demanding and that depend on self-regulation, self-reflection, and interpersonal sensitivity, should be reserved for offenders who have relatively high levels of interpersonal and conceptual functioning.

4. More directive and structured programs should be reserved for offenders who possess lower levels of interpersonal and conceptual functioning.

5. In general, highly anxious offenders respond poorly to stressful interpersonal confrontation, while less anxious offenders may profit somewhat from confrontational programs.

6. For highly restless and risk-taking offenders, a correctional program that includes novel and exciting opportunities would be an effective match.

7. For narcissistic, antisocial offenders who have many high-risk factors but little motivation for change, it is very important that treatment be readily accessible. Their total environment (family, friends, work, and the neighborhood) should be supportive of participation in the correctional program. With these types of offenders, a court order that mandates participation may be therapeutically beneficial.

8. Offenders with antisocial personalities are relatively unresponsive to rehabilitation efforts. The lack of effectiveness of treating psychopaths is a combination of their high risk-levels, multiple criminogenic needs, and responsivity deficits

that indicate a need for high levels of structure. Hence, these types of offenders would do best under intense correctional controls, intense treatment, and isolation from procriminal associates (Andrews, Bonta, and Hoge 1990).

Summary

Consistent with the theory of the psychology of criminal conduct, the individual is the unit of analysis—not society, not poverty, not self-esteem. Crime causation can be understood best by understanding the individual first and then building up (inductively) from there. The quality and character of the individual's peers (as well as parents, neighborhood, and schools) are important, as probation and parole officers have known for decades. However, the individual is most important.

Adult offenders are not a special class of creatures any more than airline passengers or hospital patients. When correctional staff honor individual differences, the quality of communication between staff and offenders will improve, the trust and rapport will increase, recidivism rates will decrease (if risk or criminogenic needs are taken into account), and the field will begin to gain some broad scale respect with the general public and policymakers.

Responsivity from the Ottawa School (Andrews, Bonta, Gendreau, *et al.*) and motivational interviewing from addiction specialists (Miller, Hester, Rollnick, *et al.*) are two critically important tools that are available to corrections practitioners now. If responsivity is used in tandem with the other two elements of the psychology of criminal conduct, risk and needs, then real progress can be made toward improving the overall efficacy of correctional intervention.

Chapter 12

Continuous Client, Staff, and Program Evaluation

Why Bother with Evaluations?

Most practitioners do not think about evaluation. This is true in the field of adult corrections just as much as it is true in education, mental health, physical health, social services, or most other human services. On the other hand, most practitioners would like to think that what they are doing is the "right thing," the "most effective thing," or at the very least, not counterproductive. Another benefit of program evaluations is that successes can be replicated and failures can be reduced or eliminated, and in so doing make stronger programs more efficient and much more cost effective (Aziz and Clark 1996).

When a correctional agency's mission includes changing the behavior of offenders, evaluations are an essential element. The best way to view evaluation is as a feedback loop. Evaluation feeds back to the practitioner what works and what is a waste of time. Without evaluation, we would still be classifying offenders by the size and shape of their heads, as was the practice in the late nineteenth century. Evaluation, then, is essential, and practitioners and policymakers alike should begin to view evaluation as an integral part of doing business.

One of the challenges of evaluation is to sift through mountains of information and isolate what is useful, what can be applied to everyday practice, and what kernel of truth can be taken to legislative hearings and shared with elected officials and others struggling with corrections policy matters. For example, an evaluation question that seems particularly timely today, since the institutional (jails and prisons) component of the corrections system more than doubled in the last decade, is the question: are prisons effective in reducing recidivism? If not, why continue to invest in failure? If prisons are effective, where is the evidence?

One purpose of this chapter is to review what the existing research literature tells us about what works. That information is presented at the end of this chapter. A second purpose of this chapter is to present an evaluation format with which to assess offender, staff, and correctional intervention programs.

A reason for highlighting and promoting evaluation is to make a contribution to the construction of a correctional consensus. With better theory, more effective programs, and a reduction in the rates of recidivism, a consensus can emerge that will unify practitioners, policymakers, and, eventually, the general public around a more realistic set of correctional goals.

There are many very sophisticated methods of collecting information and many more complex and sophisticated techniques to measure, analyze, and interpret what is collected, but those specialized methods and techniques will not be included in this chapter because the intended audiences of this chapter are practitioners, policy analysts, policymakers, public officials, and the public itself. Hence, the language used in this chapter will be geared to the lay citizen and not to technical or research audiences.

Colorado Community Corrections: A Case Example

Unless a community corrections program is serving high-risk offenders exclusively, a correctional program that has a failure rate of 40 or 50 percent or higher is not a good program. Either inappropriate offenders are being placed in the program or mistakes are being made once offenders get into the program, or both. Chart 12.1 illustrates this point. Colorado was the third state in the country (after California's Probation Subsidy Program in the early 1960s and Minnesota's in 1973) to pass legislation that provided state money to divert repeat felons from the state prison system. Colorado has been in the adult community corrections business since 1976.

CHART 12.1: Success/Failure in Colorado Community Corrections, 1985 and 1989 in Percentage

	Diversion* Clients: 1985	Diversion Clients: 1989	Transition* Clients: 1985	Transition* Clients: 1989
Successful	57	49	57	46
Failures, total	43	51	43	54
A. Failure new crimes	4	3	4	3
B. Failure: abscond, escape	20	21	7	20
C. Failure: house, technical violation**	19	27	32	31
Sample size	565	879	277	751

* A diversion client is referred by the courts in lieu of a prison sentence. A transition client is referred by prison and parole officials to a community corrections program after the offender has served most of his or her other prison sentence.

**Examples of house/technical rule violations: a client fails to clean his room, or do his in-house chores, or returns to the halfway house late on more than one occasion, or comes up with a "hot" (positive) urine, or fails to pay room and board charge.

Source: English and Mande 1991.

Community Corrections Program

The sample size is sufficiently large to make some general conclusions about the state of community corrections in Colorado. New crimes committed by offenders while in community residential programs are a very poor reflection on the quality of supervision. Happily, the rate of new crimes committed by community corrections participants is quite low. This is a good sign. However, a 20 percent abscond/escape rate and a 20 to 30 percent house/technical rule violation rate are powerful barometers of "something."

The "something" could be any number of things, which is why social scientists refer to this uncertainty as the "black box." In this case, the "black box" could be describing any of the following factors: (a) unreasonable house rules, (b) a social control orientation of staff, (c) lack of appropriate treatment services, (d) unmotivated program participants, (e) a lack of matching between offenders, staff, and program types, (f) no coordination between sponsoring agencies, resulting in conflicts in rules, regulations, expectations, or (g) a combination of these factors or a variety of other factors. Unfortunately, the information is not specific enough to isolate precisely which one or combination of these factors explains the high rate of program failure.

The purpose of Chart 12.1 is not to single out Colorado for negative scrutiny. Colorado should be praised for its commitment to evaluation. Outcome statistics for most states around the country would show a similar pattern. Colorado's evaluation findings are at least the preliminary steps to correctional enlightenment—as long as corrective action is taken to improve program performance.

One of the major omissions in evaluation of correctional programs is a careful articulation and identification of the customer. If the customer is the offender, the correctional field must be reconfigured in significant ways that emphasize the offender's needs, goals, and objectives. If the customer is the public, then corrections must be reconfigured to include ways to identify what the public wants and not interpret that through the eyes and self-interests of elected officials. At the moment, there is no consensus on this critically important matter, and correctional evaluations typically confuse and intermingle offender performance with public safety goals.

Outcome Measures

There are many ways to measure success or failure in corrections. The generally accepted measure is recidivism. Recidivism, for the most part, means reoffending in some form or fashion. However, there are more subtle measures of recidivism other than success or failure. Some examples of short-term outcome measures include the following:

1. No significant problems while in the program; moved to a less intense level of supervision or off supervision

2. Technical or house rule violation

3. Escape or abscond from the program

4. Restitution: paid, unpaid, partially paid

5. Arrest for new criminal offense

Examples of long-term outcome measures include the following:

1. Reconviction for new offense

2. Reincarceration for offense while on probation or parole

3. Relapse: alcohol, drugs, procriminal associations

Outcome measures need not be indicators of negative, antisocial behavior. Examples of positive outcome measures include the following:

1. Prosocial bonds: reconnect with family, friends, community agencies or members

2. Establish or reestablish good credit rating

3. Employment earnings; could be short- and long-term measure

This constellation of negative, positive, short- and long-term measures should be used as the outcome measures of correctional programs. As a constellation of outcome measures, program managers begin to understand how the multiplicity of factors play various roles in moving the offender away from antisocial peers or toward prosocial contacts with peers, family, employment, and other community components.

When to Evaluate Offenders and with What Measures

Another important dimension of evaluating offenders' behavior and program performance is documenting change over time. The appropriate time intervals for these assessments and reassessments are as follows:

1. Soon after arrest

2. After referral to a correctional program but prior to program intake

3. Upon entry into the corrections program

4. Every thirty days while in the program

5. Upon program termination

6. Thirty days after termination

7. At six-month intervals after program termination, for at least twelve months, up to two or three years, if possible

Different types of information should be collected at different stages of the criminal justice process. For example:

After referral to a correctional program but prior to program intake:

There are basically two types of information that should be collected at this juncture. The first is risk to the community. Much of this type of information is already available, having been collected by jail intake staff and probation officers (investigations division). Risk to the community involves measures of community stability (length of time of employment, length of time at residence, length of time in the area), a prior record (age at first arrest, juvenile history, severity of offenses), and nature and severity of the present offense.

The second type of information is on treatment needs. Jail intake officers rarely have time or specialized training to capture this type of information. Probation officers sometimes have time and skills; sometimes they do not. If possible, the types of information needed to assess treatment needs includes substance abuse history, social networks (prosocial or procriminal), and other treatment needs such as mental health, money management, and employment skills. The primary objective of evaluation at this first stage is to determine if appropriate offenders are being placed in correctional settings that match their risk level and treatment needs. As in other parts of this report, the recommendation is to make these assessments with standardized assessment forms. This standardization should include all actors across the juvenile justice and criminal justice system.

At Program Entry:

As the client enters the program, the correctional worker should have all existing information collected at jail intake and by probation staff. From this base of information, the correctional worker (sheriffs' work release, probation, private community corrections staff, or parole officers) must continue to collect the same two types of information (risk to the community and treatment needs) but do so in a much more refined and detailed manner. Correctional workers must create a relationship with the offender that results in respect and trust and encourages the offender to commit time and energy to achieve specific program goals. Hence, the measures needed at this second stage are much more focused on the unique characteristics of the offender.

The standardized measures on the fifty-four item Level of Supervision Inventory (see Chapter 9) are just the beginning of the data elements that correctional workers need to collect that will form the basis of evaluation at this stage. Additional assessments and measures may be appropriate. For example, an offender with an extensive history of substance abuse and a history of relapse should be assessed using any one of a number of the following assessment instruments: Alcohol Use Questionnaire, Drug Use Questionnaire, Adult Substance Use

Survey, Substance Use History Matrix, Stages of Change Readiness and Treatment Eagerness Scale, Situational Confidence Questionnaire, and Understanding of Alcoholism Scale. There are many other specialized instruments to assess for mental health problems, social support networks, and other needs.

It is essential that correctional workers complete a comprehensive assessment of risk and treatment needs at this second stage. Information collected at program intake is of critical importance because it establishes a baseline against which subsequent assessments and evaluations are made. Without this type of informational baseline, no credible statements can be made about offender, staff, or program effectiveness.

After program entry but before program termination:

The importance of this third stage of evaluation usually is overlooked but is very crucial. Historically, researchers have referred to this stage as the "black box" because no one carefully measured what transpired during the course of a correctional program. So, the evaluation challenge is to figure out which part of the correctional program is having an impact on the offender—while the offender is still in the program. Without this type of information, there is no way to identify specifically what caused the offender to progress (get a job or stop drinking) or regress (return to his or her procriminal friends or continue drinking).

The evaluation at this third stage is called periodic reassessment. The frequency of these reassessments will depend on the risk level and treatment needs of the offender (the higher the risk, the more frequent the reassessments) and the man or woman power resources available in the correctional agency. With medium- to high-risk offenders, the recommendation would be frequent reassessments on those particular matters (risk or need) that have shown to be problematic in the past. The reassessments should be every thirty-to-forty days for medium-risk offenders, and every fifteen-to-twenty days for high-risk offenders. The instruments needed to conduct these reassessments are the same as those for stage two.

This is a lot of assessment. This is also the ideal and may not be possible. However, the justification for numerous assessments and reassessments of offender performance is to capture change. The direction of that change is, hopefully, toward more prosocial, anticriminal behavior. Oftentimes, the direction of change is negative. If the change is negative and the correctional staffers intervene quickly, they are in much better positions to stop the negative behavior, figure out what is going on, and attempt to make a course adjustment. This is possible if the correctional practitioners have manageable caseloads, if they have proper training to conduct the assessments, and if they are motivated to do so.

After program termination:

This last stage of evaluation is where most evaluations begin. What is needed at this fourth stage is to gauge how successful the offender is after release from the correctional program. Recidivism is the universal outcome variable, but it hides more than it reveals. A variety and range of recidivism measures should be included in any evaluation. A variety of measures describe different types of activities, and they measure different things. Some are barometers for seriousness (reincarceration) that call into question the offender's behavior and others are measures of program effectiveness such as commitment to correctional goals or the effectiveness of staff.

Other information that should be collected at this stage relates to treatment services. The type and number of treatment data elements will depend on the scale of treatment needs of the offender. Examples of appropriate outcome data include the following elements:

1. total wages earned

2. length of time on the job

3. length of time at residence—stability of living

4. absence of any substance abuse problems, no tickets for driving while intoxicated, no relapse, no drinking/drug-related job absences

5. prompt payment of bills, restitution, resolution of other financial obligations

6. improvement of earnings over time

7. number and types of community resources used

Types of Research Design and Sample Construction:

The last element regarding offender evaluation is setting up the design of the research and establishing the sample. The ideal is to have matched control and experimental samples randomly selected (in research language, this is called a quasi-experimental design) and it should be adequate in size. The purpose of using a quasi-experimental design is that research findings using this design help isolate the precise factors (such as staff competencies, program philosophy, and specific treatment interventions) that lead to success. Setting up a quasi-experimental design for any human service is difficult to achieve.

In criminal justice, it is even more difficult. Generally, the prosecuting attorney wants retribution; therefore, incarceration is the preferred setting choice. Often, the defense attorney wants restorative justice; therefore, community placement is the preferred choice. The attorneys' negotiated plea usually determines correctional placement and length of stay in that placement. Neither party is interested in matched samples, and both are not supportive of random selection nor assignment. To make this happen, all the important criminal justice actors need to be informed about the long-term learning implications and importance of research.

Everyone can "win" in this research arena. All the actors: the attorneys, judges, probation officers, and everyone else has a stake in learning what works. That is the argument that needs to be presented so that matched samples selected randomly can become a reality. Yet, if there is no possibility to influence where offenders are placed for research purposes, the only thing that remains is to follow the principles of the Psychology of Criminal Conduct (see Chapter 4) and not repeat the mistakes of programs that already have demonstrated failure.

In summary, offenders need to be classified in terms of risk, needs, and responsivity. Additionally, offender status (on static and risk-related factors) and performance on a variety of dynamic factors (substance use or work) must be established initially and then reassessed at frequent intervals.

Evaluating Correctional Programs

What are the features of the correctional program that contribute to a reduction in recidivism? For example, does it make a difference if the program is located downtown or in a sparsely populated rural setting? If it is a residential program, can one-hundred residents in a single program do just as well as twenty in a program? Does the program philosophy matter? Does a tough, one-mistake-and-you're-out type program reduce recidivism more or less than a sensitive, caring, client-oriented program? Does an annual staff turnover rate of 20 percent differ in terms of offender outcome from a program with a staff turnover rate of 40 percent? Do staff ethnic or gender profiles that are congruent with the offender population get better outcomes than programs that do not have such congruence?

Some of these questions are answered in the section below, "A Review of What Works." There is scant empirical evidence to support confrontational programs, general programs, individual therapy, and intensive supervision programs (Gendreau 1994, Palmer 1996, Gendreau 1996). Cognitive, behavioral, and client-specific programs do work. These are the programs that focus on specific skills development and alter the offender's attitudes, values, and beliefs. Also, programs that structure activities which disrupt delinquency or the criminal network by placing offenders in situations where prosocial activities predominate have demonstrated efficacy in reducing recidivism. Programs that emphasize relapse prevention in community settings work (Gendreau 1994). However, not all the questions have yet been answered. More evaluations are needed. Programs and assessment of programs can be divided into structural and process components as illustrated in Chart 12.2.

CHART 12.2: Structural and Process Components of Correctional Programs

Structural Features	Process Features
Staff turnover, length of stay of staff in the program	Does the supervision match offender risk levels?
Staff to offender ratio, caseload size	Do treatment services match the identified criminogenic needs?
Overall program and/or facility size	Are offenders matched with unique skills and supervision style of staff?
Organizational incentives offered to staff for offender success	Is the case plan complete, comprehensive and measurable?
Organizational setting: noninstitutional, open institution, direct parole, closed institution, social control community program	Are reassessments of offenders done at short intervals? If so, are supervision and treatment levels adjusted accordingly?
Staff qualifications: formal education, specialized training, professional experience	Are supervision and treatment services being delivered in a timely fashion immediately after program entrance and when called for upon reassessment?
Social climate of program	Is staff performance continuously evaluated? If so, how? With what measurement tools? How frequently? If not, why not? Does the program have elaborate and extensive interagency agreements with existing human service programs in the community? Are offenders using these existing community resources and using them appropriately (such as matched with risk or needs of offenders)?

All of these structural and process features of correctional programs should be included in any program assessment. As Palmer suggests, correctional intervention programs should be viewed and evaluated as total entities, functioning wholes, or as a social system (Palmer 1996). In other words, researchers and program evaluators need to assess all the correctional components (offenders, staff, program elements, and philosophy) as well as understand the interrelationships between and among those components.

Evaluating Offender Performance

To establish a baseline of information against which certain activities can be measured, there must be a set of uniform, measurable criteria regarding the characteristics of the offender. In the pre-1980 days, the baseline offender characteristics considered in corrections placement included the following: prior record, severity of present offense, demographic factors including social history, and possibly, offender's attitude. Attitude usually meant regret or guilt for the offense committed.

Given these four factors and the subjective nature of at least three of them, there was never much agreement about the placement choices. A law enforcement or prosecutor type would interpret the four factors conservatively and recommend incarceration. A rehabilitation-oriented probation officer or judge would interpret the four factors progressively and recommend a community sanction. Unfortunately, this type of disagreement continues today.

To further complicate matters, social scientists never could agree on the most important or predictive power for baseline characteristics of the offender. Some argued that age at first arrest was most important. Others thought that the totality of the prior criminal record was of critical importance. Still others thought that substance abuse history should take precedence over other factors.

A recent attempt by elected officials to simplify this debate was seen in the "three strikes and you're out" movement in the United States (out = life in prison or a minimum of twenty-five years in some states). A primary purpose of this movement was to consider prior record the most important factor, to the exclusion of the other three factors. Oversimplification led to some bizarre results. The first offender charged under the "three strikes" law in California was a man who stole an inexpensive tool from a hardware store. When the local prosecutor was asked by the press why he chose to file a life sentence against such a minor offender, his answer was: "That's the way the legislature wrote the law. I'm just conforming to the legislature's wishes." Putting shoplifters in prison for life was not the legislative intent of "three strikes." However, the subjective language used (dangerousness) in the bill gave prosecutors enough latitude to file life sentence charges against inappropriate offenders and plenty of room for publicity and grandstanding.

A better way to develop a baseline of offender characteristics is to use a tool or scale that incorporates all of the pertinent factors that contribute to the outcome, which is some objective measure of risk to the community or recidivism. Prior record, present offense, and social history were always important factors. But the issue now is: what is the best way to format these and other factors to reduce the disagreement between the polar opposites (conservative, law enforcement versus progressive, rehabilitation perspective)?

The recommendation here is: use the Level of Supervision Inventory (LSI-Revised) to classify for charge, plea negotiation, sentence recommendation, sentence, and post-sentence supervision (institutional or community). The LSI-R has been carefully and extensively evaluated on many bases (ability to accurately predict success/failure, whether it is user friendly for correctional staff and other factors) (Bonta 1996, Jones 1996). The LSI-R is useful for general classification of offenders and should be used whether the offender is placed in jail or prison, on probation, or in any other community corrections setting. Further, the LSI-R is theory based and thus, facilitates the clear identification of the most important factors to be measured.

Using social learning principles contained in the LSI-R, offenders can be categorized into general levels of risk and criminogenic needs. These categorizations can be measured with a fair degree of accuracy, and as a result, the subjectivity of existing systems of classification can be dramatically reduced or eliminated.

The LSI-R (see Chapter 9 for a more complete description) is a fifty-four item risk assessment instrument. For probation supervision, the cutoff scores are: twenty-nine or higher = maximum-risk level; nineteen to twenty-eight = medium risk; zero to eighteen = minimum risk. Cutoff points are a combination of common sense, empirically derived conclusions, and ideology. In politically conservative locations, cutoff points may be lower for higher-risk clients. Hopefully, with education and training, cutoff points can be established independent of political ideology.

In addition to categorization for general levels of risk, the criminogenic needs (substance abuse, employment, and others) can be measured as dynamic phenomenon. Progress (or regression) toward treatments goals can be measured with the use of the following scoring table. With these types of measures, offender performance can be measured at three times: program entry, while the offender is in the program, and at program termination.

Score	Meaning of the LSI-R Score
0	A very unsatisfactory situation with a very clear and strong need for improvement
1	A relatively unsatisfactory situation with a need for improvement

2   A relatively satisfactory situation, with some
             room for improvement

3   A satisfactory situation with little opportunity
             or need for improvement

For example, when scoring offenders on the quality of their employment, a score of three would indicate that the offender expresses a strong interest in his or her job, pride in his or her ability to perform job tasks, and has received positive feedback from his or her boss for job performance. The offender's attendance on the job is very good. He or she is willing to work overtime and chooses to stay in this line of work. Conversely, a score of zero would indicate that the offender hates his or her work and finds his or her work boring, dangerous, or unpleasant. The offender complains that he or she cannot perform work tasks well. He or she only works because it is necessary to make a living and usually the job is not tolerable, even on those terms. The offender's job attendance is unreliable, and this individual is often late for work, and is prepared to quit at the earliest opportunity.

These scoring delineations offer the correctional practitioner a reasonably concise benchmark against which offender performance can be established initially and then reassessed at subsequent intervals. Remember the example of the outcome information from the Colorado community corrections system (Chart 12.1)? The outcome information was there, but there was no way to tell why the failure rate was so high and when the problems began or when they were resolved. To avoid that "not knowing" (or "black box") problem, practitioners need to specify precisely what is going on with each offender and measure this progress along a baseline that is objective and measurable. With the use of the LSI-R, it is possible to build knowledge, gain insights, and help future practitioners make more accurate case management decisions.

Evaluating Staff Performance

What role does correctional staff have in offender success or failure? Does it matter if the staff had high school degrees or college degrees? Does it matter if all or some of the staff were social-control oriented? What if the staff were group-counseling oriented, did that make a difference in offender performance? In the past, the role of staff in offender performance was never factored into the offender performance equation. As it turns out, staff qualifications, temperament, and philosophical orientation are extremely important and correlate highly to offender performance (Miller and Rollnick 1991, Palmer 1992, Gendreau 1996).

ACA Public Correctional Policy on Employee Assistance Programs

INTRODUCTION:

The most valuable resource in any correctional agency is the staff employed by that agency. Corrections is a service delivery enterprise with people as its most important product. The employees who deliver these services should be afforded all reasonable assistance to allow them to do the best job possible.

POLICY STATEMENT:

Employee assistance programs should be made available to all employees. The programs should address employee needs and requirements that will help ensure a high level of on-the-job performance. Correctional agencies should:

A. Establish employee assistance programs based on appropriate assessment of employee needs and desires.

B. Publicize program availability regularly and frequently in a variety of ways to ensure that all employees know not only what is available to them, but also how to access and participate in them.

C. Provide programs at no cost to the employee where possible. When the employee must pay some or all of the cost of the program/service, it should be an amount that does not exceed what that person could reasonably be expected to pay.

D. Provide an employee in the central/main office of the agency who would be responsible for coordinating all employee assistance programs. Each facility or major organizational unit should have one person designated as the coordinator of employee assistance programs.

E. Ensure programs and services are provided either directly by the agency or by other public or private agencies to which the employee is referred for assistance.

F. Require the Employee Assistance Program Coordinator to report at least quarterly on the level and type of activity that has occurred. That information should be used to assess the need for adding, deleting or modifying specific employee assistance programs.

G. Ensure employee requests or referrals for assistance remain confidential, unless the employee expressly elects to waive confidentiality.

This Public Correctional Policy was unanimously ratified by the American Correctional Association Delegate Assembly at the Congress of Correction in Nashville, Tennessee, August 4, 1993.

According to Palmer, probation officers, be they volunteers or professionals, who were interpersonally sensitive to conventional rules (above average on the Socialization Scale), were the most effective one-on-one supervisors. Offenders paired with these particular types of staff had lower recidivism rates and better attitudinal gains while under probation supervision. Among low-risk probationers, staff characteristics did not matter, but among high-risk probationers, staff qualities did matter (Palmer 1992).

Staff Characteristics that Contribute to Offender Performance

1. Therapists, correctional practitioners, or other staff with the following interpersonal skills are most effective with offenders:

   a) clear in their communication with offenders

   b) warm

   c) with a sense of humor

   d) open

   e) with an ability to relate affect to behavior, and

   f) able to set appropriate limits between offenders and themselves.

   With these sorts of skills, staff are effective sources of reinforcement and can competently model prosocial skills.

2. Staff have solid formal educational backgrounds (an undergraduate degree is preferable) or equivalent training on the theories of criminal behavior, and the prediction and treatment of criminal behavior.

3. Staff receive three-to-six months of formal and on-the-job internship training in the application of behavioral interventions generally and those specific to the program.

4. Staff is assessed and reassessed periodically on the quality of their service delivery.

5. Staff monitor offender change on intermediate targets of treatment (Gendreau 1996).

High mutual regard versus high mutual dislike between offenders and staff can be a critically important factor in offender performance. In one program, when there was high mutual regard, only 10 percent of the offenders failed. When high mutual dislike prevailed, 40 percent of the offenders failed (Jesness *et al.* 1975).

Matching staff characteristics with offenders is a subcomponent of overall program integrity (Gendreau and Ross 1987). Gendreau describes five important criteria regarding staff characteristics that contribute to offender performance.

This is a good list with which to select and evaluate staff performance. A number of standardized scales and instruments exist with which staff performance can be measured. A few of them include:

Correctional Institutions Environmental Scale: In 1974, Rudolf H. Moos, a researcher in Minnesota, developed a way to measure the environment of correctional programs. This was an example of an early attempt to measure staff attitudes. The Moos correctional environmental scale is a ninety-item scale that measures how offenders perceive the correctional program in terms of the number and types of rules and regulations, enforcement of rules and regulations, and staff attitudes towards offenders (Moos 1975).

Community Program Assessment Inventory: Gendreau and Andrews developed a scale to measure community corrections programs. The scale or inventory consists of several dozen items that assess correctional programs on six dimensions: program implementation, client pre-service assessment, program characteristics, staff characteristics or practices, evaluation, and a residual category. This tool documents the strengths and weaknesses of a program in each of the six dimensions and provides an overall percentage score of program quality (Gendreau 1996).

Sanctions Policy Assessment: This is a scale designed to assess staff attitudes regarding different legal and correctional sanctions. Four case examples are presented. Staff are asked how they would deal with these hypothetical cases. The scale classifies staff responses in such a way that delineations among staff types can be made (Vincent O'Leary, State University of New York at Albany, 1992).

Organizational Diagnosis Questionnaire: This is a thirty-five item questionnaire. Respondents are asked to score their organization on a scale of one to seven. The scale can be used to analyze staff or line functioning as well as to assess the thinking of different levels of management or supervision (Robert C. Preziosi, University Associates).

Understanding of Alcoholism Scale: This is a scale that measures a person's understanding of alcohol use or misuse. The scale can be used with offenders or staff in determining their knowledge and attitudes regarding alcohol use and addictions, in general. Matching of offender and staff according to shared biases is recommended (William R. Miller and Theresa B. Moyers, Center on Alcoholism, Substance Abuse and Addictions, University of New Mexico, Albuquerque, Research Division).

With the use of these types of standardized assessment instruments, staff can be classified and categorized by philosophical orientation, social control versus therapy orientation, and offender supervision styles. Making these types of distinctions is the first important step in matching particular staff with different types of offenders. This type of staff or offender matching improves offender performance.

A Review of What Works

Happily, in the mid-1990s, the general tone and direction of the literature in correctional intervention is upbeat, almost optimistic. This has not always been the case. In the late 1970s, the prevailing mood was quite the opposite. Many, if not most practitioners, questioned whether correctional intervention, in the form of treatment services, was worth the effort.

In the words of Ted Palmer (1996), a seasoned correctional research veteran of many decades:

> Knowledge about the frequency with which (correctional) intervention "works" and does not "work" has rapidly advanced in recent years, mainly due to careful meta-analyses and detailed literature reviews. Together, these studies have helped change the atmosphere surrounding correctional intervention from one of widespread gloom and frequent indifference to one of considerable hope and interest.

There have been hundreds of evaluations of individual programs, and since 1975, there have been at least twenty literature reviews and nine meta-analyses that have attempted to synthesize the evaluations. One recent effort (Palmer 1996) was an attempt to "put it all together" and synthesize as much as possible in terms of what works with particular types of offenders, specifying types of programs, and identifying specific staff characteristics and correctional settings. What follows are the conclusions that have been drawn from Palmer's literature review. The list describes types of programs, not types of offenders or staff. Palmer used recidivism as the measure of success or failure.

Confrontation Programs: Confrontation programs have not been successful. Examples of confrontation programs are Scared Straight and shock probation (jail followed by intensive probation supervision). Some of the findings indicate an actual increase in recidivism associated with certain confrontational programs (Palmer 1996).

Areawide Strategies of Delinquency Prevention: These programs, such as Project Pride in Denver during the 1970s and 1980s, are broad scope, communitywide efforts to reduce juvenile delinquency. There is no evidence indicating success with these types of programs (Palmer 1996).

Social Casework, Social Agency, or Societal Institution Approaches to Delinquency Prevention: Examples of these types of programs are child guidance clinics and public agency referrals and services. The literature is mostly negative for this type of program (Palmer 1996).

Diversion: Making a general conclusion about the effectiveness of diversion programs is difficult because of the great variety of diversion programs. Overall, the findings are not encouraging for diversion programs. A few service-oriented efforts have slightly more positive results, but, in general, diversion programs have not shown great promise (Palmer 1996).

Physical Challenge: Programs such as Outward Bound, Vision Quest, and other programs that emphasize physical challenges to offenders have had mixed reviews. Programs that have focused on life-skills training as an integral part of the overall program have had positive results, but programs that only emphasize physical challenge have not been very successful in reducing recidivism (Palmer 1996).

Restitution: Restitution programs have had modest success (an 8 to 12 percent reduction in recidivism compared to programs without a restitution requirement) (Palmer 1996).

Group Counseling/Therapy: Group counseling and group therapy programs have not had great success. Some programs that are carefully focused, behavioral, and operated within the justice system showed very modest success. In general, group counseling and therapy do not appear to provide a hopeful approach (Palmer 1996).

Individual Counseling/Therapy: Individual counseling and therapy programs have similar, mostly negative, or mixed results. The more general the counseling and therapy are, the less effective they are in reducing recidivism. The more focused and client centered they are, the more beneficial the results. Also, there is some evidence that if individual counseling is conducted within a justice system setting, it has some modest beneficial effect (Palmer 1996).

ACA Public Correctional Policy on Offender Education and Training

INTRODUCTION:

Many accused and adjudicated juvenile and adult offenders lack the basic educational, vocational, and life skills necessary to enhance community integration and economic self-sufficiency. These deficiencies may interact with other socioeconomic and psychological factors to affect the life choices made by offenders and may limit the legitimate financial and social opportunities available to these individuals.

POLICY STATEMENT:

Education and training are integral parts of the total correctional process. Governmental jurisdictions should develop, expand, and improve delivery systems for academic, occupational, social, and other educational programs for accused and adjudicated juvenile and adult offenders in order to enhance their community integration and economic self-sufficiency. Toward this end, correctional agencies should:

A. Provide for assessment of academic, vocational, and social skills deficiencies of those under their jurisdictions, including assessments to identify handicapping conditions under federal, state, and local laws and regulations;

B. Make available and provide equal access to opportunities to participate in relevant, comprehensive, educational, vocational, work study, life skills, training programs and transition and job placement activities that are fully coordinated and integrated with other components of the correctional process, the community as a whole, and the offender's family and appropriate prerelease and postrelease programs and services.

C. Ensure programs provided are taught by certified instructors in accordance with professional standards and relevant techniques;

D. Provide incentives for participation and achievement in work, education and training programs;

E. Maximize use of public and private sector resources in development, implementation, coordination, and evaluation of education and training programs and job placement activities; and

F. Evaluate the efficiency, equity, and effectiveness of program performance based on measurable goals and objectives.

This Public Correctional Policy was ratified by the American Correctional Association Delegate Assembly at the Winter Conference in Orlando, Florida, January 20, 1985. It was reviewed and amended January 6, 1991 at the Winter Conference in Louisville, Kentucky. It was reviewed without change August 21, 1996 at the Congress of Correction in Nashville, Tennessee.

Family Intervention: Family-intervention programs have had some modest success, but also have mixed results (some positive, some negative). Once again, the more focused the program, the better the results. Programs that were carefully structured, and focused on particular family problems or particular client needs, were more successful than programs without a specific focus (Palmer 1996).

Vocational Training: Vocational training programs reduced recidivism in about one out of every three programs. When vocational training programs were operated within the justice (correctional) system, there was an increase in recidivism. The general finding is that vocational training programs had mixed results (Palmer 1996).

Employment: Work experience programs had beneficial results and appear to be worth replicating and continuing. However, when employment programs are operated outside the justice system, they have not shown positive effects (Palmer 1996).

Educational Training: Educational training, which includes standard or special academic programming, remedial education, and individual tutoring has been beneficial in reducing recidivism in two out of every three studies. Like employment programs, educational training programs should be continued, but remain focused on specific skills and objectives (Palmer 1996).

Behavioral: Behavioral approaches, examples of which are contingency contracting and token economies (the level system), have produced quite positive results among a broad spectrum of studies and researchers. Behavioral programs (reinforce socially acceptable behaviors and discourage specific unwanted behaviors) are successful in their own right and have also been used successfully to implement other programs such as family intervention, and vocational or educational training. Hence, behavioral programs can be used successfully as a general approach or as a generic technique (Palmer 1996).

Cognitive-behavioral or Cognitive: Some view the cognitive approach as a subset of behavioral programs. However, whether cognitive programs are viewed separately or in combination with behavioral programs, cognitive programs have been quite successful. Cognitive programs cover a lot of ground and go under different names: interpersonal skills training, social skills training, social-cognitive interventions, and cognitive therapy. Whatever the name, cognitive programs have shown success in reducing recidivism (Palmer 1996).

Life skills: This approach, commonly referred to as life skills, skill oriented, or skill development, is a mixture of approaches. Life skills include academic or vocational training, outdoor programs, drug programs, and sometimes employment programs. These types of life skills programs have demonstrated considerable success, reducing recidivism by at least 20 percent over nonlife skills programs. When life skills programs were operated outside the justice system, they were even more successful. Specialized life skills programs had better outcomes than standard or general programs (Palmer 1996).

Multimodal: The multimodal approach was also found to be successful. Examples of multimodal programs include work/study programs with or without counseling and with or without restitution. More research and analysis must be done to isolate the precise combinations of programs and match those combinations with the specific risk and needs of offenders (Palmer 1996).

Probation and Parole Enhancement Programs: Probation and parole enhancement programs are more intensely supervised programs with more probation/parole contacts than standard supervision and oftentimes include additional social control elements such as electronic monitoring and family or employer contacts. Overall, the performance of the enhancement programs have received mixed reviews. Reduced caseloads (which results in more intense supervision) by themselves, do not seem to reduce recidivism. However, intense supervision combined with additional programs (behavioral, cognitive, life skills) elements hold some promise for recidivism reduction (Palmer 1996).

Intensive Supervision: Intensive probation and parole programs have not been successful. However, intensive probation and parole programs can be helpful if they are designed and operated as multicomponent interventions and are carefully conceptualized. This means that they should be theory based, classify for risk and needs, and match offenders to appropriate programs and staff. However, intense supervision alone does not work (Palmer 1996).

Community-based Approaches Versus Institutional Intervention: Neither community nor institutional programs were very effective in reducing recidivism with unselected, heterogeneous offender populations when offering generic programming. When offenders were carefully selected and classified and offered appropriate treatment services, community programs were more effective than institutional programs (Palmer 1996).

Palmer's list of nineteen different types of programs and their respective efficacy represents years of hard work by about eighty different researchers who deserve widespread recognition and gratitude from everyone in the field of corrections. They have moved the field of corrections forward, toward a more enlightened human service and more effective correctional interventions.

This type of evaluative information is essential to correctional practitioners for sentencing and parole recommendations and placement decisions. Without it, offenders will be misplaced or placed in programs that have little or no efficacy.

ACA Public Correctional Policy on Higher Education

INTRODUCTION:

The purposes of higher education include instruction, public service, and research. Corrections can and does benefit from academic endeavors in each of these areas.

POLICY STATEMENT:

The field of corrections in cooperation with higher education should contribute to the improvement of the professional practice of corrections. Academic programs concerned with criminal justice and corrections should:

A. Provide a pool of qualified candidates for correctional service, and assist in the delineation of dimensions of work responsibilities that may emerge as a result of changing social, economic, political, and technological trends;

B. Promote understanding, both for correctional practitioners and for the public at large, of the complex social, ethical, political and economic factors that influence all areas of corrections;

C. Challenge assumptions about crime and correction, and stimulate change when change is needed;

D. Promote and support high standards in research, planning, and evaluation in all areas of corrections;

E. Engage in public service related to corrections, including informational programs, volunteer programs, and opportunities for training such as internships and practicums to enhance the relationship between the academic community and correctional practitioners;

F. Support, through program and faculty development, the evolution of corrections as a distinct professional discipline; and

G. Implement programs in corrections at the associate degree level that can serve as a minimum requirement for full professional status as a correctional officer, and as a minimum requirement in certification.

This Public Correctional Policy was unanimously ratified by the American Correctional Association Delegate Assembly at the Winter Conference in Nashville, Tennessee, January 17, 1990. It was reviewed and amended August 9, 1995, at the Congress of Correction in Cincinnati, Ohio.

As theory becomes more accurate (better in explaining who commits crime and why) and complex (multivariable), methods to evaluate performance must mirror that complexity. Hence, the research design used for evaluation must include all the theoretical elements as well as what we know works.

Summary

All correctional programs should include a carefully constructed evaluation component. Programs without a research or evaluation component contribute little to our field of knowledge. The "what works" knowledge in the field of adult corrections has always been in high demand. In the last half decade of the twentieth century, what works information is of utmost importance. Without it, fear-driven public policy will continue to stimulate greater prison use. With it, a more rational and balanced correctional approach can be developed and perhaps our heavy reliance on incarceration can be reduced.

Chapter 13

Doing Community Corrections Right

In real estate, an industry maxim is location, location, location. When running a restaurant, the hot food should be hot and the ice cream and milk better be cold. In education, the classroom is a sacred place and should be reserved for learning, dialog, and respect for knowledge and the instructor.

The purpose of this chapter is to develop industry maxims for community corrections. To accomplish this, we describe the optimum components of community corrections.

ACA Public Correctional Policy on Community Corrections

INTRODUCTION:

Correctional programs operating in a community setting are an integral part of a comprehensive corrections system which offers a full range of options for affecting offender behavior. These include community residential facilities, pretrial monitoring, probation, parole, community service and restitution programs, and other programs that provide supervision and services for accused or adjudicated juveniles and adults. To be successful, community corrections programs must promote public safety and respond to the needs of victims, offenders, and the community as well as include a collaborative comprehensive planning process for the development of policies, programs, and services.

POLICY STATEMENT:

The least restrictive and most cost-effective sanctions consistent with public and individual safety and maintenance of social order require offenders to receive services in a community setting. It is the responsibility of government to develop, support, and maintain correctional programs and services in the community. Compliance with this principle requires that the majority of offenders receive community based sanctions. Community sanctions must utilize a screening process to select offenders most suitable for placement in light of public safety considerations. Those responsible for community corrections programs, services, and supervision should:

A. Seek statutory authority and adequate funding, both public and private, for community programs and services as part of a comprehensive corrections strategy;

B. Develop and ensure access to a wide array of residential and nonresidential services that address the identifiable needs of victims, offenders and the community;

C. Inform the public and offenders of: the reasons for community programs and services; the criteria used for selecting individuals for these programs and services; and of the fact that placement in one of these programs has several purposes, one of which is punishment;

D. Ensure the integrity and accountability of community programs by establishing a reliable system for monitoring and measuring performance in accordance with accepted standards of professional practices and sound evaluation methodology;

E. Recognize that public acceptance of community corrections is enhanced by victim restitution, community service, and conciliation programs;

F. Mobilize the participation of a well-informed constituency, including citizen advisory boards and broad-based coalitions, to address community corrections issues;

G. Participate in collaborative, comprehensive planning efforts which provide a framework for a rational criminal justice system, and;

H. Develop private, public and non-profit partnerships which acknowledge the local community as the center of the criminal justice process.

This Public Correctional policy was unanimously ratified by the American Correctional Association Delegate Assembly, at the Winter Conference in Orlando, Florida, January 20, 1985. It was reviewed and amended January 29, 1997, at the Winter Conference in Indianapolis, Indiana.

Smaller Is Better and Offender-focused Is Best

From Palmer's (1996) review of the literature, we know the following elements greatly contribute to successful outcomes in community corrections:

- Small caseloads

- Intensive, frequent, and extensive contacts with the offender

- Individualized and flexible programming

- Personal characteristics and professional orientation of the correctional practitioner

- Specific abilities and overall perceptiveness of the correctional practitioner

- Explicit, detailed guidelines for any and all correctional-intervention strategies

ACA Public Correctional Policy on Parole and Supervised Release

INTRODUCTION:

Parole or other forms of supervised release, is the conditional release of an offender from confinement before expiration of sentence pursuant to specified terms and conditions of supervision in the community. The grant of parole and its revocation are responsibilities of the paroling authority. Supervision of the parolee is provided by a designated agency that monitors and supports compliance with all requirements of the conditional release through a case management process. Since the vast majority of those incarcerated will eventually be released into the community, the public is best protected by a supervised transition of the offender from institutional to community integration. Parole offers economic and societal advantages to the public, the offender, and the correctional system by maximizing opportunities for offenders to become productive, law-abiding citizens.

POLICY STATEMENT:

The parole component of the correctional system should function under separate but interdependent decision-making and case supervision processes. Paroling authorities should seek a balance in weighing the public interest and the readiness of the offender to re-enter society under a structured program of support, supervisory management and control. Paroling systems should be equipped with adequate resources for administering the investigative, supervisory, and research functions. Administrative regulations governing the grant of parole, its revocation, case supervision practices, and discharge procedures should incorporate standards of due process and fundamental fairness. To achieve the maximum of parole supervision, full advantage should be taken of community-based resources for serving offender employment and training needs, substance abuse treatment, and other related services. The parole system should:

A. Establish procedures to provide an objective decision-making process incorporating standards of due process and fundamental fairness in the granting and revoking of parole that will address, at a minimum, the risk to public safety, impact on the victim, and information about the offense and the offender;

B. Provide access to a wide range of support services including the use of interstate compacts to meet offender needs consistent with realistic objectives for promoting law-abiding behavior;

C. Ensure any intervention in an offender's life will not exceed the minimum needed to ensure compliance with the terms and conditions of parole;

D. Provide a case management system for allocating supervisory resources through a standardized classification process, reporting parolee progress, and monitoring individualized parolee supervision and treatment plans;

E. Provide for the timely and accurate transmittal of status reports to the paroling authority for use in decision making with respect to revocation, modification, or discharge of parole cases;

F. Establish programs for sharing information, ideas, and experience with other agencies and the public; and

G. Evaluate program efficiency, effectiveness, and overall accountability consistent with recognized correctional standards and legal requirements.

This Public Correctional Policy was unanimously ratified by the American Correctional Association Delegate Assembly at the Winter Conference in Orlando, Florida, January 20, 1985. It was reviewed and amended at the Congress of Correction in Minneapolis, Minnesota, August 7, 1991. It was reviewed without change January 16, 1996, at the Winter Conference in Philadelphia, Pennsylvania.

In spite of the empirical evidence that smaller and more intense caseloads result in lower recidivism than larger less differentiated caseloads, almost half (48 percent) of all correctional halfway houses (especially for adults) in the country are quite large (50 or more beds) and one-fifth of all residential community corrections programs are extremely large (100 or more beds) (Knapp and Burke 1992). A corrections program with more than 100 beds should not be referred to as a community corrections program, but should be called what it is: a minimum-security correctional institution. Even a program with 50 to 100 beds is so large that the quality of relations between offenders and staff must be very formalized because of the scale of operations.

From Donald Andrews' (1994) meta-analysis we know:

1. Official punishment without the introduction of correctional treatment services does not work.

2. There is a need for delivery of appropriate correctional treatment service that is dependent on assessments that are sensitive to risk, need, and responsivity.

3. What works is the delivery of clinically and psychologically appropriate correctional treatment service, under a variety of settings or conditions that may be established by criminal sanction.

4. Providing correctional treatment services that are inconsistent with the principles of risk, need, and responsivity do not work.

Operating community corrections programs in the late 1990s and ignoring the lessons of Palmer and Andrews should be unacceptable correctional practice. A growing number of community corrections programs are finding out just how unacceptable and costly it is to ignore the lessons of Palmer and Andrews. Civil lawsuits have held community corrections programs legally liable for operating "shoddy" programs. "Shoddy" is defined as counter to these Palmer and Andrews principles (Lauen 1994, Sullivan and Purdy 1995, Purdy and Dugger 1996).

ACA Public Correctional Policy on Probation

INTRODUCTION:

The vast majority of adjudicated adult and juvenile offenders remain in the community. Probation is a judicial decision that assigns the responsibility for supervision and control of these offenders to community corrections.

POLICY STATEMENT:

Probation is a frequently used and cost-effective sanction of the court for enhancing social order and public safety. Probation may be used as a sanction by itself or, where necessary and appropriate, be combined with other sanctions such as fines, restitution, community service, residential care, or confinement. Agencies responsible for probation should:

A. Prepare disposition assessments to assist the court in arriving at appropriate sanctions. The least restrictive disposition consistent with public safety should be recommended;

B. Establish a case management system for allocating supervisory resources through a standardized classification process;

C. Provide supervision to probationers and, with their input, develop a realistic plan to ensure compliance with orders of the court;

D. Monitor and evaluate, on an ongoing basis, the probationer's adherence to the plan of supervision and, when necessary, modify the plan of supervision according to the changing needs of the offender and the best interests of society;

E. Provide access to a wide range of services to meet identifiable needs, all of which are directed toward promoting law-abiding behavior;

F. Ensure any intervention in an offender's life will not exceed the minimal amount needed to ensure compliance with the orders of the court;

G. Initiate appropriate court proceedings, when necessary, if the probationer fails to comply with orders of the court, supervision plan, or other requirements so the court may consider other alternatives for the protection and well-being of the community;

H. Oppose use of the probation sanction for status offenders, neglected or dependent children, or any other individuals who are neither accused nor charged with delinquent or criminal behavior;

I. Establish an educational program for sharing information about probation with the public and other agencies; and

J. Evaluate program efficiency, effectiveness, and overall system accountability consistent with recognized correctional standards.

This Public Correctional Policy was unanimously ratified by the American Correctional Association Delegate Assembly at the Winter Conference in Orlando, Florida, January 20, 1985. It was reviewed January 18, 1995, at the Winter Conference in Dallas, Texas, with no change.

Community Corrections Practice Must Be Theory Based

As explained in Chapter 4, the psychology of criminal conduct (Andrews and Bonta 1994) has emerged out of many years of theory testing and development. Today, the psychology of criminal conduct provides the adult corrections field with a powerful tool which explains why certain people commit crimes, which, in turn, provides the direction for new and more effective approaches to correctional intervention.

The psychology of criminal conduct theory can guide correctional practitioner decisions on risk assessment and help the practitioner to assess the scale and types of treatment needs. Additionally, the theory should incorporate the principles of responsivity in deciding what correctional setting (prison versus community) is best for offenders. Without a theoretical "rudder" to guide the practitioners in their decision making, decisions are made by rote, tradition, subjective judgement, and in conformance with established organizational culture. Today, this usually means punishment and incapacitation based on a culture that believes in retribution and an organizational agenda that concurs in this. A few of these established ways of doing things may be appropriate and fitting for the offender, but many clearly are not appropriate. The integration of theory into correctional practice dramatically decreases recidivism.

However, theory cannot be integrated into practice unless correctional practitioners read and learn. This learning can take place in formal academic settings, in organizationally sponsored staff training sessions, or in conferences or workshops. Either way, it takes some time and effort. Correctional managers must be committed to this effort and make it possible for staff to be relieved of their daily work responsibilities so they may read, learn, and attend special training sessions.

Evaluation Must Be an Integral Part of Community Corrections

We know as much as we do today because of previous research and evaluation efforts. Without this knowledge, we would continue to make strategic errors in calculating risk, misdiagnosing for treatment needs, not respecting individual differences among offenders, and placing offenders in inappropriate correctional settings. Fortunately, evaluation studies have provided practitioners with a wealth of knowledge.

Lessons from Evaluation Studies

1. Low-risk offenders require only low levels of supervision. If low-risk offenders receive intense supervision (ISP or residential placement), they get worse, not better (Bonta 1991).

2. High-risk offenders require intense, close supervision. If a high-risk offender receives "normal supervision" (normal probation/parole), they get worse (Bonta 1991).

3. The theoretical approach of community corrections practice should be behavioral, cognitive, and oriented toward skill development (Bonta and Andrews 1994, Palmer 1996, Gendreau 1996).

4. Lay community members should be a part of community corrections by participating in policy development, program overview and offender assistance (Lauen 1988, 1990).

These critically important lessons from previous evaluation studies provide the rationale for continuous evaluation of future community corrections programs. The community corrections field can get better only with the continuous assessment of offenders, staff, and program performance.

Management Information Systems

Ongoing program operations and program evaluation can be aided by management information systems (MIS).

> ### Rationale and Justification
> ### for Management Information Systems
>
> - Better management of information
>
> - Quicker access to information
>
> - Ability to format and reformat information for a variety of audiences, such as in-house staff, board of directors, public officials, the media, and state auditors

- Improved program capability to meet local, state and federal reporting requirements

- Ability to provide objective information to offenders (if and when appropriate) and to staff

- Facilitate information gathering, collection, tabulation for evaluation purposes

- Provide documentation for potential cost savings, assuming programs are successful

- Provide budget information needed by policymakers

The data elements needed for a community corrections management information systems include the following: (1) offender characteristics in terms of risk, needs, and responsivity; (2) number and type of offender contacts; (3) specific services needed by and delivered to the offender; (4) contacts and services of outside providers; (5) in-house work schedules; (6) records and schedules for work in the larger community; (7) money management, including rent, restitution, and work earnings; (8) a record of clinical decisions by staff; (9) termination and outcome reports for individual offenders and for staff training and performance; and (10) aggregated offender, staff, and program statistics.

All of these data elements can be collected and formatted with the use of desktop or laptop computers. Software programs now are designed specifically for community corrections clients, staff, and programs. "Credit cards" with a bar code unique to each offender can be used to document all offender movement, services received, attendance at meetings, and other program-related activity. The data collected from the offender "swipes" of his or her "credit card" is stored in computerized storage discs. This information then can be formulated into as many different forms, programs, and outcome reports as needed (Peregrine 1996).

With the use of computers, "credit cards," and automated report making capability, the need for hard copy logs virtually is eliminated. If the state, local, and program information systems are integrated, information collected at the program level simultaneously can satisfy all or most public reporting requirements.

ACA Public Correctional Policy on Correctional Information Systems

INTRODUCTION:

Timely and accurate information is a basic requirement for effective management of organizations. Such information forms a basis for sound decision making and allows for accountability in operations and program results.

POLICY STATEMENT:

For correctional staff to function effectively, they must have accurate and timely information. The design of correctional information systems must reflect combined efforts of both correctional professionals and information system specialists. To meet the diverse needs of a correctional agency, information systems should be designed that support the management processes of the agency as their primary function, and service delivery functions of the agency by providing data relevant to their efficiency and outcome, and provide sufficient flexibility to support relevant research and evaluation.

To promote development of effective information systems, correctional agencies should:

A. Clearly define the desired scope of the system, consistent with a realistic assessment of anticipated resources and technologies;

B. Involve and train correctional managers in all stages of system development and operation to ensure such managers' needs are met;

C. Prepare detailed and carefully monitored development plans to ensure systems are designed and implemented in a timely, secure and cost-effective manner;

D. Require that the system include evaluation procedures, including assessments of information needs of the users at all levels, to ensure the quality of system input and output;

E. Cooperate with correctional, law enforcement, educational, and other public agencies to provide for mutual sharing of information, consistent with legitimate concerns for privacy, confidentiality, and system security;

F. Ensure appropriate information needs of the public are met, consistent with legal requirements; and

G. Advocate provision of resources to implement and update advanced information system technologies.

This Public Correctional Policy was unanimously ratified by the American Correctional Association Delegate Assembly, at the Winter Conference in Orlando, Florida, January 20, 1985. It was reviewed and amended at the Congress of Correction in Minneapolis, Minnesota, August 7, 1991. It was reviewed January 18, 1995, at the Winter Conference in Dallas, Texas, with no change.

Use of Standardized Assessment Instruments

Community corrections decision making must be guided by informed assessments of risk, needs, and responsivity (third-generation assessments). Without objective determinations of risk, need, and responsivity, practitioner decision making is subjective, and in all probability, not very accurate.

This author recommends using the Level of Supervision Inventory (LSI-R) as the assessment instrument. While there are other instruments (CMC, RSI), the LSI-R is grounded in theory, more user friendly, and has demonstrated validity and reliability (Andrews and Bonta 1994, Bonta 1996, Jones 1996).

All the Important Steps: Screening, Assessing Risk, Outlining the Case Manager's Role, Constructing the Case Plan, Matching, Reassessing Periodically

With the use of objective assessments of risk, need, and responsivity, solid case planning and management of and with the offender is critically important. The following elements make up a comprehensive case management plan.

Offender selection at referral: Community corrections staff carefully must assess the information provided by the referral agency (state prison, sentencing court, sheriffs' office) to make sure that all prior records and other pertinent types of information are available, accurate, current, and complete. Once this information gathering and assessment are complete, decision makers decide whether to accept the offender into the program. The decision to select an offender should conform to the community corrections program's goals, objectives, and capabilities and not accede to the organizational or political agendas of the referral agencies.

Offender orientation: Offenders need to go through a program orientation, which includes a presentation and discussion of the rules of the program and expectations of the staff. The orientation is also the time when offenders are assessed for substance abuse, and social and employment history. Standardized tests (SOCRATES, Social Support, ASUS, SUHM, see Chapter 6) are available for these assessments.

Case manager assignment: After orientation is completed, the offender is assigned to, hopefully matched with, a case manager. As discussed in Chapter 11, this match should take into account the unique learning styles, motivations, and stages of change of the offender, along with the philosophical approach, experience, and case-management style of the correctional staffer. The offender should be matched with the appropriate case manager/therapist/clinician and appropriate in-house programs, referred to appropriate outside agencies and programs, and given a room assignment (if a residential program).

Continuous offender assessment: The purpose of offender assessments and reassessments is to measure progress toward the established treatment goals in the case plan. These reassessments can be improved by the use of standardized tests and instruments and measured against the dynamic treatment need factors included in the LSI-R. If another assessment instrument is used, the same type of reassessment can be conducted using the same or similar treatment needs as the baseline.

The case plan: The case plan is a road map that lays out what the offender is expected to do during his or her time in the program. The case plan also describes what others will do to assist the offender in achieving the goals and objectives of the plan. All components of the case plan must be highly individualistic and very specific, targeting risk for recidivism and criminogenic needs. Criminogenic needs should be prioritized according to their urgency.

The role of case manager: A case manager must be available to the offender at all times. During off hours (nights and weekends), the offender needs access to someone on-call. This constant, twenty-four-hours-a day, seven-days-a-week availability is necessary to keep the offender accountable to all the elements of the case plan as well as to keep the staff and program accountable to the offender and the case plan. Staff must be well trained and prepared to respond and be conducting reiterative and ongoing assessments of the offender's progress.

In-house versus outside referrals: Some of the counseling and support needed by offenders can be provided in-house or in the program if it is a nonresidential program. Offenders are community corrections clients for very short periods in their lives. Given this, one of the missions of community corrections is to tie offenders into the human services delivery system of their host community. Interagency referral agreements must be developed and maintained between the offender, the community corrections agency, and all appropriate human services. From Palmer's review of the research literature, we know that some services are better provided in-house or inside the criminal justice system, and other services are more effective if provided by outsiders. Chart 13.1 illustrates Palmer's findings.

CHART 13.1: Optimal Organizational Home: Inside or Outside the System

Programs Best Operated *Inside* the criminal justice system	Programs Best Operated *Outside* the criminal justice system
Group counseling	Vocational training
Individual counseling	Life skills programs
Employment programs	Programs for young, high-risk, unsocialized probationers

Source: Palmer 1992.

Chart 13.1 summarizes research findings, which should be used by practitioners as a general guideline and not as a professional "edict." There are exceptions. For example, the adult women's prison in Maryland had an excellent vocational program inside the state prison for women interested in becoming members of the Steel Worker's Union in the 1970s. Delancy Street in San Francisco has demonstrated that effective employment programs for offenders can be operated outside the criminal justice system.

Monitoring the case plan: Keep chronological notes in each offender's file (on a computer, hopefully) and updated frequently. Regular (weekly) meetings among case managers can provide professional peer support, review, and a critique of decisions made. A case manager supervisor or clinical director should review and evaluate all case plans periodically, at least monthly. The focus of these frequent and periodic reviews is to assess, guide, and evaluate the offender's progress and case manager's performance.

With this type of comprehensive approach to case planning and management, offenders will be supervised adequately and appropriately during their stay in community corrections. Also, a good management information system can aid greatly in collecting, tabulating, and formatting case planning information. Management information systems and case planning go hand in hand.

Matching Correctional Setting with Levels of Risk and Need

The information in Chart 13.2 presents a hypothetical situation and is meant to be advisory, suggestive, thought-provoking, but it is not an edict. The three dimensions involved in the chart are offender risk level, criminogenic needs level, and appropriate correctional setting. The idea incorporated in the chart is to realize an appropriate "fit" among the three components.

CHART 13.2: Matching Correctional Setting with Levels of Risk and Need

Risk Level	Criminogenic Needs: Low	Criminogenic Needs: Medium	Criminogenic Needs: High
Low	Monetary or day fine, no face-to-face supervision	Probation or parole plus special conditions	Intensive Supervision Programs, Day Reporting Center; two to four contacts per week
Medium	Intensive Supervision Programs, Day Reporting Center; use residential program for relapse	Start out with residential placement, move to nonresidential as quickly as possible	Start with jail or residential placement, move to day reporting center
High	Residential community placement; use jail as backup when relapse occurs	Residential placement for some offenders; incarceration for others	Incarceration for most offenders. Move to community residential program after criminogenic needs have improved.

Staff Qualifications

Ideally, community corrections staff should understand the connection between providing appropriate treatment services and a reduction in recidivism. Correctional staff must have the skills to conduct assessments, support offenders in-house, facilitate the interagency coordination on behalf of the offender, follow up to ensure that the treatment service was delivered, see that the offender participated satisfactorily, and ensure that the desired change in the offender's behavior actually is occurring.

ACA Public Correctional Policy on Correctional Staff Recruitment and Development

INTRODUCTION:

Knowledgeable, highly skilled, motivated, and professional correctional personnel are essential to fulfill the purpose of corrections effectively. Professionalism is achieved through structured programs of recruitment and enhancement of the employee's skills, knowledge, insight, and understanding of the corrections process.

POLICY STATEMENT:

Correctional staff are the primary agents for promoting health, welfare, security, and safety within correctional institutions and community supervision programs. They directly interact with accused and adjudicated offenders and are the essential catalysts of change in the correctional process. The education, recruitment, orientation, supervision, compensation, training, retention, and advancement of correctional staff must receive full support from the executive, judicial, and legislative branches of government. To achieve this, correctional agencies should:

A. Recruit personnel, including ex-offenders, in an open and accountable manner to ensure equal employment opportunity for all qualified applicants regardless of sex, age, race, physical disability, religion, ethnic background, or political affiliation, and actively promote the employment of women and minorities;

B. Screen applicants for job-related aspects of physical suitability, personal adjustment, emotional stability, dependability, appropriate educational level, and experience. An additional requisite is the ability to relate to accused or adjudicated offenders in a manner that is fair, objective, and neither punitive nor vindictive.

C. Select, promote, and retain staff in accordance with valid job-related procedures that emphasize merit and technical competence. Voluntary transfers and promotions within and between correctional systems should be encouraged;

D. Comply with professional standards in staff development and offer a balance between operational requirements and the development of personal, social, and cultural understanding. Staff development programs should involve use of public and private resources, including colleges, universities, and professional associations;

E. Achieve parity between correctional staff and comparable criminal justice system staff in salaries and benefits, training, continuing education, performance evaluations, disciplinary procedures, career development opportunities, transfers, promotions, grievance procedures, and retirement; and

F. Encourage the participation of trained volunteers and students to enrich the correctional program and to provide a potential source of recruitment.

This Public Correctional Policy was unanimously ratified by the American Correctional Association Delegate Assembly, at the Congress of Correction in San Antonio, Texas, August 23, 1984. It was reviewed January 17, 1990, at the Winter Conference in Nashville, Tennessee, with no change. It was reviewed January 18, 1995, at the Winter Conference in Dallas, Texas, with no change.

Skills, Abilities, and Knowledge Needed by Staff in Community Corrections

- Staff should have skills in one or more of the following areas:

  - employment-related skills (where and how to find vocational-interest testing, job training, job placement, development of list of sympathetic private employers)

  - substance abuse assessment, treatment and support skills and knowledge of where in the community offenders can get specialized treatment for substance abuse

  - mental health assessment and treatment (preferably outside the community corrections agency)

  - money management

  - anger management

  - social skills development

- Staff should have a working knowledge of the psychology of criminal conduct (Andrews and Bonta 1994).

- Staff should have the ability to communicate clearly and effectively in written and oral form.

- Staff should have interpersonal skills associated with effective counseling, include the following:

— using clarity in communication

— displaying warmth and openness

— relating affect to behavior

— setting appropriate limits

With these sorts of skills, therapists can be effective sources of reinforcement and can competently model prosocial skills (Gendreau 1996).

- Staff should have the ability to take directions from other, more knowledgeable people.

- Staff should possess good, functional, community ties or the ability to develop them.

- Staff should be accountable to public mandates, laws, and expectations, not just private, intra-organizational demands.

- Staff should have a commitment to stay with a program for a long enough time to both learn from more experienced staff and train others once these skills are learned.

ACA Resolution on the Term "Correctional Officer"

WHEREAS, the duties of correctional personnel whose primary responsibility are custody and control require extensive interpersonal skills, special training and education;

WHEREAS, correctional personnel are skilled professionals; and

WHEREAS, the term "guard" produces a false and negative image;

THEREFORE BE IT RESOLVED, that the American Correctional Association adopt the term "correctional officer" as the official language in all Association publications, meetings, events and communications to describe custodial/security personnel.

THEREFORE BE IT FURTHER RESOLVED: that the Association actively promote the use of the term "correctional officer" and discourage the use of the word "guard" by the media, general public, educational institutions, and publishers.

This resolution was adopted by the American Correctional Association Board of Governors on January 10, 1993, at the Winter Conference in Miami, Florida. It was reviewed without change January 16, 1996, at the Winter Conference in Philadelphia, Pennsylvania.

When community corrections staff are well qualified, offenders are better served, offender success rates are higher, staff turnover rates are lower, unit cost for offender supervision is less, and the entire community corrections effort works better. There are three critical elements of staff qualifications. They are formal education, specialized training, and prior professional experience.

Formal Education: A four-year college degree from an accredited college or university should be a minimum educational requirement (professional experience can sometimes substitute for formal education). Such a degree demonstrates the person's ability to think, reason, calculate, and decide on both abstract and concrete intellectual matters. These are skills needed in operating a community corrections program. People who specialize in criminal justice studies, learning theory, psychology, and other social sciences are going to be in greater demand than those with other areas of specialty.

Specialized Training: College degree programs do not provide the highly technical and specialized training that correctional practitioners need on a continuous basis. Specialized seminars, conferences, pre-employment training, in-service training, and other professional development sessions that correctional practitioners need are provided by: the National Institute of Corrections, professional associations (including American Correctional Association, American Society of Criminology, Academy of Criminal Justice Sciences, American Probation and Parole Association, International Halfway House Association, International Community Corrections Association), and private companies or consultants.

Examples of some of the specialized training includes: motivational interviewing, learning about relapse prevention and cognitive skill building, developing research methods, writing reports, learning about sex-offender treatment, employing clinical supervision, using basic counseling skills, and knowing how to manage client records.

A good community corrections program includes a significant budget item for staff training costs and adequate staff coverage when staff is off-site in training. Staff should receive three-to-six months of formal and on-the-job training or internship training in the application of behavioral interventions both in general and specific to the program in which they are working (Gendreau 1996).

Prior Professional Experience: Almost any prior work experience, as long as that experience is successful, is helpful and appropriate for work in the community corrections field. Like formal education, some prior work experience is more appropriate than others. Prior work experience as a probation officer is obviously more appropriate than as a steam fitter. However, if the former probation officer established work habits that were outmoded or inappropriate, that prior experience may be problematic. It is helpful to choose people to work in community corrections who already have established a solid and dependable work record. Former co-workers can verify work habits, attitudes related to work, and ability to work with others. This information is essential if good staff selection decisions are to be made.

Organizational Milieu

Administrators create an organizational atmosphere or milieu and over time, an organizational culture. This organizational atmosphere can be social-control oriented (bust heads, take no prisoners, throw away the key, and other cliches), counseling, cognitive-behavioral, legal advocacy, community organization or development, or many other types (see Palmer 1996).

The approach advocated here includes the following elements: (1) fair wages (comparable to other human service professionals in the community) and a ratio of no more than four to one between the highest- and lowest-paid staff member, (2) participatory management; which includes a strong team concept, peer review, critique, and support, (3) reasonable promotion opportunities, (4) an adequate amount of time and resources for specialized training, and (5) collaborative decision making with other community agencies.

With these particular organizational elements in place, staff turnover rates will be minimal. There will be higher levels of professional commitment within and between agencies. There will be effective supervision of offenders, and the rate of success among the offender population will be acceptably high. Reasonable rates of success should be as follows: for low-risk offenders, 90 percent; for medium-risk offenders, 70 to 80 percent; and for high-risk offenders 55 to 75 percent.

Corrections policymakers committed to greater accountability through more relevant population measures will enhance the probability for success by reviewing three broad organizational issues: commitment to an open learning organization, benchmarking, and establishing internal controls. Each of these will be discussed.

Learning Organizations

To what degree is your organization committed to evolving as a "Learning Organization"? How well is change endorsed and supported in your correctional agency? Is the status quo more valued than the outcome within the agency? To what degree is it "safe" for staff to be open about learning from mistakes, approximations, and trial and error? Standardized offender assessment may provide valuable feedback. How this idea is embraced may be critical.

Learning organizations are different from normal organizations in several ways. Chart 13.3 illustrates some of those differences.

CHART 13.3: Learning Organizations Versus Normal Organizations

Learning Organizations	Normal Organizations
Flat, egalitarian	Hierarchial, top/down organization
Decisions made in a highly participatory manner	Decisions made by top administrators, decisions sent down by memo
Minimal salary differentials; a one-to-four differential between top and bottom	Significant salary differentials from top administrators to entry-level positions
Cross training: identifying staff in other human services that have specialized expertise (such as substance abuse treatment) and recruiting them to conduct staff training in your correctional agency. Reciprocating by conducting training in their human service agency. Developing functional, reciprocal, collaborative agreements among corrections and allied agencies.	Staying in place. Not reaching out. Follow the plan. Check your flanks. Don't get into other people's business. We've got enough to do without taking on other people's problems.
The concept of mastering your craft is a real, live idea, encouraged and rewarded by the organization.	Do your job. Do not exceed the parameters of your job description. Performance reviews are pro forma.
Organizational rewards (both financial and symbolic) for innovation, staying on top of your field, bringing in new ideas to co-workers, taking the initiative.	The reward system is formal, bureaucratic, and mechanistic. Time in grade is the main element; who you know is another important element. Taking initiative is suspect.

Benchmarking

Benchmarking is establishing organizational goals and objectives through a process of careful analysis and participation among members of the organization. For example, how do agencies in the system currently conduct surveillance for new technology? Is it done proactively, aggressively, and across disciplines? Or, is new technology something to react to, close ranks behind, and minimize? How does the organizational culture promote benchmarking and reward the message carriers?

Using Internal Controls

Employing internal controls is the process (through internal audits, personnel evaluations, and other means) of assessing organizational progress. Some organizations, including new community corrections programs, have few or no internal controls. Some probation or parole organizations have internal controls but little organizational commitment to put them to use or try new approaches.

Community Linkages to Community Corrections Programs

The community produces the need, resources, and commitment for correctional programs. Hence, the first concept that should be understood by all community corrections practitioners is that the community is the host; community corrections staff and programs are the guests. Given this, community corrections staff should be deferential to long-term community members, take time to learn the community mores, customs, beliefs, and values, invite community members to visit the community corrections program, and become a part of program planning, oversight committees, offender selection committees, the state/local audit team, and other community organizations.

When community members are actively involved in community corrections, they have less fear of offenders and put themselves in a position to become advocates of community corrections programs. This involvement should be more than "window dressing." Community members should be invited to play lead roles (Lindsay 1990). Some examples of how community members can become involved are listed below.

1. Mental health staff can be a part of the offender-selection committee, interagency task force, interagency referral working group, or the board of directors of the agency. According to an American Correctional Association focus group in August 1996, including mental health staff in the correctional process is of critical importance.

2. Vocational training staff, inside community corrections programs or working in conjunction with community corrections programs (local community college, state employment and training staff, private industry trainers) can work with private-industry representatives to identify training needs, employment areas in demand, entry-level employment criteria, and in-service or retraining curriculums.

3.   Private-industry representatives can advise community cor-
     rections staff on entry-level employment criteria, provide
     positive prosocial role models for offenders, construct long-
     range business plans with community corrections admin-
     istrators, and actively promote community corrections in the
     community.

4.   Educators can volunteer to work with offenders as "coaches"
     in adult basic education, General Education Development
     test preparation and testing, serve as positive prosocial role
     models for offenders, and serve as members of the board of
     directors or advisory board members (Bayse 1993).

5.   Citizen volunteers can be recruited from churches, ads in the
     newspaper, from service clubs (such as Rotary or Kiwanis),
     and senior citizen centers. Many skilled citizens (carpenters,
     electricians, computer programmers) are eager to help
     offenders but do not know how to get involved. Once the
     connection is made, they can assist offenders with studies,
     vocational skill development, substance abuse treatment and
     support, and provide prosocial role modeling.

More community involvement by lay citizens is a "win-win" deal. Lay citizens
win by becoming more knowledgeable about crime, corrections, and offenders. In
so doing, they reduce their crime fears and increase their power. They begin to
take charge. Community corrections offenders, staff, and programs win by building a broader base of support, living and working with people who are more
knowledgeable and thereby more supportive, and gaining insights, advice, and
direct services from citizen volunteers.

The State's Role in Monitoring Local Programs

The state has an important role to play in establishing and maintaining high
quality programs, programs that meet the performance criteria outlined in this
chapter. All of the states that have community corrections programs also have
state monitoring responsibilities (Shilton 1992, Lauen 1995).

ACA Resolution on Technology and Standards

WHEREAS, the rapidly increasing confined population has necessitated an unprecedented increase in the construction of detention and correctional facilities;

WHEREAS, new and more demanding codes and statutes impose more and more demand on facilities in such areas as fire and life safety as well as in the environmental protection area;

WHEREAS, there is a plethora of new products including building materials, equipment and systems as well as relatively hi-tech products marketed to assist in meeting the challenge of accommodating the larger confinement population, special needs populations, and other groups as needed; and

WHEREAS, the vast majority of detention and correctional agencies and operations do not have the capability of evaluating and selecting suitable materials, systems and equipment which will enhance their ability to carry out their mission;

THEREFORE BE IT RESOLVED, that the American Correctional Association urges that the Department of Justice give priority to the support of the development of standards and technology as well as greater efforts to gather and disseminate information which will be helpful to correctional agencies.

THEREFORE BE IT FURTHER RESOLVED that the American Correctional Association send a copy of this resolution to the Attorney General of the United States, and appropriate agencies in the Department of Justice.

This resolution was adopted by the American Correctional Association Board of Governors on January 16, 1991, at the Winter Conference in Louisville, Kentucky. It was reviewed and reaffirmed on January 17, 1994, at the Winter Conference in Orlando, Florida.

Ideally, there should be a single state agency involved in the administration of community corrections programs. Two or more state agencies involved simply invites competition, turf-protecting tactics, and conflicts in regulations. Reducing organizational duplication and competition can be corrected by the governor and his or her cabinet and the legislature. The responsibilities of this single state agency should include the following:

1. Serving as the liaison between local programs and the state legislature.

2. Preparing the state budget and defending it in the legislative arena.

3. Establishing statewide operating standards. Several states already have promulgated statewide standards and they are available through those states.

4. Conducting program audits of all local programs frequently (at least once a year). Audits differ from evaluations in that audits are on-site assessments of program operations in relation to established program standards.

5. Providing technical assistance, training, and staffing for program evaluations and the developing of management information systems. The state should provide the leadership to integrate evaluations, report writing, and management information systems among state, county, and city or local programs.

6. Conducting staff training in specialized areas needed by practitioners to stay current in the field.

7. Enforcing state operating standards. Shoddy programs should be placed on probation and given a reasonable amount of time (no more than six months) to conform to state operating standards. If they fail to meet standards, they should be shut down.

8. Publishing and distributing evaluation findings.

9. Providing technical assistance in a variety of program areas. Some examples include the following: training new board members, developing a research design, and improving management information systems.

10. Continually restructuring funding toward meaningful outcomes and undercutting natural monopolies not based on actual public safety outcomes.

This is a tall order for most state community corrections agencies. Anything less, however, means that local programs do not have the technical, legal, and professional support they need to function optimally. State community corrections staff must convince the governor and legislators that without these state level services, program performance will suffer. It is in everyone's interest to have the state provide these types of services.

ACA Public Correctional Policy on Correctional Standards and Accreditation

INTRODUCTION:

Correctional agencies should provide community and institutional programs and services that offer a full range of effective, just, humane, and safe dispositions and sanctions for accused and adjudicated offenders. To assure accountability and professional responsibility, these programs and services should meet accepted professional standards and obtain accreditation. The use of standards and the accreditation process provides a valuable mechanism for self-evaluation, stimulates improvement of correctional management and practice, and provides recognition of acceptable programs and facilities. The American Correctional Association and the Commission on Accreditation for Corrections have promulgated national standards and a voluntary system of national accreditation for correctional agencies. The beneficiaries of such a process will be the administration and staff of correctional agencies, offenders, and the public.

POLICY STATEMENT:

All correctional facilities and programs should be operated in accordance with the standards established by the American Correctional Association and should achieve and maintain accreditation through the Commission on Accreditation for Corrections. To fulfill this objective, correctional agencies should:

A. Implement improvement as necessary to comply with appropriate standards specified or referenced in the following manuals and supplements:

Standards for Adult Boot Camp Programs

Standards for Adult Parole Authorities

Standards for Adult Community Residential Services

Standards for Adult Probation and Parole Field Services

Standards for Adult Correctional Institutions

Standards for Adult Local Detention Facilities

Standards for Juvenile Boot Camp Programs

Standards for Juvenile Day Treatment Programs

Standards for Small Juvenile Detention Facilities

Standards for Juvenile Community Residential Facilities

Standards for Juvenile Probation and Aftercare Services

Standards for Juvenile Detention Facilities

Standards for Juvenile Training Schools

Standards for Correctional Industries

Standards for Electronic Monitoring Programs

Standards for Correctional Training Academies

Standards for Small Jail Facilities

Standards for the Administration of Correctional Agencies

B. Seek and maintain accreditation through the voluntary process developed by the Commission on Accreditation for Corrections in order that, through self-evaluation and peer review, necessary improvements are made, programs and services come into compliance with appropriate standards, and professional recognition is obtained.

This Public Correctional Policy was unanimously ratified by the American Correctional Association Delegate Assembly at the Congress of Correction in San Antonio, Texas, August 23, 1984. It was reviewed January 17, 1990, at the Winter Conference in Nashville, Tennessee, with no change. It was reviewed and amended January 16, 1996, at the Winter Conference in Philadelphia, Pennsylvania.

Chapter 14

In Summary...

The purpose of this book was to describe the problems facing the field of corrections in the mid-1990s and offer suggestions for improvements. The primary focus of the book was community corrections. However, given the current "get tough" policy and the resulting crowding in the entire corrections system, it is impossible to deal with community corrections in a vacuum. Community corrections is overwhelmed by jail and prison crowding. Revocations (failures) from probation and parole have a major impact on community corrections (Spiegel 1994). Hence, the book tried to deal with the corrections system, and assumed any change in one part of the system will have an impact on other components.

The single most important recommendation is to incorporate the psychology of criminal conduct (PCC) into the assessment of risk, needs, and responsivity when offenders are arrested, filed on by prosecutors, recommended for sentencing by probation investigators, sentenced by judges, considered for release from prison by parole authorities, and considered for placement by community corrections staff. Theoretically, informed staff decisions can significantly reduce recidivism rates. A reduction in recidivism is in the best interests of crime victims, state legislators, the general public, the professionals working in the criminal justice system, and, of course, the offenders themselves.

Other major changes needed include the following: (1) the TV and print media need to change their approach to crime and punishment from exploiting heinous crime events to educating the public about the complexity of crime causation and remedies; (2) elected officials must stop exploiting the public's crime fears for their own political gain; (3) public officials need to lead, not follow, educate not react, do the right thing, and not follow the path of least resistance; (4) practitioners need to read, learn, gain new skills, be courageous and inventive, and also not follow the path of least resistance; (5) researchers and academicians need to roll up their sleeves and get involved with corrections policy and practice, be proactive with the research literature that clearly states that appropriate treatment reduces recidivism, testify at legislative hearings, and participate with the governor in corrections planning.

However, there are additional unresolved issues. The list below is a mix of unresolved problems and suggestions for action.

The Criminal Justice System Cannot and Should Not Attempt to Resolve All Sorts of Complex Social Problems

There has been a tendency within the last decade to use the criminal justice system to solve all types of complex social issues, including drunk driving, domestic disputes, and drug use. All three of these issues have their serious dimensions. Drunk driving is implicated in about 50 percent of all driving-related fatalities, which number into the thousands each year. Domestic violence, whose victims are overwhelmingly women, is a reflection of a power imbalance between women and men. The woman often is dependent economically and psychologically subservient and intimidated. The man is often a substance abuser and angry about his own unresolved psychological, occupational, and domestic problems. The last complex problem, drug use, has been and continues to be widespread among all social, economic, and racial groups in our society.

Legislators need to do a much better job of triaging, including directing public resources to the resolution of particular problems. Legislators should stop using revisions in the criminal code as a political opportunity to take advantage of the public's fear of crime. They should learn to limit the involvement of the criminal justice system to those matters that cannot be resolved in other areas, with other resources.

Reduce the Discretion and Role of Prosecutors

Publicly funded attorneys working on behalf of crime victims, sorting through police reports to "find the truth" of what happened, filing charges against offenders who have violated a criminal statute, and presenting evidence in court against the accused—all of these functions are essential for publicly funded prosecutors and for the criminal justice system. None of this should change.

What should change is the prosecutors' use of vague references to "public sentiment" and "protecting the victim" and "following the public mandate of the legislature" to justify unreasonable charges against low-risk offenders, or "stacking" (overcharging) charges, or advocating the death penalty, or playing any public role other than filing charges and presenting evidence against criminal offenders.

More specifically, what should change are prosecutors who are running for election by manipulating the public's fear of crime, prosecutors writing criminal code revisions for insecure or opportunistic state legislators, who, in turn, are manipulating the public's fear of crime, prosecutors using the loss or injury of a crime victim to further their own organizational or political gain, and prosecutors forming political alliances with prison correctional officers, crime victims, and conservative think tanks to support political campaigns, such as the "three strikes and you're out" or campaigns for particular office holders (Colvin and Rohrlich 1994, Butterfield 1995). All of these types of activities go beyond the original scope of filing charges and presenting evidence in court against criminal offenders.

Once the public is educated about how some prosecutors have misused their roles for the purposes of expanding their organizational turf, their salaries, and their political influence, the public should be encouraged to put pressure on governors and state legislators in much the same way that Mother Against Drunk Drivers (MADD) did in the early 1980s. Namely, they should initiate a public education campaign. The governors and state legislators have the power to curtail the role of district attorneys. If necessary, these changes can be incorporated into existing state statutes. Hopefully, public pressure would be sufficient to bring about this change. Families Against Mandatory Minimums (FAMM), Campaign for a More Rational Criminal Justice Policy, the trial lawyers' association, and other advocacy groups can be used to orchestrate this citizens' initiative.

Stop Using Prisons as an Economic Development Scheme

Quakers in the late eighteenth century thought that prisons should be places where criminal offenders reflected on the errors of their ways. Criminologists who followed the teachings of the Auburn (New York) prison in the early nineteenth century thought that prisons should be places where offenders worked in silence as a punishment for the errors of their ways. The positivists in the late nineteenth and early twentieth century thought that prisons were a place for rehabilitation, and rehabilitation would extinguish the errors of their ways. The "just deserts" school thought that prisons were a place for offenders to get what they deserve, namely punishment proportionate to their crime(s).

Most recently, a new justification for prisons has emerged, namely, economic development. In the words of Jim Gubetta, city council member in Weed, California, "We're dying on the vine here. The timber industry is hamstrung. In order to build an economy, you've got to have a base. If we have a prison, other industries will come" (Farragher 1994).

Is economic development a defensible justification for prisons? Is economic development better or worse than quiet reflection for one's "sins?" Both economic development and quiet reflection miss the point. The point is that offenders need to change their behavior, behavior that is harmful to themselves and others. Economic development will not change offenders' behavior because they are not the likely economic benefactors of improved economic conditions. Quiet reflection, silent labor, and other nineteenth-century ideas have not been shown to reduce recidivism. We must stick to what works and not get sidetracked with other agendas.

Suggested action: We must find other economic strategies to save American communities and stop using prisons as a rationale for economic development. State officials must be convinced that prisons are a century-long fiscal commitment of public funds that do not have an impact on the general crime rate. Further, prisons rob public funds from schools and other more important human services. Hard-nosed cost-benefit analysis must be applied to this topic. Legislative staff and investigative journalists can be helpful in this effort.

Conclusion

The field of corrections faces many challenges in the near future. The prospects for change have never been better. Factors internal to the field and external factors such as fiscal shortfalls at federal, state, and local levels are contributing to this atmosphere for change.

Some of the internal factors contributing to change include the following: the development of a much more precise and powerfully predictive theory (the psychology of criminal conduct, PCC) of crime causation, which in turn has led to much more effective methods of correctional intervention; the emergence of a small but influential group of practitioners who are committed to learning the psychology of criminal conduct theory and all that implies for improved methods of correctional intervention; a small but an influential group of prison administrators who are advocating a more parsimonious use of prisons; and a much more hopeful attitude on the part of researchers (Lipsey, Palmer, the "Ottawa School"), academicians (Alan Harlan and Kay Harris of Temple University), and policy analysts (such as Marc Maurer of the Sentencing Project) who believe in the literature findings regarding the efficacy of correctional intervention.

Some of the external factors contributing to change include the following: the lack of money to build more prisons, which in turn forces governors and legislators to reexamine their fiscal priorities; a small but growing number of educators who just now are realizing that "their" money is going to build prisons; and a small but growing number of national journalists (Neil Pierce, Anthony Lewis, and William Raspberry) who are beginning to speak out on the futility of the war on drugs and the prison construction mania.

These internal and external factors are helping to create an atmosphere for change, but by themselves, they will not alter current prison policies. Many more people inside and outside the juvenile and adult corrections system must get involved in changing the direction of corrections policy. It can be done, but it will take a very concerted effort by a much larger group of people.

References

Advisory Commission on Intergovernmental Relations. 1984. *Jails: Intergovernmental Dimensions of a Local Problem.* Washington, D.C.: Advisory Commission on Intergovernmental Relations.

Allsop, Steve and Bill Saunders. 1991. Reinforcing Robust Resolutions: Motivation in Relapse Prevention with Severely Dependent Problem Drinkers. In William R. Miller and Stephen Rollnick, eds. *Motivational Interviewing: Preparing People to Change Addictive Behavior.* New York: The Guilford Press.

American Correctional Association. 1995. Americans Overwhelmingly Support A Balanced Approach to Reducing Crime. Lanham, Maryland: American Correctional Association.

Andrews, Donald A. 1982. *The Level of Supervision Inventory.* Toronto, Ontario: Ministry of Correctional Services.

———. 1989. Recidivism is Predictable and Can Be Influenced: Using Risk Assessments to Reduce Recidivism. *Forum on Corrections Research.* Vol. 1, No. 2. (11-18).

————. 1994. An Overview of Treatment Effectiveness: Research and Clinical Principles. In *What Works: Bridging the Gap Between Research and Practice*. Longmont, Colorado: National Institute of Corrections Reference Center.

Andrews, Donald A., James Bonta, and Robert D. Hoge. 1990. Classification for Effective Rehabilitation: Rediscovering Psychology. *Criminal Justice and Behavior*. 17:19-52.

Andrews, Donald A. and J. J. Kiessling. 1980. Program Structure and Effective Correctional Practices: A Summary of the CaVIC Research. In R. R. Ross and Paul Gendreau, eds. *Effective Correctional Treatment*. Toronto: Butterworths.

Andrews, Donald A., Alan W. Leschied, and Robert D. Hoge. 1992. A Review of the Classification and Treatment Literature. Toronto: Ministry of Community and Social Services.

Andrews, Donald A. and James Bonta. 1994. The Psychology of Criminal Conduct. Cincinnati, Ohio: Anderson Publishing.

Andrews, Donald A., J. J. Kiessling, S. G. Mickus, and D. Robinson. 1983. *Some Convergent and Divergent Validities of the LSI*. Winnipeg, Manitoba: Canadian Psychological Association.

Andrews, Donald A., Ivan Zinger, Robert D. Hoge, James Bonta, Paul Gendreau, and Francis T. Cullen. 1990. Does Correctional Treatment Work? A Psychologically Informed Meta-analysis. *Criminology*. 28:369-404.

Annis, Helen M. and D. Chan. 1983. The Differential Treatment Model: Empirical Evidence from a Personality Typology of Adult Offenders. *Criminal Justice and Behavior*. 10:159-173.

Aziz, David W. and Cheryl L. Clark. 1996. Shock Incarceration in New York. In *Juvenile and Adult Boot Camps*. Lanham, Maryland: American Correctional Association.

Azrin, Nathan H. and Victoria Besalel. 1982. *Finding a Job*. Berkeley, California: Ten Speed Press.

Barak, Gregg. 1994. Between the Waves: Mass-Mediated Themes of Crime and Justice. *Social Justice*. Vol. 21, No. 3, p. 133.

Bayse, Daniel J. 1993. *Helping Hands: A Handbook for Volunteers in Prisons and Jails*. Lanham, Maryland: American Correctional Association.

Bien, T. H., W. R. Miller, and J. S. Tonigan. 1993. Brief Interventions for Alcohol Problems: A Review. *Addiction*. 88:315-336.

Blue Ribbon Commission on Inmate Population Management. 1990. A Report on Prison and Jail Crowding in California. Sacramento, California: Blue Ribbon Commission.

Blumstein, Alfred, Jacqueline Cohen, Susan E. Martin, and Michael H. Torry. 1983. *Research on Sentencing: The Search for Reform*. Washington, D.C.: National Academic Press.

Boerner, David. 1995. Sentencing Policy in Washington. *Overcrowded Times*. Vol. 6, No. 3, pp. 9-12.

Bonta, James. 1991. Correctional Halfway Houses: The Evidence on Effectiveness. *Second Annual Corrections Research Forum Proceedings*. Ottawa: Correctional Service of Canada.

———. 1996. Risk Needs Assessment and Treatment. In Alan T. Harland, ed. *Choosing Correctional Options That Work*. Thousand Oaks, California: Sage Publications.

Bonta, James and Lawrence. L. Motiuk. 1985. Utilization of an Interview-Based Classification Instrument: A Study of Correctional Halfway Houses. *Criminal Justice and Behavior*. Vol. 12, No. 3, pp. 333-351.

———. 1987. The Diversion of Incarcerated Offenders to Correctional Halfway Houses. *Journal of Research in Crime and Delinquency*. 24:302-323.

———. 1990. Classification to Correctional Halfway Houses: A Quasi-experimental Evaluation. *Criminology*. 28: 497-506.

———. 1992. Inmate Classification. *Journal of Criminal Justice*. 20: 343-353.

Bradsher, Keith. 1995. Economic Inequality on Rise in U.S. *New York Times*. April 17, 1995.

Brandsma, Jeffery M., Maxie C. Maultsby, and Richard J. Welsh. 1980. *The Outpatient Treatment of Alcoholism: A Review and Comparative Study.* Baltimore, Maryland: University Park Press.

Bratton, William J. 1996. How to Win the War Against Crime. *New York Times.* April 5, 1996.

Brown, Stephen E., Finn-Aage Esbensen, and Gilbert Geis. 1991. *Criminology, Explaining Crime and Its Context.* Cincinnati, Ohio: Anderson Publishing.

Brownstein, Henry R. 1991. Media and the Construction of Random Drug Violence. *Social Justice.* 18: 85-103.

Budiansky, Stephen. 1996. Local TV: Mayhem Central. *U.S. News and World Report.* Vol. 120, No. 9, p. 63.

Bullock, Merry L., A. J. Umen, P. D. Culliton, and R. T. Olander. 1987. Acupuncture Treatment of Alcoholic Recidivism: A Pilot Study. *Alcoholism: Clinical and Experimental Research.* 11: 292-295.

Bureau of Justice Statistics. 1983. 1983 Jail Census, Jails and Jail Inmates. Washington, D.C.: U.S. Department of Justice.

———. 1984. Time Served in Prison. Washington, D.C.: U.S. Department of Justice.

———. 1986. Jail Inmates 1984. Washington, D.C.: U.S. Department of Justice.

———. 1988. Drug Law Violators, 1980-86. Washington, D.C.: U.S. Department of Justice.

———. 1991a. Drugs and Jail Inmates. Washington, D.C.: U.S. Department of Justice.

———. 1991b. Race of Prisoners Admitted to State and Federal Institutions, 1926-86. Washington, D.C.: U.S. Department of Justice.

———. 1992. Criminal Victimizations 1991. Washington, D.C.: U.S. Department of Justice.

———. 1993. Criminal Victimization 1992. Washington, D.C.: U.S. Department of Justice.

———. 1994. Prisoners in 1993. Washington, D.C.: U.S. Department of Justice.

———. 1995a. Felony Sentences in State Courts, 1992. Washington, D.C.: U.S. Department of Justice.

———. 1995b. Jails and Jail Inmates 1993-94. Washington, D.C.: U.S. Department of Justice.

———. 1995c. Prisoners in 1994. Washington, D.C.: U.S. Department of Justice.

Butterfield, Fox. 1995. Political Gains By Prison Guards. *New York Times*. November 11, 1995, p. 1.

Byrne, James M. 1990. *Assessing What Works in the Adult Community Corrections System*. Denver, Colorado: Academy of Criminal Justice Sciences.

Campaign for an Effective Crime Policy. 1992. *Call for a Rational Debate on Crime and Punishment*. Washington, D.C.: Campaign for an Effective Crime Policy.

———. 1994. *Evaluating Boot Camp Prison*. Washington, D.C.: Campaign for an Effective Crime Policy.

Canadian Sentencing Commission. 1987. *Sentencing Reform: A Canadian Approach*. Ottawa: Canadian Criminal Justice Association.

Castle, Michael N. 1991. *Alternative Sentencing: Selling It to The Public*. Washington, D.C.: National Institute of Justice, Research in Action.

Center for Media and Public Affairs. 1994. Crime Down, Media Coverage Up. *Media Monitor*. Vol. VIII, No. 1, p. 1.

———. 1995. Media Crime Wave Continues—Crime Tops TV News for Second Year. *Overcrowded Times*. Vol. 6, No. 2., p. 5.

Center for the Study of Law and Society. 1992. *Incarceration and Crime: Facing Fiscal Realities in Pennsylvania*. State College, Pennsylvania: Pennsylvania State University.

Chaiken, William E. and Jan M. Chaiken. 1983. Crime: Trends and Targets. *Wilson Quarterly*. Spring, pp. 102-131.

Clear, Todd R. 1988. *Drug Offenders and Correctional Alternatives*. Newark, New Jersey: Rutgers University.

Clear, Todd R. and George F. Cole. 1986. *American Corrections*. Monterey, California: Brooks/Cole Publishing.

Cloward, Richard A. and Lloyd E. Ohlin. 1960. *Delinquency and Opportunity*. New York: Free Press.

Colvin, Mark and John Pauly. 1983. A Critique of Criminology: Toward an Integrated Structural-Marxist Theory of Delinquency Production. *American Journal of Sociology*. 89: 513-551.

Colvin, Richard Lee and Ted Rohrlich. 1994. Courts Toss Curves at 3 Strikes. *Los Angeles Times*. October 23, 1994.

Com Corr Coop. 1995. Proposal submitted to Boulder County Commissioners. Boulder, Colorado: Division of Community Corrections.

Cooney, Ned L., Allen Zweben, and Michael F. Fleming. 1995. Screening for Alcohol Problems and At-Risk Drinking in Health Care Settings. In Reid K. Hester and William R. Miller, eds. *Handbook of Alcoholic Treatment Approaches*. Boston: Allyn and Bacon.

Cooper, G. O., H. B. Adams, and J. C. Scott. 1988. Studies in REST: I. Reduced Environmental Stimulation Therapy and Reduced Alcohol Consumption. *Journal of Substance Abuse Treatment*. 5: 61-68.

Crossette, B. 1996. World Splitting Into a Two-Class System of Rich-Poor. *Seattle Post-Intelligencer*. July 15, 1996. (A4).

Cullen, Francis T., John P. Wright, B. Brandon, and K. Applegate. 1993. Control in the Community: The Limits of Reform? In Alan Harland, ed. *Choosing Correctional Options That Work*. Thousand Oaks, California: Sage.

Currie, Elliott. 1985. *Confronting Crime*. New York: Pantheon Books

———. 1993. *Reckoning*. New York: Pantheon Books.

Davis, F. 1951. Crime News in Colorado Newspapers. *American Journal of Sociology*. 57:325-30.

Dickey, Walter J. and Dennis Wagner. 1990. From the Bottom Up: The High Risk Offender Intensive Supervision Program. Madison, Wisconsin: University of Wisconsin Law School.

DiClemente, Carlo C. 1991. Motivational Interviewing and the Stages of Change. In Miller and Rollnick, eds. *Motivational Interviewing: Preparing People to Change Addictive Behavior*. New York: Guilford Press.

Doob, Anthony and Julian V. Roberts. 1982. *Crime and the Official Response to Crime: The Views of the Canadian Public*. Ottawa: Department of Justice.

————. 1983. *An Analysis of the Public's View of Sentencing*. Ottawa: Department of Justice.

————. 1985. The Many Realities of Crime. In Edward L. Greenspan and Anthony Doob, eds. *Perspectives in Criminal Law*. Aurora: Canada Law Book.

Drajick, K. and S. Gettinger. 1982. *Overcrowded Times*. New York: Edna McConnell Clark Foundation.

Durham, Alexis M. 1995. Images of Crime and Justice: Murder and the True Crime Genre. *Journal of Criminal Justice*. Vol. 23, No. 2, pp. 143-152.

Eisenberg, Michael. 1990. Special Release and Supervision Programs. Austin, Texas: Texas Department of Criminal Justice, Pardons and Parole Division.

Elliott, Delbert S. 1994. *Youth Violence: An Overview*. Boulder, Colorado: University of Colorado, Center for the Study and Prevention of Violence.

Elliott, Delbert S., Suzanne S. Ageton, and Rachelle J. Canter. 1979. An Integrated Theoretical Perspective on Delinquent Behavior. *Journal of Research in Crime and Delinquency*. 16: 3-27.

Empey, LaMar T. 1978. Constructing Crime: Evolution and Implications of Sociological Theory. *American Delinquency: Its Meaning and Construction*. Homewood, Illinois: Dorsey.

English, Kim and Mary Mande. 1991. *Community Corrections in Colorado: Why Do Some Clients Succeed and Others Fail?* Denver, Colorado: Colorado Division of Criminal Justice.

Fairweather, George W., D. H. Sanders, D. L. Cressler, and H. Maynard. 1969. *Community Life for the Mentally Ill: An Alternative to Institutional Care.* Chicago, Illinois: Aldine.

Farragher, Thomas. 1994. Prospects for Landing State Prison Split California Town. *The Oregonian.* July 3, 1994.

Farrington, David. 1983. Offending from 10 to 25 Years of Age. In Katherine Teilmann Van Dusen and Sarnoff A. Mednick, eds. *Prospective Studies of Crime and Delinquency.* Hingham, Massachusetts: Kluwer Nijhoff.

Federal Bureau of Investigation. 1992. Uniform Crime Reports. Washington, D.C.: U.S. Department of Justice.

Feldman, Daniel L. 1992. Prison Building Is Not Nation Building. Denver, Colorado: National Conference of State Legislatures.

Fishman, Mark. 1978. Crimes Waves as Ideology. *Social Problems.* 25: 531-43.

Fogg, Vern and Brad Bogue. 1996. *The Colorado Standardized Offender Assessment Program: A Learning Organization System for Managing Measurement, Meaning and Methods in Community Corrections.* Denver, Colorado: Office of Probation Services, Colorado Judicial Department.

Frankel, Max. 1995. The Murder Broadcasting System. *The New York Times Magazine.* December 17, 1995.

Frase, Richard S. 1993. Prison Population Growing Under Minnesota Sentencing Guidelines. *Overcrowded Times.* Vol. 4, No. 1, pp. 10-12.

Freud, Sigmund. 1950. A General Introduction to Psychoanalysis. New York: Permabooks.

Fuller, R. K. 1995. Antidipsotropic Medications. In R. K. Hester and W. R. Miller, eds. *Handbook of Alcoholism Treatment Approaches.* Boston: Allyn and Bacon.

Gallup. 1989. The Gallup Report. Number 285. Princeton, New Jersey: Gallup Poll.

Garrett, C. 1985. Effects of Residential Treatment on Adjudicated Delinquents: A Meta-analysis. *Journal of Research in Crime and Delinquency.* 22: 287-308.

Gendreau, Paul. 1994. The Principles of Effective Intervention with Offenders. In A. Harland, ed. *What Works in Community Corrections*. Thousand Oaks, California: Sage Publications.

――――. 1996. Offender Rehabilitation: What We Know and What Needs To Be Done. *Criminal Justice and Behavior*. Vol. 23, No. 1, pp. 144-161.

Gendreau, Paul and Claire Goggin. 1996. Correctional Treatment: Accomplishments and Realties. In P. Van Voorhis, D. Lester, and M. Braswell, eds. *Correctional Counseling*. Cincinnati, Ohio: Anderson Press.

Gendreau, Paul and Robert R. Ross. 1979. Effective Correctional Treatment: Bibliotherapy for Cynics. *Crime and Delinquency*. 25: 463-489.

――――. 1981. Correctional Potency: Treatment and Deterrence on Trial. In Ronald Roesch and Raymond R. Corrado, eds. *Evaluation and Criminal Justice Policy*. Beverly Hills, California: Sage.

――――. 1987. Revivification of Rehabilitation: Evidence from the 80's. *Justice Quarterly*. 4: 349-407.

General Accounting Office. 1992. *Asset Forfeiture*. Washington, D.C.: U.S. General Accounting Office.

Gest, Ted. 1996. Diversity on the Bench. *U.S. News and World Report*. Vol. 120, No. 6, p. 40.

Glick, B. and A. Goldstein, eds. 1995. *Managing Delinquency Programs That Work*. Lanham, Maryland: American Correctional Association.

Glueck, Sheldon and Eleanor Glueck. 1950. *Unraveling Juvenile Delinquency*. Cambridge, Massachusetts: Harvard University Press.

Goldkamp, John S., Michael R. Gottfredson, and Doris Weiland. 1988. The Utility of Drug Testing in the Assessment of Defendant Risk at the Pretrial Release Decision. Philadelphia, Pennsylvania: Temple University.

Gordon, D., and J. Arbuthot. 1987. Individual, Group, and Family Interventions. In Herbert C. Quay, ed. *Handbook of Juvenile Delinquency*. New York: John Wiley.

Gottfredson, Michael and Travis Hirschi. 1995. National Crime Control Policies. *Society*. January, p. 31.

Gottfredson, Stephen D. 1995. Fighting Crime at the Expense of Colleges. *Chronicle of Higher Education*. January 20, 1995.

Gottfredson, Stephen D. and Sean McConville. 1987. *America's Correctional Crisis*. New York: Greenwood Press.

Gottfredson, Stephen D. and Ralph B. Taylor. 1982. Attitudes of Correctional Policymakers and the Public. In Stephen D. Gottfredson and Sean McConville, eds. *America's Correctional Crisis*. New York: Greenwood Press.

Gottschalk, R., W. Davidson, L. Gensheimer, and J. Mayer. 1987. Community Based Interventions. In Herbert C. Quay, ed. *Handbook of Juvenile Delinquency*. New York: John Wiley.

Graber, Doris. 1980. *Crime News and the Public*. New York: Praeger.

Guydish, J. R. 1987. Self Control Bibliotherapy as a Secondary Prevention Strategy with Heavy-drinking College Students (Unpublished). Spokane, Washington: Washington State University.

Harris, P. W. 1988. The Interpersonal Maturity Level Classification System: I-level. *Criminal Justice and Behavior*. 15: 58-77.

Havassy, Barbara E., Sharon M. Hall, and David A. Wasserman. 1991. Social Support and Relapse: Commonalities Among Alcoholics, Opiate Users, and Cigarette Smokers. *Addictive Behaviors*. 16: 235-246.

Heather, N., J. Kissoon-Singh, and G. W. Fenton. 1990. Assisted Natural Recovery from Alcohol Problems: Effects of a Self-help Manual with and without Supplementary Telephone Contact. *British Journal of Addiction*. 85: 1177-1185.

Hester, Reid K. and William R. Miller, eds. 1995. *Handbook of Alcoholism Treatment Approaches*. Boston: Allyn and Bacon.

Hindelang, Michael J. 1981. Variations in Sex-Race-Specific Incidence Rates of Offending. *American Sociological Review*. 46: 461-474.

Hirschi, Travis. 1969. *Causes of Delinquency*. Berkeley, California: University of California Press.

Hoffman-Bustamonte, Dale. 1973. The Nature of Female Criminality. *Issues in Criminology*. 8: 117-136.

Holley, Joe. 1996. Should the Coverage Fit the Crime? *Columbia Journalism Review*. May/June, p. 27.

Huizinga, David, Finn-Aage Esbensen, and Delbert S. Elliott. 1988. *The Denver Youth Survey: Project Overview. Project Report #1*. Boulder, Colorado: Institute of Behavioral Sciences.

Hunzeker, Donna. 1992. Bringing Corrections Policy into The 1990's. *State Legislative Report*. Vol. 17, No.5. Denver, Colorado: National Conference of State Legislatures.

Immarigeon, Russ. 1985. Private Prisons, Private Programs, and Their Implications for Reducing Reliance on Imprisonment in the United States. *The Prison Journal*. Vol. 65, No. 2., pp. 60-74.

Izzo, R., and Robert R. Ross. 1990. Meta-analysis of Rehabilitation Programs for Juvenile Delinquents: A Brief Report. *Criminal Justice and Behavior*. 17: 134-142.

Jesness, Carl F. 1975. Comparative Effectiveness of Behavior Modification and Transactional Analysis Programs for Delinquents. *Journal of Consulting and Clinical Psychology*. Vol. 43.6, pp. 758-779.

Jones, Peter R. 1996. Risk Prediction in Criminal Justice. In Alan T. Harland, ed. *Choosing Correctional Options That Work*. Thousand Oaks, California: Sage Publications.

Justice Education Center. 1991. Offender Profile Study: A Comparison of Criminal Justice Clients in Prison and in the Community. Hartford, Connecticut: Chief Court Administrator's Office.

Kalish, C. B. 1988. International Crime Rates. Washington, D.C.: U.S. Department of Justice.

Keane, T. M., David W. Foy, B. Nunn, and R. G. Rychtarik. 1984. Spouse Contracting to Increase Antabuse Compliance in Alcoholic Veterans. *Journal of Clinical Psychology*. 40: 340- 344.

Kendall, Phillip C. and Steven D. Hollon, eds. 1979. *Cognitive-behavioral Interventions: Theory, Research, and Procedures.* New York: Academic Press.

Keve, Paul. 1996. *Measuring Excellence: The History of Correctional Standards and Accreditation.* Lanham, Maryland: American Correctional Association.

Knapp, Kay. 1976. *Community Corrections, Widening the Net of Social Control.* St. Paul, Minnesota: Minnesota Department of Corrections.

Knapp, Kay, Peggy Burke, and Mimi Carter. 1992. *Residential Community Corrections Facilities: Current Practice and Policy Issues.* Washington, D.C.: National Institute of Corrections.

Kopel, David B. 1994. *Prison Blues: How America's Foolish Sentencing Policies Endanger Public Safety.* Golden, Colorado: Independence Institute and Washington, D.C.: Cato Institute.

Labaton, Stephen. 1993. Seized Property in Crimes Cases Causes Concern. *New York Times.* May 31, 1993.

Lauen, Roger J. 1988 and 1990. *Community-Managed Corrections and Other Solutions to America's Prison Crisis.* Laurel, Maryland: American Correctional Association.

———. 1994. Community Corrections in Colorado. *Community Corrections Report.* Vol. 1, No. 5, pp. 3-9.

———. 1995. *A Critique of a Criminal Justice Reform Effort: Community Corrections in Colorado.* Boston: Academy of Criminal Justice Sciences.

Lerner, K., Greg Arling, and S. Christopher Baird. 1985. Client Management Classification Strategies for Case Supervision. *Crime and Delinquency.* 32: 254-271.

Lieb, Roxanne. 1993. Washington Prison Population Growth Out of Control. *Overcrowded Times.* Vol 4, No. 1., pp. 13-14.

Lindsay, Margot C. 1990. *A Matter of Partnership: Public Involvement in Residential Community Corrections.* Washington, D.C.: National Institute of Corrections.

Lipsey, Mark W. 1989. *The Efficacy of Intervention for Juvenile Delinquents.* Reno, Nevada: American Society of Criminology.

————. 1990. Juvenile Delinquency Treatment: A Meta-analytic Inquiry into Variability of Effects. Newbury Park, California: Research Synthesis Committee, Russell Sage Foundation.

Loeber, R. and Magda Stouthamer-Loeber. 1987. Prediction. In Herbert C. Quay, ed. *Handbook of Juvenile Delinquency.* New York: John Wiley.

Logan, Charles H. and Bill W. McGriff. 1989. Comparing Costs of Public and Private Prisons: A Case Study. *NIJ Reports,* No. 216. September/October. Washington, D.C.: U.S. Department of Justice.

Marlatt, G. Allen. 1978. Craving for Alcohol, Loss of Control and Relapse: A Cognitive-behavioral Analysis. In P. Nathan, *et al.,* eds. *Alcoholism: New Directions in Behavioral Research and Treatment.* New York: Plenum Press.

Martin, John A. 1989. Drugs, Crime, and Urban Trial Court Management: The Unintended Consequences of the War on Drugs. *Yale Law Review.* Vol. 8, No. 1, p. 117.

————. 1990. Responding to Substance Abuse in Boulder County: Interpreting the United Way Needs Assessment. Boulder, Colorado: Division of Research and Evaluation.

Martinson, Robert. 1974. What Works? Questions and Answers About Prison Reform. *The Public Interest.* 35: 22-54.

McDonald, Douglas C. 1989. *The Cost of Corrections: In Search of the Bottom Line, Research in Corrections.* Omaha, Nebraska: Kutak Foundation and Washington, D.C.: National Institute of Corrections.

————. 1992. *Private Penal Institutions.* Chicago: University of Chicago Press.

Miami Herald. 1996. The Rich Get Richer. February 18, 1996.

Miller, W. E. and D. E. Stokers. 1963. Constituency Influence in Congress. *American Political Science Review.* Vol. 57: 46-56.

Miller, William R. 1994. Addiction: A Whole New View. In Joann Ellison Rodgers, interviewer. *Psychology Today.* September/October, p. 36.

Miller, William R. and Reid K. Hester. 1980. Treating Problem Drinkers: Modern Approaches. In William R. Miller, ed. *The Addictive Behaviors: Treatment of Alcoholism, Drug Abuse, Smoking and Obesity*. Oxford: Pergamon Press.

Miller, William R. and Theresa B. Moyers. [no date] Center on Alcoholism, Substance Abuse and Addictions, University of New Mexico, Albuquerque, Research Division.

Miller, William R. and Stephen Rollnick. 1991. *Motivational Interviewing: Preparing People to Change Addictive Behavior*. New York: The Guilford Press.

Miller, William R. and V. C. Sanchez. 1993. Motivating Young Adults for Treatment and Lifestyle Change. In George Howard, ed. *Issues in Alcohol Use and Misuse by Young Adults*. Notre Dame, Indiana: University of Notre Dame Press.

Minnesota Sentencing Guidelines Commission. 1984. *The Impact of the Minnesota Sentencing Guidelines, Three Year Evaluation*. St. Paul, Minnesota: Minnesota Sentencing Guidelines Commission.

Monti, Peter M., D. B. Abrams, J. A. Binkoff, W. R. Zwick, Michael R. Liepman, Ted D. Nirenberg, and D. J. Rohsenow. 1990. Communication Skills Training with Family and Cognitive Behavioral Mood Management Training for Alcoholics. *Journal of Studies on Alcohol*. 51: 263-270.

Moos, Rudolph H. 1975. *Evaluating Correctional and Community Settings*. New York: John Wiley.

Murphy, T. J., Robert R. Pagano, and G. Allen Marlatt. 1986. Lifestyle Modification with Heavy Alcohol Drinkers: Effects of Aerobic Exercise and Meditation. *Addictive Behaviors*. 11: 175- 186.

National Center for Education Statistics. 1994. *Literacy Behind Prison Walls: Profiles of the Prison Population from the National Adult Literacy Survey*. Washington, D.C.: Government Printing Office.

National Council on Crime and Delinquency. 1987. *It's About Time, Solving America's Prison Crowding Crisis*. San Francisco, California: National Council on Crime and Delinquency.

National Institute of Justice. 1985. *The Private Sector and Prison Industries*. Washington, D.C: U.S. Department of Justice.

_____. 1990. Drug Use Forecasting Annual Report. *Drugs and Crime in America*. Washington, D.C.: U.S. Department of Justice.

New York Times. 1996. State Prisons Find a New Source of Financing: Their Inmates. July 7, 1996, A-11.

Nieman Reports. 1994. Too Many Crime Stories: Not Just the Wrong Emphasis. Manchester, New Hampshire: Harvard University.

O'Farrell, Timothy J., ed. 1993. *Treating Alcohol Problems: Marital and Family Interventions*. New York: Guilford.

Office of Planning and Budgeting. 1990. Untitled report. Denver, Colorado: State Office of Planning and Budgeting.

O'Leary, Vincent. State University of New York at Albany, 1992.

Onken, Lisa Simon, Jack D. Blaine, and John J. Boren. 1993. Behavioral Treatments for Drug Abuse and Dependence. Washington, D.C.: National Institute of Health.

Palmer, Ted. 1965. Types of Treaters and Types of Juvenile Offenders. *Youth Authority Quarterly*. 18: 14-23.

_____. 1967. Personality Characteristics and Professional Orientations of Five Groups of Community Treatment Project Workers: A Preliminary Report on Differences Among Treaters. Sacramento, California: California Youth Authority.

_____. 1973. Matching Worker and Client in Corrections. *Social Work*. Vol. 18, No. 2, pp. 95-103.

_____. 1992. *The Re-emergence of Correctional Intervention*. Newbury Park, California: Sage Publications.

_____. 1996. Programmatic and Nonprogrammatic Aspects of Successful Intervention. In Alan T. Harland, ed. *Choosing Correctional Options That Work*. Thousand Oaks, California: Sage Publications.

Parent, Dale G. 1993. Boot Camps Failing to Achieve Goals. *Overcrowded Times*. Vol. 4, No. 4, pp.12-14.

Pasewark, Richard, Deborah Seidenzahl, and Mark Pantle. 1981. Opinions Concerning Criminality Among Mental Patients. *Journal of Community Psychology.* 9:367-70.

Pear, Robert. 1996. Many States Fail to Meet Mandates on Child Welfare. *New York Times.* March 17, 1996.

Peregrine. 1996. "Credit Card" Management Information Systems. Lakewood, Colorado: Peregrine, Inc.

Petersilia, Joan. 1995. How California Could Divert Nonviolent Prisoners to Intermediate Sanctions. *Overcrowded Times.* Vol. 6, No. 3.

Prendergast, Alan. 1996. The Sins of Youth. *Westword, a Weekly Newspaper.* July 18-24, 1996, pp. 18-19.

Preziosi, Robert C. Organizational Diagnosis Questionnaire. University Associates.

Prochaska, James O. and Carlo C. DiClemente. 1982. Transtheoretical Therapy: Toward a More Integrative Model of Change. *Psychotherapy: Theory, Research and Practice.* 19: 276-288.

Project Match. 1997. Matching Alcoholism Treatment to Client Heterogeneity. *Journal of Studies on Alcohol.* 58:7-29.

Purdy, Matthew W. and Celia W. Dugger. 1996. Legacy of Immigrants' Uprising: New Jail Operator, Little Change. *New York Times.* July 7, 1996, p. 1.

Ramirez, Anthony. 1994. Privatizing America's Prisons, Slowly. *New York Times.* August 14, 1994.

Randall, D., L. Lee-Simmons, and Paul Hagner. 1988. Common Versus Elite Crime Coverage in Network News. *Social Science Quarterly.* 69: 910-29.

Read, Edward M. 1996. *Partners in Change: The 12-Step Referral Handbook for Probation, Parole and Community Corrections.* Lanham, Maryland: American Correctional Association.

Reback, Donna. 1993. Special Report on Corrections in Select States. *Overcrowded Times.* Vol. 4, No. 1.

Rimmele, Carl T., Matthew O. Howard, and Martin L. Hilfrink. 1995. Aversion Therapies. In Reid K. Hester and William R. Miller. *Handbook of Alcoholism Treatment Approaches*. Boston: Allyn and Bacon.

Roberts, John. 1997. *Reform and Retribution: An Illustrated History of American Prisons*. Lanham, Maryland: American Correctional Association.

Roberts, Julian V. 1992. Public Opinion, Crime, and Criminal Justice. *Crime and Justice: A Review of the Research*. Vol. 16, pp. 99-179.

Roberts, Julian V. and Michelle G. Grossman. 1990. Crime Prevention and Public Opinion. *Canadian Journal of Criminology*. 32: 75-90.

Rogers, Carl. 1959. A Theory of Therapy, Personality, and Interpersonal Relationships as Developed in the Client-centered Framework. In Sigmund Koch, ed. *Psychology: The Study of Science*. 3:184-25.

Rummler, Geary A. and Alan P. Brache. 1990. *Improving Performance: How to Manage the White Space on the Organization Chart*. San Francisco, California: Jossey Bass.

Sacco, Vincent. 1995. Media Constructions of Crime. *The Annals, American Academy of Political Science*. Vol. 539.

Salahi, David L. 1994. California University Costs. *Los Angeles Times*. March 29, 1994.

Sannibale, C. 1988. The Differential Effect of a Set of Brief Interventions on the Functioning of a Group of "Early Stage" Problem Drinkers. *Australian Drug and Alcohol Review*. 7:147-155.

Schein, Edgar H. 1990. *Career Anchors: Discovering Your Real Values*. San Diego: Pfeiffer and Company.

Schlesinger, Phillip and Howard Tumber. 1994. *Reporting Crime: The Media Politics of Criminal Justice*. Oxford: Oxford University Press.

Schoen, Kenneth F. 1995. The State-Centered Program: Toward a Balanced System of Corrections. *Overcrowded Times*. October, p.13.

Seattle Post-Intelligencer. 1995. Chain Gangs Crushing Rock Under a Searing Sun Coming to Alabama. July 29, 1995. A4.

Select Committee on Narcotics Abuse and Control. 1982. Health Questions About Marijuana. 97th Congress, Second Session. Washington, D.C.: U.S. Government Printing Office.

Sentencing Accountability Commission. 1991. Untitled report. Wilmington, Deleware: Sentencing Accountability Commission.

Sentencing Project. 1995. *Americans Behind Bars: A Comparison of International Rates of Incarceration.* Washington, D.C.: The Sentencing Project.

————. 1995. A Special Report on Correctional Policies and Their Impact on African-Americans. Washington, D.C.: The Sentencing Project.

Shapiro, Bruce. 1996. How the War on Crime Imprisons America. *The Nation.* Vol. 262, No. 16, p.14.

Sheley, Joseph and C. Ashkins. 1981. Crime, Crime News, and Crime Views. *Public Opinion Quarterly.* 45: 492-506.

Shilton, Mary K. 1992. *Community Corrections Acts for State and Local Partnerships.* Laurel, Maryland: American Correctional Association.

Simourd, L. and Donald A. Andrews. 1994. Correlates of Delinquency: A Look at Gender Differences. *Forum on Corrections Research.* 6:32-35.

Spiegel, Claire. 1994. Half of Inmates Are Sent to Prison as Parole Violators. *Los Angeles Times.* October 24, 1994.

Staples, Ben. 1995. The Chain Gang Show. *New York Times Magazine.* September 17, 1995, pp. 62-63.

Statistics Canada. 1992. *The Daily.* March 3, 1992.

Stern, Henry. 1995. Prison Population in U.S. Tops 1 Million, Reports Says. *The Oregonian.* August 10, 1995. A6.

Sullivan, John and Matthew Purdy. 1995. In Corrections Business, Shrewdness Pays. *New York Times.* July 23, 1995.

Terblanche, Stephen. 1995. Sentencing in South Africa. *Overcrowded Times.* Vol. 6, No. 2., pp. 10-12.

Thornsberry, T. P. and M. Farnsworth. 1982. Social Correlates of Criminal Involvement: Further Evidence on the Relationship Between Social Class and Criminal Behavior. *American Sociological Review.* 47:505-518.

Tittle, Charles R., W. J. Villimez, and D. A. Smith. 1978. The Myth of Social Class and Criminality: An Empirical Assessment of the Empirical Evidence. *American Sociological Review.* 43:643-656.

Toner, Robin. 1996. Time Present, Time Past. *New York Times Book Review.* January 28th, 1996.

Tonry, Michael. 1994. Racial Disparities Getting Worse in U.S. Prisons and Jails. *Overcrowded Times.* Vol. 5, No. 2, pp. 1, 16-17.

Tornudd, Patrik. 1993. Fifteen Years of Decreasing Prisoner Rates in Finland, Helsinki: National Research Institute of Legal Policy. *Overcrowded Times.* Vol. 5, No. 5, pp. 1, 11-13.

Treaster, Joseph B. 1993. It's Not Legalization, but a User-Friendly Drug Strategy. *New York Times.* December 19, 1993.

U.S. Census Bureau. 1994. The Rich Get Richer. *Miami Herald.* February 18th, 1996.

West, Donald J. 1985. The Politicization of Delinquency. In David P. Farrington and John Gunn, eds. *Reactions to Crime: The Public, the Police, Courts, and Prisons.* New York: John Wiley and Sons.

Wideman, John Edgar. 1995. Doing Time, Marking Race. *The Nation.* October 30, 1995, pp. 504-505.

Wiebush, Richard G., Christopher Baird, Barry Krisberg, and David Onek. 1994. *Risk Assessment and Classification for Serious, Violent and Chronic Juvenile Offenders.* San Francisco: National Council on Crime and Delinquency.

Wilkins, Leslie. 1967. A Survey of the Field from the Standpoint of Facts and Figures. In *The Effectiveness of Punishment and Other Measures of Treatment.* Strasbourg: Council of Europe.

Will, Jeffry A. and John H. McGrath. 1995. Crime, Neighborhood Perceptions, and the Underclass: The Relationship Between Fear of Crime and Class Position. *Journal of Criminal Justice.* Vol. 23, No. 2, pp. 163-176.

Wisconsin Department of Health and Social Services. 1989. Reducing Criminal Risk: An Evaluation of the High Risk Offender Intensive Supervision Project. Madison, Wisconsin: Office of Policy and Budget.

Wolfgang, Marvin E. and Franco Ferracuti. 1967. *The Subculture of Violence.* London: Social Science Paperbacks.

Wright, John Paul, Francis T. Cullen, and M. B. Blankenship. 1995. The Social Construction of Corporate Violence: Media Coverage of the Imperial Food Products Fire. *Crime and Delinquency.* Vol. 41, No. 1, pp. 20-36.

Young, Warren and Mark Brown. 1993. *Cross-national Comparisons of Imprisonment, Crime and Justice: A Review of the Research.* Vol. 17. Chicago: University of Chicago.

Index

A

ACA. *See* American Correctional Association
Academic community. *See* Researchers
Academy of Criminal Justice Sciences, 214
Accountability of system, 132
Accreditation, 26, 221-22
Acupuncture, 157
Adams, Stuart, 102
Adult Substance Use Survey (ASUS), 130, 141, 178-79, 207
AFDC. *See* Aid to Families with Dependent Children
African-Americans
    in prison, 88-92, 93
Aid to Families with Dependent Children (AFDC), 24
Alcohol and alcoholism, 81, 82-85. *Also see* Substance abuse
Alcohol Dependence Scale, 130, 139
Alcohol Positive Outcome Expectancy Test, 142
Alcohol Use Questionnaire, 178
Alcoholics Anonymous (AA), 83, 152, 157, 165
American Correctional Association (ACA), 102, 214
    boot camps, 72
    policies and resolutions. *See* American Correctional Association Policies and Resolutions
    standards and accreditation, 26
American Correctional Association Policies and Resolutions
    Classification, 115-16
    Community Corrections, 197-98
    Correctional Industry, 20-21
    Correctional Information Systems, 206
    Correctional Officer, term, 213
    Corrections, purpose of, 28-29
    Crowding and Excessive Workloads in Corrections, 13-14
    Drug-free Correctional Workforce, 80
    Education and Training, offender, 191
    Employee Assistance Programs, 186
    Fiscal Responsibility for Correctional Legislation, 24-25
    Higher education, 194
    Juvenile Justice, 60-61
    Parole and Supervised Release, 199-200
    Private Sector Involvement in Corrections, 21-22
    Probation, 201-02
    Recruitment and Development, correctional staff, 211-12
    Research and Evaluation, 97-98
    Sanctions and Controls, appropriate use of, 107-108
    Sentencing, 6-7
    Standards and Accreditation, correctional, 221-22
    Substance Abuse, offender's, 76
    Technology and Standards, 219
    Violence Reduction, 40-41
American Probation and Parole Association, 102, 103, 214
American Society of Criminology, 214
Andrews, Donald, 103, 120, 151, 163, 167, 168, 201
Antabuse, 156, 157, 165
Antidipsotropic medications, 156
Asians, 92
Assaults, 107
Assessment. *See* Classification
ASUS. *See* Adult Substance Use Survey
Attorneys, 100, 181, 224-25
Auburn, New York school of criminology, 135, 225
Audits, 220
Australia, incarceration rate in, 15
Aversion therapies, 156

B

Baird, Christopher, 120, 144
Baltimore Sun, 45
Bandura, Albert, 69
Beccaria, Cesare, 31-32
Blacks. *See* African-Americans
Bonta, James, 103, 120, 151, 160, 167, 168
Boot camps, 72, 169
Boston University Stress Exam, 141
Boulder, Colorado, 101
Bradley, William, 33
Bratton, Chief of Police, 53-54
Brief Intervention, 155
Broad-spectrum skill training, 155
Bush, President George, 2

C

California
    correctional expenditures in, 25
    crime rate in, versus South Africa, 89
    incarceration in, versus South Africa, 90-92
    Probation Subsidy Program, 174
    three strikes and you're out legislation, 183
Cambridge Study on Delinquency Development, 32
Campaign for a More Rational Criminal Justice Policy, 225
Campaign for an Effective Crime Policy, xiii-xiv
Canada. *Also see* Ottawa school
    incarceration rate in, 15
    murder rate in, 55
    violent crime in, 35
Career Anchors, 153
CASAS. *See* Comprehensive Adult Student Assessment System
Caseload, 96
CAT. *See* Client Assessment Treatment
Center on Alcoholism, Substance Abuse and Addictions, 189
Chain gangs, 135
Clark Foundation, Edna McConnell, 105
Classification. *See also* Risk assessment
    ACA Public Correctional Policy on, 115-16
    Case Management Classification System (CMC), 144, 167
    drug-use typology, 79
    I-Level system, 166-67
    Level of Supervision Inventory as a tool for, 184
    offenders, low-risk, 113-15
    restrict prison use, 108
    triage approach to, 122-23
    uniform system, 114-15
Client Assessment Treatment (CAT), 142
CMC. *See* Classification, Case Management Classification System
Cocaine Positive Outcome Expectancy Test, 142
Cognitive-behavioral Treatment, 150-51, 155, 192
Collaboration, 98-102
Colorado
    community corrections in, 174-76, 185
    correctional expenditures in, 25
    criminal statutes for murder in, 10
    lengthening prison terms in, 10
    Probation Services, Office of, 101
    risk assessment in, 124
    Standardized Offender Assessment Program (SOAP), 101-02, 130

statewide classification system, 109-10
Communication among practitioners, policymakers, and
    researchers, 95-103
Community corrections
    ACA Public Correctional Policy on, 197-98
    American Probation and Parole Association, 102
    appropriate treatment programs in, 161
    case management of, 207-09
    civil lawsuits, 201
    Colorado and, 174-76, 185
    community involvement in, 217-18
    crowding, reduction of, 107
    Delaware and, 109-10
    employment and, 154
    evaluation of programs, 175-77, 181-83, 203-12
    International Association of Residential and Community
        Alternatives (IARCA), 102
    International Community Corrections Association (ICCA), 102,
        214
    internship, 101, 214
    juveniles and, 109
    Management Information Systems (MIS) for, 204-05
    Minnesota and, 110–11
    organizational atmosphere, 215-17
    Palmer, Ted, 102
    parole for minorities, 106
    parole, uniform classification system, 114
    population increase in, xi-xii
    private programs in, xii, 27
    Probation Services, Colorado Office of, 101
    Probation, ACA Public Correctional Policy on, 201-02
    programs, size of, 200-01
    Psychology of Criminal Conduct and, 203
    risk assessment and, 124-27
    screening offenders, 207
    software programs, 205
    staff qualifications for, 210-15
    state's role in monitoring, 218-20
    successful elements of, 199, 201
    supervision strategies, 95
    theory and, 203
    work experience for, 214-15
Community involvement, 115, 217-18
Community Program Assessment Inventory, 188
Community support network, 150
Comprehensive Adult Student Assessment System (CASAS), 152
Confrontational approaches, 156
Connecticut, jail population, 114
Construction
    funding, 106
    halting, 106, 109
    Washington (State), 111
Contingency contracting, 157, 158
Correctional Industry, ACA Public Correctional Policy on, 20-21
Correctional information systems
    ACA Public Correctional Policy on, 206
    assessment and, 124
    community corrections, 204-05
    data elements needed for, 205
    reasons for, 204-05
    state's role in, 220
    treatment integrity and, 158
Correctional Institutions Environmental Scale, 188
Correctional placement. See Risk assessment
Corrections
    ACA Public Correctional Policy on Purpose of, 28-29
    Auburn, New York school of, 135, 225
    costs associated with, xi, xiv, 24-26, 226
    economic development and, 226

ideology and, 32-33
    public expectations of, 33-34
    theory and, 32-33, 203
Costs. See Corrections, costs associated with
Crime
    age and, 58-62, 63, 165
    corporate, 42-43, 45
    gender and, 58-59, 165
    measuring, methods for, 63
    media presentation, vii, 39-45, 223-24
    police reports of, See Police reports of crime
    policy construction, 53-55
    race and, 165
    rates, self-reports of, 68-69
    reduction of, as viewed by law enforcement, 53-54
    social class and, 63-64, 166
    trends in, 56-62
    white collar, 51, 64, 68
Criminal conduct, major risk factors, 71-72
Criminological theory
    Cultural Deviance Theory, 64
    Differential Association Theory, 66
    integrated, 68, 69
    Labeling Theory, 67
    Middle-class Subculture Theory, 65
    Psychology of Criminal Conduct. See Psychology of Criminal
        Conduct
    Radical Theory, 67
    Social Control Theory, 66
    Strain Theory, 65
    Symbolic Interactionist Theory, 65
    use of, 54-55
Crowding
    ACA Public Correctional Policy on, 13-14
    effect on corrections, 223
    overcapacity, 37
    reduction of, 107
CSOAP. See Colorado Standardized Offender Assessment Program
Currie, Elliott, 89, 103

D
Dade County, 81
Data collection, 132
Death penalty, 225
Delaware
    prison reduction in, 109-10
    statewide classification system, 109-10
Delinquency. See Juveniles
Denver, Colorado, 190
Disadvantaged position and crime, 63
District attorneys, 99, 100
Domestic violence, 224
Domestic Violence Behavioral Checklist, 142
Drug abuse. See Substance abuse
Drug Abuse Screen Test, 130, 139
Drug Use Questionnaire, 178
Drugs, war on, 80
Drunk driving, 224
Due process, 120

E
Economics, 16-17, 32
Edna McConnell Clark Foundation, 105
Education
    Adult Basic Education Test, 152
    community corrections staff and, 214
    Comprehensive Adult Student Assessment System (CASAS),
        152
    correctional costs' effect on, xi, xiv, 24-26, 226

employment assistance, 152
General Education Development (GED), 153, 218
Higher Education, ACA Public Correctional Policy on, 194
learning organizations, 215-16
Offender Education and Training, ACA Public Correctional Policy on, 191
public preference for, 36
staff, 101
training, academic and vocational, 54, 152-54, 192, 214
Elected officials. See Policymakers
Electronic monitoring, 73, 165, 169, 193
Elliott, Delbert, 103
Employee Assistance Programs, ACA Public Correctional Policy on, 186
Employers, private, 153. Also see Private Industry Councils (PICS)
Employment
    as an outcome measure, 180
    assistance, 152
    community corrections and, 154
    Level of Supervision Inventory and, 185
    programs, 192, 209
England, incarceration rate in, 15
Enlightenment Period, 31
Ethnic incarceration rates, 91-92
Evaluation
    ACA Public Correctional Policy on Research and, 97-98
    benefits of, 173-74
    collecting information for, 174
    community corrections programs, 175-77, 181-83, 203-12
    correctional programs, 189-93
    offender, 177-81, 183-85
    outcome measures used for, 176-77
    quasi-experimental design for, 180-81
    research design for, 180-81, 195
    risk to the community, 178
    staff performance, 185, 187-89
    system, 132
    treatment needs, 178
Excessive Workloads, ACA Public Correctional Policy on, 13-14

F
Families Against Mandatory Minimums (FAMM), 225
Family Therapy. See Marital/Family Therapy
FAMM. See Families Against Mandatory Minimums
Fees charged to inmates, 26
Females. See Women
Finland, prison reduction in, 112-13
Fiscal Responsibility for Correctional Legislation, ACA Resolution on, 24-25
Focus groups, 115
Ford, Betty, clinic, 157. Also see Milieu therapy
FRAMES, 118, 144, 149-50
France, incarceration rate in, 15
Freud, Sigmund, 166

G
GED. See Education, General Education Development
Gender. See Crime, gender and
Gendreau, Paul, 103, 120, 145, 168, 188
Germany (West), incarceration rate in, 15
Glueck, Sheldon and Eleanor, 69, 166
Godlis, Jeff, 49
Gubetta, Jim, 226

H
Halfway house clients, 110, 200
Hares Checklist for Psychopathy, 142
Hirschi, Travis, 69
Home confinement clients, 110

Homicide. See Murder rate
Horton, Willie, 2
Hypnosis, 157

I
ICCA. See International Community Corrections Association
Indiana, correctional expenditures in, 25
Information systems. See Correctional Information Systems
Intensive Supervision Programs, 84
International Community Corrections Association (ICCA), 102, 214
International Halfway House Association, 214
Internship, 101, 214
Intervention, correctional. See Treatment
Inventory of Drinking Situations, 159
Italy, incarceration rate in, 15

J
Jails, risk assessment and, 106, 114
Job Finder's Club, 154
Justice, Department of. See National Institute of Corrections
Juveniles
    Cambridge Study on Delinquency Development, 32
    causes of delinquency, 62-63, 84
    deinstitutionalization of, in Massachusetts, 108-09
    Juvenile Justice, ACA Public Correctional Policy on, 60-61
    programs, 190

K
K-EYE-TV (television station), 49
Kiwanis Club, 100, 218
Kneeland, Carole, 49
KVUE-TV (television station), 49

L
Legislation, 72-73, 84, 95, 99, 100
    construction, 106
Legislators. See Policymakers
Level of Supervision Inventory-Revised, 130, 178
    benefits of, 144-45, 207
    components of, 127-29
    employment and, 185
    history of, 120
    as a needs assessment instrument, 140-41
    scoring, 184-85
    sentencing and, 184
    use with low-risk offenders, 114, 115
Lewis, Anthony, 227
Lombroso, 55
Lorton Prison, 87
LSI-R. See Level of Supervision Inventory-Revised

M
MADD. See Mothers Against Drunk Drivers
Management Information Systems (MIS). See Correctional Information Systems
Mandatory sentencing laws, 110
Marijuana. See Substance abuse, marijuana
Marijuana Positive Outcome Expectancy Test, 142
Marital/Family Therapy, 155
Massachusetts, juveniles, deinstitutionalization of, 108-09
Matching. See Responsivity
Maurer, Marc, 227
McFeaters, Cathy, 49
Mead, George Herbert, 69
Media
    crime news, sources, 46-47
    crime presentation, vii, 39-45, 123-24
    journalists, 226
    news, slanting and distortion of, 47-50

Mempa v. Rhay, 120
Mental health, services for, 159
Meta-analysis, 120, 189, 201
Mexican-Americans, 89
MI. See Motivational Interviewing
Miechenbaum, Donald, 69
Milieu therapy, 156-57
Miller, Jerome, 108
Miller, William, 103, 147
Minnesota
    incarceration rate in, 110
    prison reduction in, 110-11
    Probation Subsidy Program, 174
    risk assessment in, 124
Minnesota Multi Phasic Inventory (MMPI), 127
Mischel, Walter, 69
MMPI. See Minnesota Multi Phasic Inventory
Moos, Rudolph, H., 188
Mothers Against Drunk Drivers (MADD), 225
Motiuk, Lawrence, 120
Motivational Interviewing (MI)
    defined, 147
    practitioners' use for, 86, 118, 172
    specialized training, 214
    theoretical basis for, 148
Motivational Inventory, 142
Murder rate, 55, 90

N

Narcotics Anonymous (NA), 153, 157, 165
National Council on Crime and Delinquency (NCCD), 105
National Crime Survey, 68
National Institute of Corrections (NIC), 214
Native American Indians, 89
NCCD. See National Council on Crime and Delinquency
Needs assessment, 106
Netherlands, incarceration rate in, 15
New Zealand, incarceration rate in, 15
NIC. See National Institute of Corrections
Norway, incarceration rate in, 15

O

Offender assessment. See Risk assessment
Offender classification. See Classification; Risk assessment
Offenders
    employment assistance for, 152
    employment history, 123
    evaluation, 177-81, 183-85
    high risk, 123, 124, 161, 204, 215
    low risk, 122-23, 124, 132, 162, 204, 215
    marital status, 123
    moderate risk, 122, 124, 215
    screening for community corrections, 207
Ohio, violent crime in, 35
Organizational Diagnosis Questionnaire, 188
Ottawa school, 69, 86, 103, 172
Outward Bound, 190
Overcrowding. See Crowding

P

Palmer, Ted, 102, 166, 189, 201
Paraprofessional, 132
Parole. See Community corrections
Parole and Supervised Release, ACA Public Correctional Policy on, 199-200
Pelican Bay Prison (California), 87

Pennsylvania
    correctional expenditures in, 19
    crime rate in, 18-19
Petersilia, Joan, xv
Philadelphia, crime rate in, 55
Pierce, Neil, 227
Pilot projects, 95, 99
Placement. See Risk assessment
Police reports of crime, 68
Policymakers
    fear of crime, exploitation of, 224
    rehabilitation, view of, 159-60
    relationship with practitioners and researchers, 95-103
    three strikes and you're out movement, 183
Political context of corrections, 31-38
Practitioners, relationship with policymakers and researchers, 95-103
Prison admission, 87
Prison construction, 106
Prison reduction
    benefits of, 107
    Delaware and, 109-10
    Finland and, 112-13
    Massachusetts and, 108-09
    Minnesota and, 110-11
    Washington State and, 110-12
Prison reform, 110
Private Industry Councils (PICS), 153-54
Private Sector Involvement, ACA Public Correctional Policy on, 21-22
Privatization, 19-23, 27
Probation. See Community corrections
Project Pride, 190
Prosecutors
    fear of crime, manipulation of, 225
    role of, 224-25
    three strikes law, use of, 183
Psychology of Criminal Conduct, 64, 86, 172
    findings of, 70-71
    history of, 69
    importance for changing corrections, 223, 226
    objectives of, 69-70
    practitioners' use for, 117, 181, 203
    staff knowledge of, 212
Psychotherapy, 156, 157
Psychotropic medications, 156
Public policy, 136
Publication of research, 99, 220
Pung, Orville, 28

Q

Quakers, 225
Quality control, 26-28, 132

R

Race
    African-Americans in prison, 88-92
    disproportionalness, 87-88, 106
    drug use and, 88
    incarceration and, xi, 87-93
    parole preference and, 106
    whites, prison admission of, 87, 88
Rape, 90
Raspberry, William, 227
Reagan, Nancy, 82
Recidivism
    as an outcome measure, 176, 180
    criminogenic needs and, 142-44, 172

factors causing, 120
higher-risk offenders, 121, 162
length of prison stay and, 84
low-risk offenders, 162
offense of conviction and, 165
predictors of, 121-22, 165, 183
reduction of, 223
risk assessment, 125, 126
treatment and, 136, 160-61, 210
Recruitment and Development, Correctional Staff, ACA Public
    Correctional Policy on, 211-12
Rehabilitation. See Treatment
Relapse prevention, 81, 158-59, 182, 214
Relapse Strategy Test, 142
Research. See Evaluation
Research and Evaluation, ACA Public Correctional Policy on,
    97-98
Researchers, 95, 97, 101, 102-03, 224
Responsivity
alcohol treatment approach, 83-84, 86
boot camps and, 169
defined, 167-68
development of, 128-29, 166-67
matching, 158, 166, 168-69
program features inconsistent with, 169-70
summary of research, 171-72
Restitution, 190
Restorative justice, 181
Revocation, 114, 223
Risk assessment
changing, suggestions for, 95, 131
Colorado Standardized Offender Assessment Program,
    101-02, 130
dynamic risk factors, 126
first-generation, 124-25, 127
FRAMES. See FRAMES
history of, 119-20, 127
mistakes with, 119
offenders, high-risk and, 106, 119, 120, 123
offenders, low-risk and, 106, 118, 119, 122-23
organizational implications, 130-32
prison use lowering by, 106
purpose of, 121
second-generation, 125
stages of criminal justice, 129
static risk factors, 125
third-generation, changes to, 123, 126, 127, 131
Risk Supervision Inventory (RSI), 140
Robberies, 90
Rogers, Carl, 156
Rollnick, Stephen, 147
Rotary Club, 100, 218
RSI. See Risk Supervision Inventory
Russia, 64

S

Safer Foundation, 154
Salient Factor Score, 120
San Francisco, 209
Sanctions and Controls, Appropriate use of, ACA Public
    Correctional Policy on, 107-108
Sanctions Policy Assessment, 188
SAQI. See Substance Abuse Question Inventory
Scared Straight, 190
Scotland, incarceration rate in, 15
SCQ. See Situational Confidence Questionnaire
Sensory deprivation, 157

Sentencing
ACA Public Correctional Policy on, 6-7
Finland, 112
legislative guidelines, 113-14
lengthening prison terms and, 10-11, 84
Level of Supervision Inventory and, 184
public knowledge of, 35
recommendations for, 118
Washington (State), increase in, 111-12
Sentencing Project, 227
Sex offenders, 111
Situational Confidence Questionnaire (SCQ), 141, 159, 179
Skill training. See Treatment, Cognitive behavioral approaches to
Skinner, B. F., 69
Social class and crime, 64-65
Social Support Network (SSN), 140, 151
Social Support Questionnaire (SSQ), 140, 152, 159
Sociological theories of crime, 65-68
South Africa
crime rate in, versus California, 89
incarceration in, versus California, 90-92
South, prisons in, 87
SSN. See Social Support Network
SSQ. See Social Support Questionnaire
Staff
Drug-free Correctional Workforce, ACA Resolution on, 80
Employee Assistance Programs, ACA Public Correctional
    Policy on, 186
evaluation of, 185, 187-89
evaluation of treatment needs, 178
learning organizations, 215-16
matching skills and styles with offenders, 169, 189
mental health, 217
personnel policy, 108
qualifications, 210-15
Recruitment and Development, ACA Public Correctional Policy
    on, 211-12
state training for, 220
stress reduction for, 107
theory, learning, 203
Stages of Change Readiness and Treatment Eagerness Scale
    (SOCRATES), 140, 179, 207
Standardized Offender Assessment Program, 101-02, 130
Standards, 26, 220, 221-22
State Sentencing Guidelines Commission (Minnesota), 110-11
Steel Workers' Union, 209
Substance abuse
adolescent, drug control, 79
African-Americans and, 88
alcohol. See Alcohol and alcoholism
cocaine, 75, 81, 82
Cocaine Positive Outcome Expectancy Test, 142
crack, 82
drug offenders, classification of, 78-79
Drug-free Correctional Workforce, ACA Resolution on, 80
drugs, impact on criminal justice, 77-80
European experiences, 77-78
general population and, 82
hallucinogens, 82
heroin, 81
inhalants, 82
jail inmates, 81-82
marijuana, 75, 81, 82
Marijuana Positive Outcome Expectancy Test, 142
Offender's, ACA Public Correctional Policy on, 76
relapse prevention, 81, 158-59
stimulants, 82
tobacco. See Tobacco
treatment strategies for, 154-59

Substance Abuse Question Inventory (SAQI), 144
Substance Use History Matrix (SUHM), 130, 141, 179, 207
SUHM. *See* Substance Use History Matrix
Suicides, 107
Sutherland, Edwin, 51
Sweden, incarceration rate in, 15

T

TABE. *See* Test of Adult Basic Education
Technical schools. *See* Education
Technology and Standards, ACA Resolution on, 219
Tenure, 101
Test of Adult Basic Education (TABE), 152
Texas, parolees in, 167
Three strikes and you're out legislation
    California and, 183
    movement across the United States, 37
    policymakers and, 183
    prosecutors' use of, 183, 225
    public support for, 136
    Washington State and, 112
Tobacco, 81
Tocqueville, Alexis de, 92
Training. *See* Education
Treatment. *Also see* Motivational Interviewing
    cognitive behavioral approaches to, 150-51, 155, 192
    community resources, importance of, 150
    compared with punishment, 136
    developing a plan for, 144-47
    identifying levels of, 102
    identifying the needs for, 136-44
    individualization of, 136-39
    ineffective program characteristics, 147
    needs assessment instruments for, 106, 139-42
    program success, 160-62
    rehabilitation, public acceptance of, 136
    risk level and, 161-62

Stages of Change, 118, 148-49, 158
    substance abuse, 154-59

U

Understanding of Alcoholism Scale, 179, 189
United States
    crime rates in, 55-60
    incarceration rate in, x, 15-16
    wealth distribution in, 16-17
University of Rhode Island Change Assessment (URICA), 140
URICA. *See* University of Rhode Island Change Assessment
Urinalysis, 165

V

Vermont, risk assessment in, 124
Victimization, 57
Violence Reduction, ACA Public Correctional Policy on, 40-41
Violent offenders, 118
Vision Quest, 190
Vocational schools. *See* Education
Volunteers, 152, 187, 218

W

Washington (State), prison reduction in, 111-12
Watson, Elizabeth, 49
Weed, California, 226
Welfare. *See* Aid to Families with Dependent Children
White collar crime, 51, 64, 68
Whites, prison admission of, 87, 88
Wisconsin Risk Assessment Scale, 167
Wisconsin, risk assessment, 120, 142
Women
    domestic violence and, 224
    on federal bench, 92
    incarcerated, 87
Workloads, 95

Index of Authorities Cited

A

Ageton, Suzanne S., 68
Allsop, Steve, 159
American Correctional Association, 34, 36, 72
Andrews, Donald A., 54, 63, 64, 69, 86, 117, 120, 128, 136,
    143, 151, 155, 156, 159, 163, 165, 166, 167, 168, 169, 170,
    172, 201, 203, 204, 207, 212
Annis, Helen M., 156
Applegate, K., 84, 132
Arbuthot, J., 150, 155
Arling, Greg, 167
Ashkins, C., 43
Aziz, David W., 173
Azrin, Nathan H., 139, 154

B

Baird, Christopher, 121, 167
Barak, Gregg, 42, 43, 44, 50
Bayse, Daniel J., 218
Becker, 67
Besalel, Victoria, 139, 154

Bien, T. H., 155, 156
Blankenship, M. B., 42, 48
Blue Ribbon Commission on Inmate Population Management,
    24, 90, 91, 92
Blumstein, Alfred, 136
Bogue, Brad, 102
Bonta, James, 54, 63, 64, 69, 86, 107, 113, 114, 117, 122, 123,
    124, 128, 136, 143, 144, 145, 151, 156, 159, 160, 162, 165,
    166, 167, 168, 169, 170, 172, 203, 204, 207, 212
Bordua, 66
Bradsher, Keith, 16
Brandsma, Jeffery M., 157
Bratton, William J., 53
Brown, Mark, 15, 16
Brown, Stephen E., 54, 58, 68
Brownstein, Henry R., 44
Budiansky, Stephen, 39
Bullock, Merry L., 157
Bureau of Justice Statistics, x, 8, 9, 10, 11, 12, 13, 56, 57, 75,
    77, 82, 87, 88, 89, 91, 92
Burke, Peggy, 200

Butterfield, Fox, 23, 225
Byrne, James M., 84

C

Campaign for an Effective Crime Policy, xiii, 106
Canadian Sentencing Commission, 35, 36
Canter, Rachelle J., 68
Castle, Michael N., 110
Center for the Study of Law and Society, 19
Chaiken, Jan M., 39
Chaiken, William E., 39
Clark, Cheryl L., 173
Clear, Todd R., 78, 109, 135, 144
Cloward, Richard A., 65, 68
Cohen, Albert K., 65
Cohen, Jaqueline, 136
Cole, George F., 109, 135
Coleman, 65
Colvin, Richard Lee, 225
Com Corr Coop, 151, 157, 159
Cooley, 67
Cooney, Ned L., 81
Cooper, G. O., 157
Cressey, Donald R., 65, 66
Cressler, D. L., 159
Crossette, B., 17
Cullen, Francis T., 42, 48, 84, 132
Currie, Elliott, 16, 17, 55, 63, 89

D

Davis, 65
Davis, F., 43
Dickey, Walter J., 132
DiClemente, Carlo, 118, 140, 148, 149
Doob, Anthony M., 35, 43
Dugger, Celia W., 27, 201
Durhan, Alexis M., 43, 48

E

Edna McConnell Clark Foundation, 105
Eisenberg, Michael, 132
Elliott, Delbert S., 68, 87
Empey, LaMar T., 64
English, Kim, 175
Erickson, 67
Esbensen, Finn-Aage, 54, 58, 68

F

Fairweather, George W., 159
Farnsworth, M., 63
Farragher, Thomas, 226
Farrington, David, 62
Federal Bureau of Investigation, 55, 56, 57, 62
Feldman, Daniel L., 24
Ferracuti, Franco, 68
Fishman, Mark, 48
Fleming, Michael F., 81
Fogg, Vern, 102
Frankel, Max, 44
Frase, Richard S., 111
Freud, Sigmund, 166
Fuller, R. K., 156

G

The Gallup Report, 36
Garrett, C., 150, 155
Geis, Gilbert, 54, 58, 68

Gendreau, Paul, 72, 84, 120, 135, 147, 156, 167, 168, 169, 170, 181, 182, 185, 187, 188, 204, 213, 214
General Accounting Office, 80
Gest, Ted, 93
Glaser, W. 65
Glick, Barry, 59
Glueck, Eleanor, 166
Glueck, Sheldon, 166
Goggin, Claire, 72
Goldkamp, John S., 81
Goldstein, Arnold, 59
Gordon, D., 150, 155
Gottfredson, Michael, 68, 82
Gottfredson, Stephen D., 25, 34, 105
Gottschalk, R., 150, 155
Graber, Doris, 43
Grossman, Michelle G., 36
Guydish, J. R., 158

H

Hagner, Paul, 43
Hall, Sharon M., 151
Harris, P. W., 167
Havassy, Barbara E., 151
Heather, N., 158
Hester, Reid K., 83, 84, 85, 138, 139, 154, 155, 156, 157, 159, 168
Hilfrink, Martin L., 156
Hindelang, Michael J., 58, 165
Hirschi, Travis, 60, 66, 68
Hoffman-Bustamonte, Dale, 58
Hoge, Robert D., 54, 156, 159
Holley, Joe, 49
Hollon, Steven D., 150, 155
Howard, Matthew O., 156
Hunzeker, Donna, 24

I

Immarigeon, Russ, 23
Izzo, R., 151, 155

J

Jesness, Carl F., 188
Jones, Peter R., 207
Justice Education Center, 114

K

Kalish, C. B., 55
Keane, T. M., 158
Kendall, Phillip C., 150, 155
Keve, Paul, 26
Kiessling, J. J., 170
Knapp, Kay, 110, 200
Kopel, David B., 80
Krisberg, Barry, 121

L

Labaton, Stephen, 80
Lauen, Roger J., 19, 23, 27, 201, 204, 218
Lee-Simmons, L., 43
Lemert, 67
Lerner, K., 167
Leschied, Alan W., 54
Lindsay, Margot C., 217
Lipsey, Mark W., 136, 150, 155
Loeber, R., 120
Logan, Charles H., 23

M

Mande, Mary, 175
Marlatt, G. Allen, 159
Martin, John A., 79, 80
Martin, Susan E., 136
Martinson, Robert, 136
Maultsby, Maxie C., 157
Maynard, H., 159
McConville, Sean, 105
McDonald, Douglas C., 21, 23
McGrath, John H., 42
McGriff, William W., 23
McKay, Henry D., 64
Mead, George Herbert, 65
Media Monitor, 42, 43, 44
Miller, W. E., 33
Miller, William R., 83, 84, 85, 86, 118, 138, 139, 147, 148, 149, 151, 154, 155, 156, 157, 159, 168, 185, 189
Minnesota State Sentencing Guidelines Commission, 111
Monti, Peter M., 158
Moos, Rudolph H., 188
Motiuk, Lawrence L., 107, 114, 122, 123, 128, 145
Moyers, Theresa B., 189
Murphy, T. J., 157

N

National Center for Education Statistics, 63
National Council on Crime and Delinquency, 105
National Institute of Justice, 20, 75
New York Times, 26
Nieman Reports, 45

O

O'Farrell, Timothy J., 155
O'Leary, Vincent, 188
Ohlin, Lloyd E., 65, 68
Onek, David, 121

P

Palmer, Ted, 151, 155, 169, 170, 181, 182, 185, 187, 189, 190, 192, 193, 199, 204, 209, 215
Parsons, 65
Pasewark, Richard, 34
Petersilia, Joan, xv, 106
Prendergast, Alan, 48
Preziosi, Robert C., 188
Prochaska, James O., 118, 140, 148
Purdy, Matthew W., 23, 27, 201

Q

Quinney, 67

R

Ramirez, Anthony, 23
Randall, D., 43
Read, Edward M., 152
Reback, Donna, 110
Rimmele, Carl T., 156
Roberts, John, 20, 135
Roberts, Julian V., 35, 36
Rogers, Carl, 156
Rohrlich, Ted, 225
Rollnick, Stephen, 118, 147, 148, 149, 151, 159, 185
Ross, Robert R., 151, 155, 167, 188

S

Sacco, Vincent, 44, 45, 46, 50
Salahi, David L., 25
Sanchez, V. C., 118, 149
Sanders, D. H., 159
Sannibale, C., 156
Saunders, Bill, 159
Schein, Edgar H., 153
Schlesinger, Phillip, 50
Schoen, Kenneth F., 34, 115
Select Committee on Narcotics Abuse and Control, 75
Sentencing Project, 87
Shapiro, Bruce, 55
Shaw, Clifford R., 64
Sheley, Joseph, 43
Shilton, Mary K., 218
Simourd, L., 120
Smith, D. A., 63
Spiegel, Claire, 223
Staples, Ben, 135
Statistics Canada, 55
Stokes, D. E., 33
Stouthamer-Loeber, Magda, 120
Sullivan, John, 23, 201
Sutherland, Edwin H., 65, 66

T

Tannenbaum, 67
Taylor, Ralph B., 34
Terblanche, Stephen, 89, 90, 92
Thornsberry, T. P., 63
Tittle, Charles R., 63
Toner, Robin, 33
Tonigan, J. S., 155, 156
Tonry, Michael H., 88, 136
Tornudd, Patrik, 112
Treaster, Joseph B., 78, 80
Tumber, Howard, 50

U

United States Census Bureau, 17

V

Villimez, W. J., 63

W

Wagner, Dennis, 132
Wasserman, David A., 151
Welsh, Richard J., 157
West, Donald J., 32
Wideman, John Edgar, 88
Wiebush, Richard G., 121
Wilkins, Leslie, 84
Will, Jeffry A., 42
Wisconsin Department of Health, 132
Wolfgang, Marvin E., 68
Wright, John Paul, 42, 48, 84, 132

Y

Young, Warren, 15, 16

Z

Zinger, Ivan, 151, 155
Zweben, Allen, 81